William B. Cushing
in the Far East

Portrait of W. B. Cushing by A. Bradish.

William B. Cushing in the Far East

A Civil War Naval Hero Abroad, 1865–1869

JULIAN R. MCQUISTON

McFarland & Company, Inc., Publishers
Jefferson, North Carolina, and London

Photographs by kind permission of Chautauqua County
Historical Society, Westfield, New York, unless otherwise noted.

LIBRARY OF CONGRESS CATALOGUING-IN-PUBLICATION DATA

McQuiston, Julian R., 1926–
William B. Cushing in the Far East : a Civil War naval hero
abroad, 1865–1869 / Julian R. McQuiston.
p.   cm.
Includes bibliographical references and index.

ISBN 978-0-7864-7055-6
softcover : acid free paper ∞

1. Cushing, William Barker, 1842–1874 — Travel — East Asia.
2. Ship captains — United States — Biography.   3. United States.
Navy — Officers — Biography.   4. United States — Relations — East Asia.
5. East Asia — Relations — United States.
6. Fredonia (N.Y.) — Biography.   I. Title.
E467.1.C98M35 2013   973.7'58092 — dc23   [B]   2012045766

BRITISH LIBRARY CATALOGUING DATA ARE AVAILABLE

© 2013 Julian R. McQuiston. All rights reserved

*No part of this book may be reproduced or transmitted in any form
or by any means, electronic or mechanical, including photocopying
or recording, or by any information storage and retrieval system,
without permission in writing from the publisher.*

On the cover: *The Maumee,* Cushing's ship to the Orient, photograph
by A. Thomas, Yokohama, July, 1868, and William Cushing on his
wedding day (both photographs courtesy Chautauqua County Historical
Society, Westfield, New York); Kate Cushing just after her wedding day
(courtesy Darwin R. Barker Historical Museum, Fredonia, New York)

Manufactured in the United States of America

*McFarland & Company, Inc., Publishers
Box 611, Jefferson, North Carolina 28640
www.mcfarlandpub.com*

Table of Contents

Acknowledgments vi

Preface 1

Introduction 3

1. The Challenge of a Pacific Empire   13
2. Cushing Embraces a Fredonia Sweetheart   20
3. Route to the Far East by Sail and Steam to Match the Power of Ocean Water   34
4. Cruising on the Troubled Waters of the Far East   49
5. From Tropical Heat to Northern Turbulence   85
6. Wandering Among the Crumbling Remnants of the Celestial Empire   109
7. Imperial Japan   131
8. Surveying the Landscape and the Inhabitants of Japan   156
9. A Lingering Farewell to the Far East   174

Notes   207

Bibliography   217

Index   220

Acknowledgments

I wish to acknowledge several colleagues who provided useful material. Mary B. Sievens explained the erudite religious convictions that flourished within the sturdy communities on the frontier. Markus Vink translated an account of Cushing's arrival in Indonesia. The staff of the Reed Library at SUNY Fredonia was consistently supportive. Jack Ericson, archivist of the library's Special Collections, gave me his office and secretary for a little more than a month to examine Cushing manuscripts deposited in the local archive of the Chautauqua County Historical Society at Westfield, which was then supervised by the Nixon family. John Paul Wolfe, present curator of the society, with the aid of Niles Dening, helped with photographs and illustrations. Douglas Shepard provided the editorial revision of footnotes, and Sylvia Peterson, Nancy Wojcik, and Theresa Dispenza assisted with typing. James Boltz was an indispensable aid, providing considerable editorial assistance and support in many ways. Finally, I wish to dedicate this book to my wife, Patricia, who gave me constant encouragement not to drop my paddle.

Preface

    Several years ago, when I was still chairman of the History Department at SUNY Fredonia, the Chautauqua Historical Society asked me to sort and index a collection of papers it had purchased from the estate of the widow of Commander William Barker Cushing, a celebrated Civil War hero. Cushing had put together a remarkable record as a daring young naval officer and accepted the challenge to destroy a Confederate ironclad ram, the *Albemarle*. Cushing sought the aid of technicians at the New York Navy Yard, where he submitted a scheme to construct a light, steam-driven craft that could swiftly approach the *Albemarle* and strike it with a torpedo, which would be suspended from the bow of the light steamer.

    Executing his daring plan with determination, Cushing received accolades nationwide. In a navy composed predominately of graying officers, Cushing was the youthful exception, a heroic young conqueror. He was resolved to pursue a naval career, which gave him an exceptional opportunity to escape from the limitations of an isolated farming community. The paradox, however, was that although Cushing heaped scorn on his rural antecedents, he kept returning to them, although he did not linger long among the familiar surroundings of his youth. In one of these hasty ventures he encountered Katherine Forbes, the daughter of a prosperous grocer. The ensuing courtship provides this narrative with a romance that balances the overview of the rigors pertaining to the daily chores and challenges of sailing a naval ship in strange seas.

Introduction

As this narrative unfolds, the initial setting (and, indeed, the most consistent one) is the village of Fredonia, a small community situated in the last county, Chautauqua, in western New York before reaching Pennsylvania. It is separated from Lake Erie by a larger neighbor, the City of Dunkirk. At the end of the Civil War, Dunkirk had a population of some 6,000 inhabitants; Fredonia contained approximately 2,000. Dunkirk was a bustling mercantile center, which prospered from the commerce associated with Lake Erie. Fredonia was essentially a farm-market town. The fruit and grape industry was still in an embryonic stage; wine presses had not yet become prevalent. The village of Fredonia sprawled on a fertile lake plain. It was difficult to fix any definite boundary, for it merged gradually into the meandering lanes that led to clusters of houses, sheds, and barns that dotted the countryside.

There is, however, one indisputable boundary: the escarpment that rises precipitously from the lake plain to a series of rolling hills that eventually join the Allegheny mountain range, through which flows a river also named Allegheny. These hills have an outstanding attribute: they form a generously sized basin for Lake Chautauqua, which empties into a small channel that flows into the Allegheny River. This geographic configuration made possible a portage

Rendering of downtown Fredonia showing Johnson House, the Baptist church, Fredonia Academy and the Presbyterian church.

trail from Lake Erie to Lake Chautauqua, which has at its head the escarpment overlooking Lake Erie and stretches some eighteen miles to its mouth. It empties into a small channel that drains into the Allegheny River, which in turn joins the Monongahela River to form the Ohio River at Fort Duquesne (Pittsburgh).

The earliest explorers of the region were French. Alarmed by the accelerating French military penetration into a region claimed by the colony of Virginia, the governor of that province dispatched a young officer in the colonial militia, Major George Washington, to protest the French incursion. The major was politely received by the commandant and given a fine French dinner, undoubtedly with much tempting wine, but Major Washington was lucky to return alive. The Indians stole his horse, and he had to trudge footsore through snow-packed trails.

Kate Forbes, a schoolgirl at the academy in Fredonia, had undoubtedly heard this tale, and certainly she had read accounts of the celebrated naval hero William Barker Cushing, who left Fredonia at the age of fourteen in 1855 to be a page to Francis Smith Edwards of Fredonia, elected to serve in the House of Representatives. In 1857 Cushing entered the Naval Academy at Annapolis on the nomination of Congressman Edwards, who also helped Cushing's younger brother, Alonzo, to

Top: Cushing at 14, just before going to Washington, D.C., with Congressman Edwards to be a page in the House of Representatives. *Bottom:* Midshipman Cushing, age 14, in 1856, his first year at Annapolis.

Portrait of the young Kate copied by McLaren.

receive an appointment to the United States Military Academy at West Point. From this time onward, William Barker Cushing's visits to Fredonia were infrequent, but facilitated by the Buffalo and Erie Railroad, which had a station in nearby Dunkirk. This station was Fredonia's vital link to the world beyond its circumscribed horizon. It became the nucleus of the communications network that kept Kate Forbes and William Barker Cushing united, despite the

Zattu Cushing, William's grandfather, was the first permanent settler in what eventually became Fredonia. He was the first Chautauqua County Court judge.

two very different spheres in which they confronted the challenges of their lives.

The modest number of inhabitants in Fredonia and the nature of their agricultural pursuits contributed to a stable society that attracted only a limited number of new families. However, the name Cushing was well known, for a principal founding pioneer of the village and surrounding territory had been William Barker Cushing's grandfather, Zattu, who became a judge. In fact, his jurisdiction initially stretched through much of western New York, from Niagara Falls to the Pennsylvania border. In addition to his legal career, Judge Cushing was a prosperous farmer and an astute land speculator. His eldest son, Milton, attended Hamilton College, became a physician, and migrated to Ohio, where he practiced medicine. Contracting tuberculosis, he abandoned medicine to attempt merchandising and land investments, in which he had modest success. His wife died from tuberculosis, as did eventually their two sons.[1]

In 1836 Milton took a second wife, Mary Barker Smith, who came from Salem, Massachusetts. Her ancestry was impeccable. The family arrived in Massachusetts in 1630, and by the time revolutionary agitation gained momentum, members of the family had acquired a steady reputation for political leadership. Mary Smith earned a distinguished record in the Boston schools, which was recognized when John Adams, who had supported revolutionary calls for separation from England and had served as the second president of the fledgling republic, presented her with a medal in 1822 commemorating her academic achievement. Possibly because she came from a family of six girls, she was encouraged to teach on the frontier, where educational opportunities were, as a rule, marginal. At any rate, she followed a popular path among young New England women professing scrupulous morality and deep immersion in sacred and educational principles. She obtained a teaching position at Columbus, Ohio, where she married Milton Cushing. She then gave birth to Milton, her eldest son, who eventually became a paymaster in the United States Navy.[2]

Mother Mary Barker Cushing with her four Civil War sons: Alonzo Hereford, William Barker, Howard Bass and Milton Buckingham.

Mary Barker Cushing and her husband moved farther west. They made their way to Chicago, then northward to Milwaukee, Wisconsin. Their ultimate destination was an uninhabited site, except for a scattering of Indians, ultimately called Delafield. Their cabin was the first building in a community approximately 30 miles west of Milwaukee. In this primitive cabin on the edge of the wilderness in 1842, William Barker Cushing was born. On account of his father's deteriorating health, Cushing missed an opportunity to recall any playmates from nearby Indian villages, but he did have the companionship of his slightly younger brother, Alonzo, likewise born at Delafield. There were also two sisters of Mary Barker who came to Delafield in search of husbands, a venture in which they found success.³

Alonzo Cushing, William's brother and West Point graduate, entered the military academy in June 1857 at the age of 16. He served with Union forces in the Civil War and became a hero at Gettysburg where he was killed in 1863.

Slowly, the Cushing family wandered back toward Ohio in search of a salubrious climate for the elder Milton. They did pause at Chicago, where Milton briefly resumed his medical practice. However, he was compelled by his continued ill health to abandon his profession once again. He did not, on the other hand, abstain from romantic stimulation. William Barker Cushing's surviving sister, Mary Isabel, was born in Chicago.

Milton Cushing left shortly thereafter to travel to Vicksburg, Mississippi, to test the climate, but it was not congenial. His condition had become truly desperate. He died in 1847 at the home of a brother in Gallipolis, Ohio, a town on the Ohio River. Mary Barker Cushing was now on her own.[4]

Whatever merit Milton Cushing may have demonstrated as a physician or as a businessman, he seems to have neglected to provide for the welfare of his wife and children. The two sons from his first marriage soon perished from the disease that killed their father; their sister married and lived in Wilmington, North Carolina. As a result, Mary Barker Cushing came to Fredonia, largely because it was a place where her husband's family lived, but she was a complete stranger seeking to rear her family in an environment where she had no roots. With plucky spirit, she succeeded. She eventually witnessed the marriage of her daughter, Mary Isabel, in Trinity Episcopal Church, where a winsome young bridesmaid, Kate Forbes, caught the wandering eye of Lieutenant Commander Cushing, who had returned to celebrate his sister's wedding and to assist in the selling of his mother's house before she moved to her ancestral surroundings in Boston and its environs.

William Barker Cushing here about 17 years old.

Above: Profile of Cushing when he was in command of the *Monticello*. *Opposite, bottom:* The *Monticello*, Cushing's favorite ship during the Civil War.

Cushing at age 19 before receiving command of the *Ellis* in 1861.

Cushing had achieved a stunning reputation in the Civil War. His most sensational feat had been the sinking of a Confederate ironclad ram at Plymouth, North Carolina. This event was the capstone of a remarkable series of operations against foreign and Confederate attempts to disrupt the Union blockade of southern ports. Cushing was invited to the White House to provide President Lincoln with information on riverine strategy. After the climactic destruction of the Confederate ram *Albemarle*, Lincoln recommended that Congress enact a resolution congratulating Cushing for his heroic service to his country. Cushing had become a great American hero.[5]

In 1876, two years after Cushing's premature and tragic death, Gideon Welles, Lincoln's secretary of the Navy, observed "that the great chief of the American Navy, [David Glasgow] Farragut, who was endowed with like heroism, and for whom *alone* the office of Admiral was created and its honors intended, said to me, that while no Navy had braver or better officers than ours, 'young Cushing was the hero of the war.'" Theodore Roosevelt made a similar comment when he declined Kate Cushing's invitation to write a biography of her husband: "I am very much complimented by your letter. No one could help being pleased at being singled out to write a history of a man who, in my opinion comes next to Farragut on the hero roll of American naval history, but it is not possible for me to undertake such a work at this time."[6]

Kate Cushing, who had accepted Cushing's impulsive attentions during his visit at Fredonia on the occasion of his sister's nuptials, found quickly that she had permitted herself to be the recipient of a marriage proposal. Eventually, she too would be married in the same church where she had served as bridesmaid to the woman who became her sister-in-law. By 1898 Kate Cushing dedicated much of her time and energy to perpetuating the memory of her deceased husband. She solicited the aid not only of Theodore Roosevelt but also of Alfred Thayer Mahan, both of whom were advocates of naval power and preoccupied with the might of the battleship in enforcing the American national interest. The dramatic performance of the American Navy against Spanish squadrons in the Philippines and Cuba during the decisive destruction of the remnants of an ancient colonial empire revealed that a brand new power now challenged the hegemony of the traditional European powers. The Great White Fleet, of which Theodore Roosevelt was so proud, guaranteed respect for the United States on the high seas.

However, Cushing's relative and colleague, Admiral Albert Barker, cautioned that although Captain Mahan's name comes readily to the forefront "as a writer of great preeminence," Cushing's career apparently did not appeal to Captain Mahan in a way that would bring out his best efforts. Admiral Barker reminded Marie Cushing, "Your father was never Commander-in-Chief of a great fleet, operating against a foreign foe and hence never had an opportunity to act on a large scale and show to the world his full capabilities." Barker added, "Now Mahan makes the *world* his study, and as you know he is at his best when dealing with actions and events which affect the destiny of nations."[7]

Barker's commentary on the reaction of Mahan to a biography of Cushing was accurate. Mahan had a lackluster career until Theodore Roosevelt guided him to naval studies. Mahan was the antithesis of Cushing. Although both had served with the Asiatic Fleet at approximately the same time, Cushing's curiosity was open to the challenge of strange customs, puzzling social conventions, and exotic cultural artifacts. Mahan, however, was bored with sea duty, particularly in foreign climes. He was fortunate to have been befriended by Theodore Roosevelt and to have analyzed Nelson's naval strategy and tactics at a time when the ship of the line was reappearing in the form of the battleship.[8]

At any rate, Mahan revealed his tepid interest in any biography of Cushing when he authorized his publisher to respond to Kate Cushing that he would be willing to review the feasibility of undertaking the project only if Kate would organize her papers according to topic and arrange them in a chronological sequence. Then he would decide if he was interested in pursuing the project. Clearly, Mahan was not enthusiastic.[9]

William Barker Cushing, profile at the end of the Civil War.

One must feel compassion for Kate Cushing that her search for a knowledgeable and sympathetic biographer for her husband proved to be a disheartening venture. At first she had enlisted the service of Captain E. P. Dorr, a former naval officer who lived in Buffalo, New York, and was a prominent member of the historical society of that city. Unfortunately, Dorr's death brought an abrupt end to that undertaking. Kate next solicited the aid of H.H. Huntingdon, a well-known Chicago writer, primarily on literary topics.[10]

When David Parker, whose friendship with Cushing could be traced back to their youthful days in Fredonia, wrote to Kate Cushing to request her support for a proposal to write a book on Cushing, she replied that Huntingdon now had her support. However, Kate assured Parker that Cushing had on many occasions related fond recollections of happy times with Parker. In particular, Kate remembered how much pleasure Cushing received from the companionship of Fanta, the little black and tan dog Parker had given him on the eve of his departure from the naval yard at Norfolk.[11] Kate also explained that she had been reading some of the letters that Cushing had written to her when he was the captain of the USS *Maumee*. "By the way," she added, "these letters I speak of—embracing his voyage from the U.S.—Hampton Roads, almost around the world—namely—to Brazil—Cape Town—Indian Ocean—Java—all along the coast of China—Japan to San Francisco & then by the new railroad just finished, would make a delightful book. They are so full of

The *Maumee*, the reconditioned gun boat Cushing took to the Orient, photograph by A. Thomas, Yokohama, July 1868.

incident & adventure & bearing on every page the stamp of individuality & enthusiastic nature."[12]

Now, approximately 130 years after Kate penned her wistful conviction of the inestimable value of her husband's correspondence while serving with the Asiatic Squadron, her observation is now open to a reading public far removed from the time and milieu of Commander William Barker Cushing. On the other hand, debate on the fundamentals of naval strategy and tactics continues. Although ships and weaponry may change radically, and although national interests may differ in succeeding generations, there is always the need for the maverick hero. Kate Cushing has introduced well the letters that form the backbone of this chronicle of an ambitious and heroic naval officer, his love for a small-town girl, and his pride in his sparkling ship, the USS *Maumee*.

Chapter 1

The Challenge of a Pacific Empire

At the end of the American Civil War, the United States Navy could focus once again on its primary obligation to protect the mercantile pursuits of its citizens, as well as the representatives of the federal government and a growing number of citizens who sought to advocate their religious convictions in newly acquired lands that were exposed to Western influence. The horrendous conflicts of the inland deltas and rivers of the Confederacy were no more.

William Barker Cushing had achieved his heroic stature in littoral operations. Anxious to continue his career in the Navy, he sought to prove that he could master the responsibilities of naval command on the waters of the ocean. The American republic, now reunited, confronted entrenched mercantile competition and frequently an indifferent, if not outright hostile, reception from foreign societies that flourished well beyond its oceanic frontiers.

In 1853 Commodore Perry had forced a scornful Japanese regime to yield to compelling pressure. As a result, the Japanese were required to abandon two centuries of isolation from foreign intercourse and open several ports where their products could be exchanged for cargoes from the United States. This treaty was predicated on the ability join in the comfortable commerce of tea and coffee. The bulk of ocean trade had previously been fixed on whales to provide liquid for lamps, but whale liquid was soon replaced by coal oil.

In America cotton from the southern plantations was sent to provide suitable material for weaving in gigantic buildings stuffed with racks of looms, ready to transmit bolts of material. The American blockade of southern ports had promoted widespread poverty in textile regions of Great Britain, while Perry's success had attracted competition from British, French, and Russian mercantile interests. Naturally, American traders, either from New England or from the Pacific coast, now sought to renew their significant position in Japan. On March 11, 1854, Commander Perry and Japanese authorities formally ratified the Treaty of Kanagawa, which recognized that, for the moment, Japan would limit trade with American ships.

At this time the mills of the cotton industry in the southern region of prosperous Lancashire, where bales of raw cotton from the American cotton plantations provided the essential material, had faded as conflict drifted Great Britain and the United States into hostile rivalry.

A revival of American naval presence in the Far East would protect American commerce with China and Japan and reinforce diplomatic initiatives in those countries. There was also an obligation to protect ubiquitous missionaries whose fervent devotion to their cause often occasioned an angry rebuke from well-installed Buddhist institutions and their champions.

When he was assigned to the USS *Lancaster*, the flagship of the Pacific squadron, in June 1865, Cushing was introduced to the issues and challenges of the Pacific region. The *Lancaster* was one of the more impressive "steamers" of the Navy. It belonged to the Hartford class, the name of the flagship of Admiral Farragut during his celebrated campaigns on the Mississippi River and along the Gulf Coast. Like her sister ship, the *Lancaster* had a screw propeller and a steam engine, but her hull was constructed of timber, and masts and sails were still considered indispensable to reliable navigation. Her main battery of 24-inch Dahlgren guns made her a real threat to any opponent. The *Lancaster* and her sister vessels were worthy expressions of naval strength in a period in which the revolutionary design and armaments of monitors had yet to be advanced to practical operations on the high seas.[1]

Cushing not only gained experience on a major ship that was still relatively new (the *Lancaster* had been commissioned in 1859–1860) but he also became acquainted with the Pacific and its western shores. Within two months after the end of the Civil War, the Navy reorganized from being essentially a coastal and riverine fleet, returning to a policy of deploying squadrons in the Caribbean and South Atlantic, Mediterranean, Pacific, and Far Eastern waters. Cushing joined his ship at Aspinwall, a port on the Atlantic coast of Panama, which he identified as belonging to a Spanish province called "New Grenada." Although this title summons memories of the halcyon days of imperial Spain, sadly the images that Cushing encountered were those that displayed the tattered reality of the once great colonial empire. Cushing informed his mother that the port of Aspinwall "is a City that illustrates the decay of Spain's glory and fame as well as anything could." He observed that the population consisted mostly of "Spanish negroes." Wherever he looked, Cushing could gaze upon "the old walls, the scores of great churches fast going into decay; the quaint streets and houses all remind me of history and romance." On the other hand, he lamented, "But to think that such a miserable people should be permitted to hold this magnificent country, and to call themselves a nation is too much for me." His final comment was that "we could land a good ship's crew and take the whole of Central America."[2] It appears that Cushing was the unwitting herald of Theodore Roosevelt.

Eventually, Cushing and the *Lancaster* ventured to Hawaii, then called the Sandwich Islands and governed by an independent king. Cushing informed his mother that the *Lancaster* was the first American warship to visit these islands in eight years and, consequently, the considerable number of Americans who lived on this strategically important collection of islands was especially elated. However, during the prolonged absence of the U.S. Navy, the British had increased their visits and were courting the king. Also, they had invited the king's mother to visit London, where she would be presented to Her Imperial Majesty, Queen Victoria.[3]

Cushing was well aware of the mounting competition between British and American interests, both naval and commercial, for control of the Sandwich Islands. "We are expecting the English Flag Ship in," he wrote, "and when she comes, won't there be rivalry!" He told his mother that when the English ship made her previous visit, Americans had been insulted with impunity. "A party from the British ship," he revealed, "took our consulate Eagle down in the night and carried it off." The American consular staff had protested vigorously and demanded an appropriate apology. As a result, Cushing explained that Lord Beresford, "the young officer who did the deed was sent ashore to nail it up again—while our minister, an old Lincolnite, stood directing it." Apparently, the elderly American had a wonderful time guiding the thoughtless young British naval officer, who received considerable instructions: "A little higher! A little to the right! Not quite so far, Sir! &&." Unfortunately, the American revenge did not end the frequent serenading of American houses with rebel tunes.[4]

Cushing did not allow the endless diplomatic rivalry among Western powers over hegemony in the Sandwich Islands (which would eventually become the focus in the Pacific of the United States Navy) to divert his immediate attention from the spectacular panorama of volcanic explosions and the numerous streams of molten lava. To satisfy his exuberant curiosity, Cushing attempted to reach the rim of Kilauea, the highest and most spectacular of the active volcanoes on the main island of Hawaii. Unfortunately, his horse stumbled, and Cushing was tossed under his prostrate horse. Injured by a broken shoulder, he had to be carried in a litter on a 35-mile trip back to his ship.[5]

However, he arrived ultimately in a mended state at San Francisco, where he was lionized by the local citizens. The youthful hero of the Civil War became caught up in the social whirl of the season. "The parties are just opening," he informed his mother. "A grand one was given at Gen. Halleck's a few days since which I attended and had a splendid time," and he also confessed that "I find that it is impossible to keep out of flirtations."[6]

"The ladies here," he cheerfully reported, "are exceedingly pretty and the admitted belle of the City is very charming in every way." As a consequence of his social acclaim, Cushing wrote, "I am therefore engaged in the dangerous amusement of escorting her everywhere and have cut out all competitors." Yet Cushing recognized the limits of his successful forays, for "if she were not a young lady who knows full well how to look out for herself, I would not enter the lists." "As it is," he pointed out, "no harm can come to either side." Cushing's denial of serious romance was plain. The simple excuse was that "I cannot, now, afford to marry." Meanwhile, he could console himself with the honorary accolade of the Freedom of the City of Francisco bestowed upon him by the Board of Supervisors.[7]

"I have had a glorious time in San Francisco," he acknowledged, "but I find it very expensive." In the second half of this letter, he echoed a mounting concern that his future might well be constrained by financial stringency. He revealed further alarm at learning that "my prize money first turned out so small," and he "felt very shaky about it." Cushing had been awarded $6,000 in May 1865 in prize money for sinking the *Albemarle*. However, he explained that "when I had that $2800 taken from me, I got worse." There was additional disappointment to bear, for Congress had suspended further funding for claims involving prize money. "If the Supreme Court decides against our claims," Cushing predicted the loss of several thousand more dollars.

The real cause for Cushing's misery over his shrinking fortune was that he had acquired a fiancée. "I would not have become engaged, if I had anticipated so much misfortune," he lamented, and declared that "I have not enough to support a wife — with my habits." He concluded, "I can only remain at Sea and wait for something to turn up."[8]

He then informed his mother that "I have made up my mind not to go East, or if I do to start another Cruise at once." He had already stated his resolve emphatically to his fiancée and that he suspected there was much discord in her household. However, "I said that, frankly, that with all the misfortunes that had come upon me I could not afford to marry for years to come, and that I intended to remain at Sea." If his fiancée, Maggie, was willing to wait for such a prolonged period, then their engagement could remain in place. Cushing, however, did not believe that such a strategy would work. "I don't know," he mused, "what they will say or think in Chelsea." Possibly, the verdict would be that he had succumbed to a "fit of the blues." Having reached this decision after much thoughtful reflection, he was determined to remain fixed in his resolve. "I can't *and will not*," he vowed forcefully, "live a life of poverty with a wife."[9]

Undoubtedly, Cushing had encountered Maggie during his excursions to Boston and its environs. The earliest of these ventures took place in June 1861. On that occasion he wrote to his cousin Mary Edwards, the daughter of the congressman who had sponsored his admission to the Naval Academy, that "I have been having a grand time in Boston, while waiting for the *Colorado* to sail." "You know maybe," he informed Mary, "that mother's relations all live in Boston." He acknowledged that "I have not been there since I was four years old," but "I did not know much more about them." "I found," he admitted, "some handsome young lady cousins there, but everything was so different from New York." Cushing had apparently reconciled himself to unfamiliar social conventions, for he announced that "I never enjoyed myself so much in my life."[10]

In a letter from 1863, Cushing, in answering a query from his mother, advised her to sell her house in Fredonia and then to live in a boarding establishment. He promised that he was able to provide some additional money "so that you can board in good style. I want you to live some where in good quarters where I can bring my friends, and need not be ashamed." He added, "It is my duty first to see that you are comfortable."[11]

He likewise suggested that his sister Mary should sell her piano to help with the change in the household's living arrangements. As he vowed to live a spartan regimen and to give primary consideration to his mother's welfare, it is clear that Fredonia was not a major landmark on his horizon. In spite of his matrimonial uncertainties, Boston and its neighborhood were the beacons that guided Cushing to his domestic home port. His mother retained well-rooted links with her native soil, and Cushing had formed close ties with his mother's family. The strength of this bond is revealed in a letter to Mary Edwards from June 1863. Cushing's ship, the USS *Commodore Barney*, had been so badly battered in recent engagements that it had to be sent to Baltimore for extensive repairs, which provided Cushing with an opportunity to spend almost three weeks in Boston, where his mother was staying with some friends. "I must say that I never have enjoyed myself before as I did there," he claimed. He reported that "I had a dozen engagements a day, laughed, talked, smoked, and enjoyed the society of ladies and some grand rides, good fishing, and splendid dinners on the sea beach."[12]

So taken with the pleasures and amenities of Boston was Cushing that he pronounced cheerfully that "if ever I am afflicted with a better half," that city "shall be the place where she shall serve out baked beans and bread to hungry juvenile Cushings."[13] Clearly, Cushing was contemplating enlarging his romantic horizon with the warm embrace of domesticity.

There were also persuasive professional motives for focusing on the Atlantic coast, for the Navy was still essentially an Atlantic fleet. Its major shipyards, such as those at Boston and New York, were located on the East Coast. Moreover, Annapolis was the center for naval instruction and research and, of course, Washington was the headquarters of naval administration. Obviously, in Cushing's mind, Fredonia had been a temporary haven for his mother. There she could live quietly and economically as she reared her children in a setting that honored her husband's memory. That chapter in their lives was now over, and his future was on Atlantic shores, where his mother could be sheltered comfortably within her family circle.

His concern for his mother's welfare and his wish to see her installed in her native surroundings was not a sudden impulse, as Cushing contemplated a lengthy career in the postwar Navy. In April 1863, after relating some of the dramatic and terrifying moments of his recent encounters with Confederate batteries on the Virginia and North Carolina coasts, Cushing replied to his mother's suggestion that she might settle in Washington. "As to the project of moving to Washington," he counseled, "I decidedly object to it," for "it is not a fit place for anyone to live in these times." Cushing was prepared, however, to rescind this decided opinion, "if Milt wishes it." "My wish has been for you to live in Fredonia," he explained, "until Mary has completed her Seminary course, and then take a house (a nice one) in Boston or Chelsea."[14]

As his term of service in the Pacific came to an end, Cushing made the long journey home, where he would help his mother settle her affairs, then go on with her to Boston. His knowledge of Fredonia and its society must have been limited, for after leaving for Annapolis at the age of fourteen, he did not return until seven years later, on which occasion he had confided to his mother his project for destroying the *Albemarle*. That visit had been brief, as had an equally short three- or four-day trip to receive the acclamation of the citizenry of Fredonia for his heroic success in sinking the Confederate ship. On March 20, 1865, he became a Mason at Chelsea and then went to Fredonia. He had approximately a two-month leave after the end of the Civil War. Possibly a good part was occupied with his relatives in Boston, and certainly with Maggie, while only a modest amount of time was spent in Fredonia. Yet, despite the considerable attraction that Boston exercised on him, he had kept up correspondence with family and friends in Fredonia. However, it is plain that his focus was fixed on the Atlantic shores. Fredonia had become an urn for childhood memories.

However, the contemplations of April 1866 had been side-tracked, at least temporarily, by the marriage of his sister Mary Isabel to E. F. Gayle in Trinity Episcopal Church in Fredonia on June 6, 1866. Gayle, it should be noted, is recorded in the parish register as a resident of Salem, Massachusetts. Obviously, despite the long time in mail delivery between coasts, Cushing could have received several letters informing him of the forthcoming wedding of his sister. On March 11, 1867, he had been detached from the USS *Lancaster*, which was at Norfolk, and he was ordered to the Brooklyn Navy Yard. Yet there is no reason to suggest that he would abandon his intention to settle his mother in Boston, where he could share her hearth. He purchased his mother's house in Fredonia for six hundred dollars on May 3, 1867. Two months later, on July 1, 1867, he sold the house for nine hundred dollars. With that tidy profit, he severed his link with his boyhood home and dissolved tangible bonds with all those who shared the memory of his father.

It can be reasonably argued that Cushing was in Fredonia during the first week in May, when he negotiated the purchase of his mother's house. A month later he attended his sister's wedding, in which Kate Forbes participated as a bridesmaid. Less than a month later he proposed to Kate on the same day that he sold his mother's house. Four days afterward Cushing was ordered to resume active service. Within two months Cushing had peremptorily discarded his vow not to consider marriage until an adequate income had been secured and his professional goals realized. It would appear that with cavalier nonchalance he had walked away from the axioms to which he had sworn unyielding loyalty.

Undoubtedly Kate Forbes was a vivacious and attractive young woman. At the age of twenty she was a sterling illustration of radiant feminine charm and youthful beauty. However, Cushing had encountered any number of handsome and vivacious young women. Kate was, moreover, a country belle. Her background was that of a winsome young miss, who had been reared in comfortable circumstances by a well-respected family. Her father, David Forbes, who had commanded a regiment in the Civil War, was a prosperous merchant who bought and sold foodstuffs. She had received a sound education in the customary language and mathematical skills provided to the children of affluent parents at the same academy that Cushing had attended.

Kate had been reared in a rural background. She was the product of an insular and self-contained community that had yet to explore those heretofore remote and strange regions that the rush of railroad construction was opening up. Cushing, however, had become a member of the growing society of cosmopolitan men and women who dwelt in an environment far removed from the raw social structure and rudimentary conventions of a citizenry that still clung to its primitive origins. Cushing was an heir to the legacy of the Civil War; through his mother's family he had become familiar with the intellectual momentum of the Boston intelligentsia, and he had been introduced to the polished and urbane society of successful politicians and merchants, especially those belonging to his material relatives. He had become immersed in Boston and its New England heritage.

His alliance with Kate, therefore, was a contradictory move. Cushing had responded to impulse, not only in his naval career, but also in his private affairs. Apparently on impulse, he succumbed to her charms. Any lack of knowledge about Boston and its environs or the political ferment of Washington could be readily remedied. He gambled on the hope that the country girl would soon master and even delight in the bustle of Washington politics and the learned polemics of New England savants.

Chapter 2

Cushing Embraces a Fredonia Sweetheart

On July 1, 1867, Cushing wrote the first of a lengthy series of letters to his newly christened fiancée. "My darling Kate," he exclaimed. "It is four days now since I have seen you—and long long days! To day our ship went into commission, and in a short time she will sail—and where to, think you?" Cushing then supplied the answer to his question. "Contrary to all expectation," he revealed that, "she is going to the Brazils [sic] and not to China." There was a good chance that Albert Barker, a cousin from Salem, and he would be serving together once again. Cushing's ship, the *Quinnebaug*, was a wooden-screw sloop armed with five three-inch rifled-bore muzzle-loading guns.[1]

On July 21 Cushing informed Kate that the next day he would begin living on the *Quinnebaug*, where he would supervise the remaining preparations for departure. However, he hoped to travel to Fredonia over the weekend. He planned to reach Fredonia on Saturday afternoon, and he intended to remain until Monday evening. Meanwhile, he had gone to a theater in the Bowery that provided vaudevillian drama to an audience that included a considerable contingent of Irish youths, many of whom were newsboys. After a noisy theatrical performance, Cushing and a friend went to the Delmonico Restaurant.[2]

Abruptly, Cushing dramatically changed his plans. He sent Kate a letter from Washington in which he announced that "I concluded not to go out in the *Quinnebaug* and I told the Secretary [of the Navy, Gideon Wells] that I did not like her, and I disliked the station—I am detached, and will probably command the *Penobscot* in the Asiatic Squadron." If Cushing received his orders the next day, he intended to travel to New York on the evening train. Clearly he was unable to take his trip to Fredonia as soon as he had anticipated, but hoped that he would be able to stay for several days in the company of Kate.[3]

Cushing's instructions were unusual by ordinary canons. The *Penobscot* had disappeared in the West Indies. She had been sailing on the customary route taken by sailing vessels proceeding to India and Southeast Asia. When

Cushing found her, he was to relieve her captain, Lt. Commander Fleming, of his post and deliver him to the commander of the South Atlantic Squadron at Rio de Janeiro. Then Cushing should sail the *Penobscot* to Hong Kong to join the Asiatic Squadron. Obviously, Cushing would have to take a commercial steamer to St. Thomas in the Virgin Islands, then still in the possession of Denmark. If Cushing could not locate Fleming and his ship on any of the other islands in the Caribbean, he should take passage on a French or English steamer sailing to Rio de Janeiro. However, if the *Penobscot* had left Rio de Janeiro, Cushing should consult with the commander of the South Atlantic Squadron on the feasibility of returning to the United States or accepting a position in the South Atlantic Squadron.[4]

On July 31, 1867, Cushing proclaimed glad tidings of great joy to Kate. His departure had been postponed until August 22. Accordingly, he would be able to be with Kate for several weeks. He intended to spend several days with his sister Mary at Salem, and then he would hasten to Fredonia to see his mother and Kate.[5]

On August 21 Cushing wrote a brief note to Kate from the Astor House in New York to say that he was leaving for the tropics and China, as he had advised in his letter of July 31. Evidently, he had made two trips to Fredonia, for he now suggested that she might have seen him a third time, because on his way to the train station in neighboring Dunkirk his carriage had turned over, and he had to return to the stable to hire a replacement.[6]

Despite a hectic travel schedule during his unexpected break, Cushing did sail for St. Thomas, a Danish colony in the Virgin Islands. There he discovered that the missing ship might be on a small island called Santa Cruz (St. Croix), which was approximately forty miles from St. Thomas. Cushing then became a passenger on a small ship that was formerly a pilot boat in New York. He commented that it was "commanded by a black Captain; and with a crew that would make a black spot on a Sea of ink." He was careful to reciprocate the gracious deference that his host bestowed upon him, and as a result Cushing received the "very best quarters on board, much coveted by the passengers," which consisted of a small house on deck, called a dog house — "just large enough to sleep in; but with plenty of fresh air."[7]

During the night, Cushing received several good soakings from tropical showers, which he found refreshing. When daylight awakened him, he was greeted by a picturesque view of the harbor of Santa Cruz. He discovered Captain Fleming to be very ill and unable to walk. After breakfast at the hotel, Cushing went directly to the *Penobscot*, which was anchored in the harbor, and took command. The much relieved crew and officers were ordered to prepare for departure the following morning.[8]

Cushing then left the ship to spend the rest of the day and evening exploring the island. At five in the afternoon Cushing and his paymaster took a horseback ride on which they were accompanied by two attractive ladies who had traveled extensively in the United States. They rode, Cushing wrote, "over the finest roads that I ever saw." His account contained an almost lyrical description of the scenery that they encountered: "We rode some twenty miles through nothing but rich sugar plantations and the most picturesque of sugar villages. The roads were bordered on both sides by tall cocoa nut trees, set out some ten feet apart — and were worthy of belonging to the Ancient Romans."[9]

The next morning Captain Fleming was brought on a portable cot to the *Penobscot* and carried on board, and the ship sailed to St. Thomas, where the flagship *Susquehanna* and the sloop *Monongahela* were anchored. Admiral Palmer took charge of the prostrate Captain Fleming, leaving Cushing free to return to the United States, which he did four days later after loading five hundred tons of coal onto his ship, as well as an ample number of boxes of magnificent cigars and several cases of well-aged Santa Cruz rum.[10]

As his ship sailed steadily toward the naval yard at Washington, Cushing rigorously drilled the crew in managing sails, operating the guns, and using the cutlass effectively. Such constant practice also kept the officers on edge, for they would be held accountable for slovenly performance. "The officers all say that the men work twice as well since I took command," Cushing announced cheerfully, "and seem to be trying to do their very best." He added with a touch of pride that his exacting standards had caused him to be "detested in the Navy."[11]

In his effort to acquaint Kate with the routine and structure of the Navy, his pedagogic instruction provides useful insight for the modern student of the post–Civil War steam fleet. Cushing started with time. He lectured that daily time was anchored on eight bells, which was noon. However, when he announced that the time was eight bells, Cushing had to give that time his official recognition. The duty officer had to be told that the captain of the ship had stated that the correct time was definitely eight bells. If delayed, the arrival of noon would come later (or possibly not at all) on that particular day.[12]

On land, Sunday was devoted to rest, religious services, and family pursuits. In the Navy it was a time of inspection. At ten in the morning, there was a drum beat announcing a call to quarters, "and soon thereafter the executive officer came to the Cabin and reported that the 'ship is ready for inspection Sir.'" Cushing would reply, "Very well Sir." Then he reported, "And on deck I go in full uniform. I walk over the white decks and past shining cannon, followed by my staff; and along the line of sturdy seamen all dressed in white, with their rolling blue collars, and raked flat caps. As I man the line the officer of division orders 'Present Arms!' and the long row of gleaming cutlasses and the swords of the officers come up to a salute."[13]

Adhering to this procedure, Cushing proceeded through the entire ship. If he discovered a negligent "Jack Tar" whose shoes were not shined or whose neck handkerchief was missing, that luckless sailor was condemned to shovel coal, to scrape and clean the deck, and to clean the "bright work," which included the ornamental brass work on the deck and superstructure. After the inspection concluded, there was a general muster of the ship's company on the quarterdeck, where Cushing read the "Articles of War." At the conclusion of this reading each sailor, when his name was called, had to present himself with his cap in hand to the captain for another rigorous examination, and then he passed in review of a line of officers standing on the starboard side of the ship. Then the first lieutenant was commanded to "Pipe Down," which was the signal that the ship's company was dismissed. Sunday was over, and Cushing would retire to the solitude of his cabin, where he could gaze upon a small picture of Kate.[14]

He had ample opportunity to complete his educational lectures on naval customs and operations. He also tackled the problem of reliable communication on a ship. At this time, the advent of modern communication was still on the horizon. The most reliable and commonly used instrument remained the simple whistle, which sounded a "peculiar trill." Cushing explained, "These whistles are termed 'calls' and talk to a sailor in the fiercest storm, when the human voice could not be heard." He clarified that "a way up aloft is Jack — may be — in the black of night, and howling gales, amidst thunder and sleet, working for life, as the mast whistles through the air, and when his safety may depend on one rope made fast or let go at the proper second." Moreover, Cushing asserted that the sailor's "voice would not reach the deck amidst that terrific din — but high up through the streaking rigging and amidst the creaking spars rises to his anxious ears a shrill pipe that he knows at once and in a moment he comprehends his duty, and is safe." Cushing listed several other signals: one particular trill called the men to their meals; another to haul in some rope; another to stop hauling; and so on for hundreds of orders. Shipboard signals were largely the same as those employed in the age of Nelson.[15]

One is forced to speculate carefully on Cushing's sudden and unexpected affection for the young woman he met by chance at his sister's wedding in Fredonia. Until that time, as previously noted, he had pledged that he did not have the financial resources to contemplate marriage. For that reason, he had been anxious to disavow an alliance with a fiancée at Salem. It may well have been that the youthful and innocent Kate had awakened within him the passion of true love. If such is the case, he may have been blind to the awkward, and possibly embarrassing, position that she now occupied as his fiancée. Cushing's naval career had separated him from Fredonia for most of his adolescence and youthful manhood. He was literally a stranger. It was easy for him to define Fredonia as a backward rural community. Hence he wrote to Kate that "I often wonder if the social insects of Fredonia are through with their buzzing yet." He cried, "Poor little thing!" He charged that "it seems a pity that the place

Painting of Fredonia by Julia Parker Wilson Clarke showing the Common and the academy where the Cushing boys went to school.

has so little population; so they have so few reputations to attack." He added sharply, "At the rate they go on, their mutual characters will turn out of the battle very much in the condition of the famous fighting Kilkenny cats, nothing left on either side but a small piece of fur."

He told Kate, "You are like the ten men required saving Sodom from destruction. You are all that prevents me from leaving it for ever."[16] "Otherwise, if ever I saw a dirty mangy dog I would name it 'Fredonia,' if I discovered any particular mean, low creeping trick or lie I would make 'Fredonia' the adjective to describe it," he proclaimed. "And if any one asked me if I came from there I would lie in self defense and say no." Cushing concluded his diatribe with this declaration: "One has a right to preserve his life in any way — why not his reputation?"[17]

It may be surmised that Kate was bewildered by Cushing's intemperate outburst. As for Cushing, he should have recognized that he was engaged to a country sweetheart who might well be upset by some scurrilous gossip about her liaison with a dashing naval hero, who in the eyes of many of the righteous citizens was yet another Civil War upstart prone to tell tales of adventure and survival. However distressed Kate may have been at the jeers of some stalwarts of society, Fredonia and its environs were native territory. It was the world that she knew. Cushing ought to have offered her tender understanding and sympathy, not vitriolic sermons. Moreover, he should not have affirmed his integrity and honor. If they were obvious, they required no public defense from him. He did observe that Kate had become more reserved in her expressions of affection, and he noticed that she frequently charged Mary White as a major architect of malicious gossip. Mary White's uncle was a distinguished entrepreneur and doctor in Fredonia. He had prospered, and today his large home still serves as a fashionable hotel and inn, with portraits of Squire White and his wife displayed in the main entrance. Mary White claimed a close attachment to Cushing. If true, they must have engaged in a genuine juvenile fling. Throughout her courtship with Cushing, Kate continued to be tormented by Mary White, who ultimately gave up and married a local prospect.[18]

On the evening of September 10, after sailing approximately five days, Cushing was awakened abruptly from a pleasant slumber by a deck officer who informed him that the ship was caught in a furious squall. Cushing had to abandon any prospect of a sound night's sleep to shout orders necessary to keep the ship on course and afloat. When morning came, he had been able to navigate away from the powerful Gulf Stream of the Atlantic into sheltered waters in an inland passage guarded by the barrier islands of Hatteras. Although Cushing had escaped from the storms of the Atlantic, the persistent cloudy weather prevented him finding his actual location by use of a sextant. To be certain of the depth of the water, he used a "deep sea lead," which also dredged up sand and shells that suggested the particular section of the islands they were passing. Cushing remarked, "My judgment is that we are about thirty miles south of the stormy Cape Hatteras; or about one hundred and forty miles from Chesapeake Bay, where I wish to enter."[19]

On September 21, an anxious and "blue" Cushing wrote to Kate from Washington that he had not heard from her, but his mother had written to inform him that she had been told Kate was in Buffalo. Cushing confessed that "I shall indeed be sad, for I realize more and more daily, how much I love you — and I long to see you again." He claimed, "It is a craving of the heart that can only be satisfied, now that I am in the United Sates, by a visit to Fredonia." However, he could obtain a leave of absence only for a week; therefore, his visit to Fredonia would be short. He suggested that "between the 20th and 30th of this month," Kate could expect him. Then Cushing reported the all-important news: he had been given command of the reconditioned gunboat, the USS *Maumee*, which he was to sail to the Far East. From now on until the end of his assignment with the Asiatic Squadron, Cushing's cruise with the *Maumee* was intertwined with his romance with Kate Forbes.

Cushing did have a final rendezvous with Kate in Fredonia at the end of

September and into the first days of October. He returned to Washington on October 5. His visit to Fredonia was probably five or six days in duration. On October 6 he wrote to Kate to inform her that he would not be able to squeeze in any additional days to make yet another hasty trip to her side. Instead, it was more prudent that he should remain at the Navy Yard, where he could supervise the final preparation of the *Maumee* for her long voyage to the Far East.[20]

Before he made his trip, an apprehensive Cushing had sought to discover the cause for Kate's tepid response to his ardent declarations of enduring love for her. "You say," he lamented, "that you are overflowing with unpleasant Buffalo gossip, of which I presume I am the hero, but what they could manufacture there I certainly do not know — probably imported by Miss Mary White." He then confronted his nemesis by exclaiming, "May the Lord in his *infinite* mercy pardon that hopeless liar!" Cushing speculated that "there seems to be a strong and well-organized force that, from various motives, are determined to separate us, and are willing to risk their own Souls to do it — but as the Devil, in his own good time, will get them all, I can wait until final accounts are settled." He added, "Time will prove whether a gentleman and man of honor can rise above the fetid and envenomed clouds of falsehood and malice."[21]

Cushing did not hesitate to champion his integrity, for he charged that "if any person living dare to my face, to charge me with any act unbecoming in an officer and a gentleman — to impugn my courage, my truth or my morals, can look me in the eye and declare that I ever violated the dignity of manhood by drunkenness or vice — if any can affirm that there is any reason why I should not offer an untarnished hand and heart to you, a pure and good woman — then I will take off a uniform that I will be unworthy to wear, and will admit that I have sunk to the low grade of the moral bankrupts who malign me."[22]

Meanwhile, Cushing did find some relief from the torments of romance and the chores associated with preparing the *Maumee* for her commissioning. He was invited to dine with General Grant, and Governor Fenton of New York called on him. In addition, Cushing had a pleasant chat with General Hancock, who commanded the artillery unit in which his brother Alonzo had served at Gettysburg. He also mentioned that his younger brother Howard was in Washington arranging for his transfer to a cavalry regiment that was slated to be sent to fight belligerent Indian tribes. Cushing joked that he asked for a cutting of Howard's hair in case he got scalped. Tragically, Howard did perish in a gun battle against a band of hostile Indians.[23]

On October 7 Cushing assumed the command of the USS *Maumee*, another gunboat of a genre similar to that of the *Penobscot*. The *Maumee* belonged to the Kansas class of gunboats that had been constructed in 1862–1863. They all had steam engines, although of varying designs, and one funnel.[24]

The *Maumee* had been decommissioned on June 17, 1865. However, on October 9, 1867, she was recommissioned at the Washington Navy Yard, where she was being prepared to join the Asiatic Squadron of the Navy. Although the *Maumee* had been designed originally as a two-masted sloop, she had received an additional mast after the Civil War. She had a displacement of 836 tons and a crew of 154. Her length was 179 feet and her beam was 30 feet. Her Ericsson steam engine, which operated on a vibrating-lever principle, provided steam for a single cylinder with two pistons that moved in tandem. It was a simple and efficient machine, but required careful maintenance. However, it could deliver a speed of eight to eleven knots. The *Maumee*'s bunkers could store 120 tons of coal. After the Civil War, her principal armament was an 11-inch Dahlgren gun that was placed on a pivot between the funnel and foremast. On her broadsides there were two 32-pound smoothbore guns. A note in the Cushing papers states that the *Maumee* had fourteen portholes for guns and that she carried eight guns of various calibers. She drew 12 feet of water and was 31 feet wide. (This brief description is in the handwriting of Kate Cushing.)[25]

Cushing continued to supply Kate with information on his imminent departure on the *Maumee*. He announced cheerfully, "My carpets and furniture came down today from the City; all very nice — and I am going to take great comfort in my cozy cabin," adding that "my cook proves to be a good one, and my Steward is a model." There was, however, a snag on the appointment of a secretary. Houghton Wheeler declined an invitation for the position. Consequently, Cushing revealed that "I have sent on the appointment to Mr. Higgins — who will have to be here in a week if he wishes to go."[26] Charles Higgins was the son of a wealthy engineer who had made a fortune in rebuilding destroyed rail lines in southern states as Union armies acquired greater control. He now constructed and managed successful street-car systems in local communities. His family lived in a commanding residence at the head of the most prominent street, Central Avenue, in Fredonia.

Cushing hinted that quite probably his route to the Far East would be directed to the Cape Verde Islands and then turn directly toward the West to Rio de Janeiro. This was a time-honored route for sailing ships, for it took advantage of prevailing currents and wind patterns. He was sufficiently sure of this routing that he advised Kate to send her letters to Rio de Janeiro, where he could collect them. Three days later he reported that he had invested most of the day receiving several survey boards and also reviewing a respectable number of official documents. He informed Kate, "My preserved fruit and vegetables consisting of five hundred and twenty eight cans came on yesterday. The expense charges were about fifty dollars." Once more, he wrote, "My cabin is being elegantly furnished — mirrors, carpets, chairs and all are selected by me at Government expense." He, moreover, revealed that he continued to be the recipient of many dinner invitations, but he accepted only a few. He was now anxious to commence his journey.[27]

Cushing calculated that he had a roster of twenty officers, including himself, and he cordially saluted them as a "very good set ... though," he gushed, "let me modestly state that the Captain is the best of the lot, in consequence of his training under a certain dear Admiral in Western New York." There seems to have been an uneasy relationship in Cushing's mind between the two pillars of his devotion — his naval career and his love for Kate. A few days later he angrily berated Kate, rebuking her with a harsh accusation that "I just intend to write a note today to say that that I don't think you are very kind to me." He whined, "Why do you not write? Do you think that, when so near you, I can live upon one letter in eight or ten days? Or is croquet so very fascinating that your time is entirely occupied?" He queried, "Do my frequent letters 'bore' you, and is your silence a hint to me not to be troublesome?" Cushing declared that "I can take a hint, as the man said when he was knocked down — but if you do not regret such treatment your heart must be made of stone."[28]

Cushing's truculent tone was undoubtedly prompted by a severe cold and sore throat, a malady that was to haunt him throughout his Asian tour. As for Kate's stone heart, Cushing was probably unable to comprehend that a 20-year old innocent in rural Fredonia would have considerable difficulty in abandoning a croquet match to become acquainted with the science and routine of the Navy of the United States.

It may be that Cushing had rashly attempted to unite two diametrically opposed propositions and make them the cornerstone of his future. When he succumbed to the youthful beauty of a vivacious Kate Forbes during the month of June 1867, he was negotiating for a ship command, which would advance his naval career. By moving forward in rank and experience, his compensation would increase. However, such an ambition could well be threatened if a wife wished him to remain on land for an extended period. Advancement was on the ocean blue for a young and ambitious officer. Cushing had enlisted the aid of S.P. Lee, a senior Navy commander under whom he had served during the Civil War, and Admiral Josh Smith, a cousin belonging to his New England connection. Gideon Wells, still the secretary of the Navy, was inclined favorably to aid Cushing. Probably, Cushing recklessly counted on the same dramatic initiative that had served so well during the Civil War to carry him safely through any confrontation between the two dominant institutions of his future.[29]

On October 16, 1867, Cushing received from the Department of the Navy his order for sailing to the Far East. His destination was Hong Kong, where he was to report to Admiral Bell. His order stipulated, "You will proceed via the Cape Verde Islands, Rio de Janeiro and the Cape of Good Hope — using sail to the best possible advantage and resorting to steam only in case of necessity or in the calm regions near the equator. When you use coal you will exercise strict economy, and note in the steam log in accordance with Section 6 Regulation circular 6, the reasons for resorting to steam and the amount of coal used."[30]

Cushing wrote that very day to Kate to instruct her to send letters to Rio de Janeiro by the steamer that would depart from New York on November 22 for the Brazilian capital. Somewhat sheepishly, he added, "I retract my late growling note written ten days after I left you, and when I had heard from you but once, and was actually longing to get a letter." Cushing advised Kate to send several more letters to Washington, because his departure was being delayed for at least a week. A test of his machinery had not been satisfactory, and repairs would proceed slowly, thanks to red tape.[31]

On a happy note, Cushing announced that "Mr. Higgins and his Son illuminated Washington by their presence night before last — and were at the Navy Yard yesterday." Moreover, Cushing wrote that young Higgins was exploring the recently enlarged national capital. However, Cushing revealed that Charles Higgins "would in a short time be in uniform and living onboard." Cushing commented further, "The adverse opinion of Fredonians rather seems to elevate the young man in my opinion, than otherwise." He concluded his report on the citizenry from Fredonia by emphasizing that once again he was dining with the Risley family, which was prominent in Fredonian society.[32]

Turning to the events in Washington, Cushing observed that the city was filling up with members of Congress and their partisans. His reporting is a reminder that he shared many of the commonly accepted platitudes of his day, which have been repudiated in contemporary American society. He should not be judged by today's more enlightened standards, but rather as an ordinary supporter of the conventional mores of his age, as in his claim that "Rebels want laws made; niggers want every thing from land and votes up to a darkey President; and women are on the rampage about female suffrage."[33]

Cushing reinforced his latter assertion with an anecdote. He had been staying at a Washington hotel while work was being completed on his ship. A porter delivered a message from a visitor who was waiting to see him in the hotel lounge. Hastily, Cushing made himself presentable. "Imagine my dismay," he wrote to Kate, "when encountered by a strong minded female of about twenty-five sweet summers who declared herself an agent of the female and universal suffrage association, and who immediately demanded in the name of Woman that I should subscribe $5 to the noble Cause which she represented."[34]

Flummoxed, Cushing at first reacted with a thought that "I strongly urge upon her the propriety of going home to nurse the babies, if she had any, or if not to look diligently after an affinity; but what I <u>did</u> let the enclosed receipt declare — I surrender at discretion." He contributed, but he remained fearful that a newspaper would print his name in a list of those who had endorsed this organization and its mission. Although he allowed himself to be caught in such a predicament, on account of his inability to resist importunities from attractive ladies, happily, his weakness had little occasion to strike in Washington. "The ladies of Washington are a very impolite set," he complained. He explained his vexation by writing that "I got up nine times the other evening in one trip from the Navy Yard to give nine ladies my seat in the horse car; and was not once thanked." He revealed that his response in the future would be "to get seated alongside of the blackest darkey in the car." Consequently, he was certain that "the delicate wearers of crinoline [would] decline to accept the Sacrifice with a toss of the head that is reverse of graciousness."[35]

Cushing, however, was far too preoccupied with the hectic activity associated with the impending departure of the *Maumee* to concentrate on any reformation of the feminine population of the national capital. Although he continued to accept the hospitality of the Risley family from Fredonia, he reduced his social activity to a marginal level. He did appreciate the amusing commentary from Kate on the cursory account that Charles Higgins had written on Cushing's recent activity. Cushing gave Kate carte blanche to continue her intelligence work. "If I had feared it, in the least," he explained, "I trust that I am smart enough to have left said Charles at home." Yet Cushing warned, "But if his Mama repays my kindness to her Son by indulging in the manufacture of any gossip, it will go hard with the family heir." Cushing suggested to Kate that "if you know Mr. Higgins, and talk to him, he can tell you all about my ship." Proudly, Cushing boasted, "She is a beauty; and in every respect a good one."[36]

Cushing was unable to push the intrusion of Fredonia gossip aside. Probably, he should have sought someone from his Salem and Boston connections. It would be a responsible conjecture that he hoped to erode an undercurrent of skepticism and envy of the Civil War valor of a parvenu branch of the Cushing dynasty. Kate had received her information from a local tailor, Philo Stevens, who had made a tidy fortune by selling inexpensive suits to discharged veterans of the Civil War. Stevens thought well of himself and emerged as a source of confidential news and counsel. "Your informant, Mr. Stevens, was not correct in stating that Mr. Higgins was in my State Room," Cushing wrote. Instead, Cushing explained, "He is going to mess in my Cabin, and is on my Staff—but his stateroom is one of two which I have." Cushing commented further that "he seems to be a very nice, quiet, unobtrusive fellow, and will, I doubt not give satisfaction." "Of course," Cushing confided, "I treat him as kindly as I can and I am not as strict with him as with those who better understand the discipline and etiquette of the Service." Cushing concluded his narration with a boast that does not ring true: "It may be vanity in me, but I am not afraid to have a reporter of all my doings onboard or in foreign ports—as I am not one of those who is a gentleman only when he is known—I shall be proud of criticism."[37]

As his ship was virtually ready to sail, the *Maumee* became a centerpiece for Washington social excursions. Cushing found himself in the role of a gracious host who made polite conversation to countless charming young ladies as he served cold salads and glasses of wine. On the other hand, he was careful to tell Kate that his pleasure in the convivial festivities was muted by the vision of the face that he really wished might be found in the crowd. His melancholy did not prevent him from grooming Kate for her eventual attendance at such polished social gatherings. He insisted that she be careful to avoid speaking in rural vernacular; pure enunciation was mandatory in cosmopolitan society. Moreover, she should be attentive to Miss Star's piano instructions. Cushing was on a perilous course in lecturing Kate on decorum, for there is an axiom that women resent masculine advice on their behavior and mannerisms.

The following day was cold and rainy, but Cushing could not escape his social chores. A crowd of insistent young ladies demanded that they should be permitted to board the *Maumee*. For the whole day they occupied Cushing's cabin, where they consumed ample portions of chicken salad accompanied by fruit, and Cushing observed that "champagne was not naturally repugnant to their feelings."[38]

On October 30, 1867, the *Maumee* was inspected and declared ready for duty. On November 1 Cushing left Washington, and on the following morning he arrived at the Norfolk Navy Yard, where the engine of the *Maumee* was to be repaired. Cushing did explore some of his former haunts on shore, where he "was surprised at the changes which peace has brought about." He recorded, "Instead of the old depressed and ruined City that I left three years ago I found streets filled with a bustling busy crowd, and all was life and action." Unfortunately, Cushing observed that "the majority of the people are returned rebels, and 'the man who sank the Albemarle' caught many a glance that might have been dangerous if changed into a sword thrust." Cushing responded to hostile stares by moving proudly through the well-populated streets. Moreover, he allowed Higgins to visit Richmond. Cushing did receive a cheerful and unexpected letter from Kate, who had boldly sent it to Norfolk, though she feared that the dead letter office would be its ultimate destination.[39]

Cushing preferred to remain on the *Maumee*, where he could greet his former comrades, among whom were many who had been his classmates at Annapolis. He was shocked to learn that in a class of one hundred and twenty, only fourteen remained true to their calling after eleven bitter years.

It is surprising that Cushing remembered fondly his days at the Naval Academy, for he had been compelled to retire on the eve of completing his studies. Many of the pranks that his compatriots and he had staged had the character of juvenile behavior. On the other hand, the academy was still in its infancy, and the revolutionary changes in technology were still a glimmer on the horizon. When they became undeniably apparent, curriculum and instruction at Annapolis would be transformed.

Cushing and his guests reviewed the official Register of Naval Officers, which revealed that "some had long since retired; others turned traitor to their flag; many had died abroad; and, here and there a few had recorded — 'Killed in battle' — Fourteen out of a hundred and twenty!" Musing on this startling statistic, Cushing wrote, "It seemed strange to us that we should be of the few who, in the vicissitudes of eleven years, have held true to the path into which so many joyous hearts entered. — And I am sure that their hearts warmed as mine did into a more than brotherly affection, as we saw how time had spared us in the general sense." An undoubtedly tearful Cushing announced, "And so we parted; and when we meet again, some of us will be old and gray; and more gone from the old 'Class of 57' — but I shall not soon forget the comfort I have felt today, in clasping the strong, manly hands of those whose inmost nature I know; and whose honor is above suspicion — brothers — not in blood — but in study and association in gale and in battle — and last but not least in loyalty to the grand old flag we loved and honored in boyhood. God bless them! say I."[40]

On November 4 Cushing celebrated his 25th birthday on the *Maumee*. It was a somewhat subdued affair, since he had promised Kate that he would abstain from alcoholic beverages. Evidently, she had been caught up in a fervent temperance movement, during which a number of passionate crusaders smashed kegs found in the village saloons. Cushing honored the tradition of naval hospitality, and kept his pledge to his fiancée by a sleight of hand. He ordered his steward to fill a carafe with cold tea, which he identified as sherry wine to his guests, claiming that it was a select vintage he reserved for his private use. He soberly wrote in his diary, "My birthday. I am now twenty-five years old. I must give a jolly dinner upon so important a day, but as I do not drink wine or liquor, I am afraid that my jollity would not be in pace with my intended guests who do." He confessed that "I get bantered a great deal about refusing to drink so I have my steward make a decanter of cold tea, which looks just like Sherry wine." Cushing admitted ruefully that it was "a shameful trick but I must keep my promise to myself and to 'somebody else.'"[41]

Several days later, Cushing received a visitor, a merchant in Norfolk, who had served as an officer on the *Albemarle*. Minutes before Cushing had had an opportunity to launch his torpedo, he had come under fire, and he responded with his pistol. One of his bullets grazed the head of a Confederate officer, who later recovered. The merchant wanted to see the Union hero as a curiosity of recent history. He had no wish for revenge; his interview was a pleasant exchange of opposing narratives of events during that dramatic engagement. As Cushing was chatting with his guest, his chief engineer appeared to announce that his machinery had been installed. The *Maumee* was ready to sail.[42]

As he prepared to start his long journey, Cushing stated, "I have commenced to keep a journal of the Cruise, and intend to continue it; and if you are a good girl," he admonished Kate, "and write me a great many nice letters you shall read it when I get back."[43]

The next day, November 8, he wrote a brief farewell letter to Kate in which he reported, "It is just coming on night, and we are going out upon old Ocean. In the morning a hundred miles will separate me from my Country; and those will grow into thousands rapidly. This is goodbye, my precious love — my last to any one before sailing." Cushing cried that "at this last moment it tears my heart to leave you — If my eyes do not shed tears my soul does." He added a short commentary: "Oh Kate, dear darling Kate! May God bless and keep you — yes — us — until we meet again. All my hopes are bound upon you, and with all my heart I ask you to love and remember me." He stopped his letter with a crisp note that it was time to drop the pilot.[44]

Chapter 3

Route to the Far East by Sail and Steam to Match the Power of Ocean Water

At 7:00 P.M. the *Maumee* entered the Atlantic. The following day the sea was exceptionally violent. A number of the crew succumbed to seasickness, including Cushing's steward and the paymaster. Glassware was broken and crockery smashed. It was virtually impossible for one to eat on a table without spilling the contents of one's plate on nearby companions. During the next several days the sea became tranquil and a stormy sky gave way to sunny rays. Cushing wrote, "Ceased steaming this afternoon, am much pleased with the handsome manner that the *Maumee* sails and behaves in so rough a sea."[1]

Two days later, on November 12, Cushing stated that he had "overhauled and over board most of my old letters." Obviously caught up in a swirl of passionate reminiscences, he bade "good bye to the flirtations that they chronicled—I did not waste a sigh upon them." He added piously, "The measles, whooping cough and flirtations are all incidental to the various stages of youth." On the same day he had his mustache shaved off and his hair cut short. He noted that "my officers, most of whom with their age and braids, might be taken for the personal friends of Noah, seem quite astonished at my juvenile appearance this afternoon." Cushing speculated that "if the nineteen of them were thrown up with me at their head, and a stranger came aboard, I wonder whom he would select as Captain."[2]

Cushing noted that the *Maumee* was nearly eight hundred miles from Fort Monroe and that during the previous night the ship had sailed past the "Bermuda Islands." Although Cushing was confident that he had the respect of his officers and crew, and he was pleased with the performance of his ship, he could not dismiss the image of Kate. "Read 'somebody's letters,'" he confided to himself, and then promised that "I wouldn't part with them if the box containing them would be filled with diamonds in exchange." Then he coyly hinted that "of course 'somebody' is a 'he'— and I will think of 'him' often as I smoke my pipe through the long tropical evenings."[3]

Several days later the sea was sufficiently calm for Cushing to order a cannon and small arms drill for the crew, on which occasion he estimated that the ship had averaged over 180 miles a day. On November 19 he recorded a pleasant day and the news that the crew and ship continued to perform creditably. "Here way out in the Ocean," Cushing mused, "free from the World of Nations, I have a World of my own, moved and govern[ed] by my will with none to check it." Weather, however, could prove to be a decisive check. "I am, indeed," Cushing proclaimed, "Monarch of all I survey," but "with one exception — this fickle wind, which like a woman's changeful fancies [sic] scorning all control blows where it listeth."[4] On Thanksgiving Day he wrote that he had enjoyed a good dinner and a pleasant day. On the first day of December he recorded that the *Maumee* had passed the Cape Verde Islands, and a week later that "we are only a few hundred miles from the coast of Africa — Thirty days out from Chesapeake Bay."[5]

On December 11 the *Maumee* crossed the equator, which provided a perfect excuse to celebrate with the customary visit of Neptune and his retinue to seek out and punish those who had not given him homage on a previous occasion. Cushing chronicled this raucous event in detail. The liturgy of this ceremony seems to have been firmly established, for the proceedings were quite similar to those still performed on the decks of modern ships. There are variations in paint and costumes, but splashing and dunking are consistent elements of the ritual.[6]

On December 21 Cushing gave permission to the crew "to organize a troop of 'Nigger Minstrels' for the entertainment of guests etc." "The leader of them was 'middle man' in a company of them ashore," Cushing had learned. "I don't know how he came to ship as 'coal heaver'— but he is a comical fellow."[7] Six days later Cushing wrote, "Christmas come and gone, and not yet in Rio." Happily, that afternoon Cape Rio came into sight. Hence Cushing expected to anchor early the following morning "after a voyage of 49 days." Alas, however, the mail steamer on its homeward journey passed the *Maumee* as she slipped toward her anchorage. Anticipating the arrival of the *Maumee* and her complement at Rio were the flagship *Guerriere* and the sloops *Pawnee, Huron, Quinnebaug, Idaho* and *Wasp*.[8] An hour after arriving on December 28, the flagship, accompanied by the *Wasp* and *Quinnebaug*, left to sail to Montevideo, the Falklands, and then the Cape of Good Hope. Cushing "was much disappointed, as I especially expected to have a good time with the officers — especially Barker." He consoled himself, however, by receiving courtesy visits from officers of the French and English warships in the harbor. In the evening he went to see a French opera. He noted that the prima donna had a good voice and a "pretty" face. After the performance, Cushing went to the Hotel aux Freres Provencal to dine. He wrote that "the Carrerona salad was superb."[9]

On Sunday December 29, the senior naval officer of the squadron, Captain Woolsey, and the captains of the *Huron* and *Idaho* called on Cushing, who later went ashore to dine at the same hotel that he had visited the night before. He again attended the opera and then had a late "supper," during which he recalled that it was "hard work to keep from drinking, but did not take a drop 'for all that.'"[10] On the following day he supervised the reloading of empty coal bunkers and barren storage bins with provisions. Seventy-eight pounds of beef and vegetables were loaded on to the *Maumee*, and it received 80 tons of coal from a tender. Eighteen tons of coal had been carried on the previous day. While this activity was under way, the commanding officer of HMS *Egremont* paid a courtesy visit.[11]

The hustle and bustle of supplying his ship with the necessities of ocean voyaging did not dampen Cushing's relish in the ceremonial obligations of port etiquette. He put on full dress uniform and called on English and French admirals: "Was much amused with the old Coons astonishment at so young an Officer being in command of a foreign cruiser. Patched up my conversation with the Frenchmen in English, Spanish and French and had quite a jolly time."[12]

He also made an excursion to the public gardens, which he found quite beautiful. He observed, moreover, that the outskirts of Rio were well planned, with wide streets and well-constructed houses. "The contrast between the wide, clean streets there, and the dirty narrow ones of the business portion," he acknowledged, "was enough to correct one from any former opinion that no one in Brazil knew how to live." Initially, Cushing had been very censorious of the mean ambiance of Rio, writing to Kate, "There are none of the wide streets that characterize other modern cities; and shade trees are an unknown luxury." He had also observed that "the paved roads slope down to a channel in the middle; and through this runs all the dirt and refuse of the Brazilian Metropolis — generating an odor that American tongues, influenced by American noses, refuse to compliment."[13]

Cushing likewise encountered strange social customs. At the opera house, which was called the Alcazar, one could enjoy operettas and burlesques, "but while all the first men go there, few or none of the elite of your sex attend." "The women spectators," he had observed, "are generally black-eyed Spanish 'Delilahs' who laugh and chat with any one — Some are handsome and public attendance upon them by men of standing is a matter of no surprise or comment." He did notice, however, that "the inhabitants are decidedly mixed — English Americans, the melancholy-looking Spaniards, the homely Portuguese, and the class — larger than all — made up of a mixture of Portuguese, Africans, native Indians, and assorted minorities — generally called a Brazilian." Cushing was also impressed with the generous variety of tropical fruit, much of which was alien to the diets of those who lived on the prairie plains of North America. Pomegranates, pineapples, bananas, grapes, and oranges were ordinary staples that were both luxuries and exotic fruits to be savored as a rare treat.[14]

While exploring the market, Cushing came upon a remarkable collection of exotic birds and small animals. As a result, he made an impulsive purchase of a small monkey, which he hoped would be a good companion for Fanta, a small black and white terrier that was the gift of David Parker, a Fredonian who had been in the U.S. postal service in Northern Virginia, but who had been relieved of his office by President Johnson, probably on the pretext that he was too closely associated with the Republican Party. Cushing wrote to Kate, "I bought a small monkey as a playmate for my pup Fanta — and they are fast friends now." For Kate, he was sending some earrings that were made of polished green beetles, obviously dead, encased in gold mounts. Cushing claimed that they were very popular in Rio.[15]

Despite a favorable impression of Rio, after his extended survey of the city's environs, New Year's Day proved to be disagreeable. "It is too hot to enjoy life in Rio," Cushing complained, and he further proclaimed that "I am anxious to get under way; as society is all broken up and it is dull." The New Year was not given much honor by the citizens of Rio, he commented, but the emperor, Don Pedro, had returned to the capital. On inspecting the emperor, Cushing reported that "he is a fine looking man — and a smart and scientific one." Meanwhile, he supervised the loading of 14 tons of coal, and later he received 125 tons of anthracite coal. His first and second engineers confirmed an invoice for this shipment.[16]

His gloomy reaction to the passing scene did not discourage Cushing from purchasing a number of photographs of the city and environs. He did not neglect to provide for the feminine contingent of his family circle, for in addition to the celebrated "Brazilian Bugs," he added a fan displaying feathers from hummingbirds.[17] On January 2, he received on board a delegation of officers from English and French ships "who had just found out who I am, and came to congratulate me on my position and my success during our war."[18] The next day Cushing "let the men buy a dozen musical instruments to form a band and a Negro Musical troop." He also had the opportunity to ride out into the countryside, where he was "charmed by the beauty of the plantations and tropical verdure."[19]

Unfortunately, his pleasant meandering and jolly receptions with colleagues in his own fleet, as well as those from foreign navies, were marred by the necessity of suspending his executive officer "for neglect of duty." "He is about 35," Cushing recorded, "and one of the kind that whitens around the gills when he gets in a passion." However, he allowed half of his crew to have a 24-hour shore leave.[20] On January 3 he acquired two additional crewmen to replace several members of the crew who preferred not to renew their contracts, and he was compelled to dispatch a launch to return a straying seaman, a mission that was successful. On January 5 Cushing wrote in the log book that three warring members of the crew had failed to return to the *Maumee*.[21] These skirmishes with thoughtless members of the crew did not prevent Cushing from granting shore leave for 48 hours to 27 crewmen on January 6.[22]

Before he left Rio de Janeiro, Cushing had an unusual opportunity to exercise his flair for the flamboyant impulse. On stepping from his gig to gain the dock, a cutter carrying several Brazilian officers unexpectedly rammed into the side of Cushing's launch. He immediately returned to the *Maumee* to put on his dress uniform and returned to land to seek out the culprits, who proved to be Brazilian officers involved in a court martial. On finding the site of this proceeding, Cushing entered the room to demand an apology. The officers replied that they regretted the incident, but they were unaware of the provenance of the launch or the rank of its passenger. Cushing's retort was that the flag of the United States of America was on the stern and that on the bow was a commander's pennant. He promptly received a full apology.[23]

On January 9, 1868, at five in the afternoon, Commander Cushing and his complement bade farewell to Rio de Janeiro as they exchanged cheers with the USS *Pawnee* and the French warship *Magicienne*. From the *Pawnee* came the hymn "Hail Columbia" as the *Maumee* departed on a 4,000-mile voyage to Cape Town. For Cushing, sadly, the disappearing outline of the spectacular harbor of Rio de Janeiro did not spark pleasant reminiscences of his visit: "I am disgusted with the big City of Rio and its 500,000 people, because of numerous things—and I don't want to see it again."[24]

Probably Cushing's disenchantment with Rio de Janeiro and its inhabitants contributed to his barbed response to Kate's request for guidance on the propriety of Oliver Wendell Homes' celebrated *The Autocrat of the Breakfast Table* as appropriate literature for young women. Apparently, Kate had been censured by the Reverend Mr. Arey, the rector of Trinity Church, who had questioned the wisdom of her reading this popular series of lectures by the distinguished professor at Harvard University. Unfortunately, this book had been given by Cushing to Kate. "I must say that I am astonished at Mr. Arey's objection to Oliver Wendell Holmes and the 'Autocrat'—I thought Mr. A had more common sense." Cushing admitted, "My advice to you conflicts most forcibly with his; for I say read it—and you will find many a good moral."[25]

"Holmes' Professor at the breakfast table," Cushing acknowledged, "treats sacred or theological subjects, and might perhaps be objectionable to a strict Churchman; but the Autocrat is simply a jumble of good things—little literary appetizers—that can do no more harm than a hearty laugh." Cushing went on the offensive. He charged that "at least Mr. Arey, in order to juge [*sic*] books, must have read them — and by his advice treats you as a weaker mind than his own — forgetting the Socratic business that gagged him long since." Cushing delivered his counsel in a pithy summation. "I want you to let me know," he said, that "since you ask my advice, whose influence you yield to — I am more interested in you in every way than he can ever be and I feel insulted at his remarks about a book that I gave you." However, Cushing concluded his lecture on a conciliatory note: "And so, Mademoiselle, you can do as you please." He concluded softly that "I trust however that in thinking it over you will exonerate me from a charge of ill temper."[26]

There was no opportunity for his melancholy to disappear on the following day. On becoming ill, his steward inadvertently dropped overboard almost a full bushel of Cushing's much-prized collection of oranges and limes. While he was at dinner, his newly acquired monkey "came suddenly down the Skylight, plumps into my soup plate, and from there with a leap into my butter." It was, Cushing thought, "a strong hint to me about his dinner and my impoliteness at not inviting him down." The matter was settled promptly when Cushing "thrashed the little villain with a pen handle, and trust that my hint was as good as his."[27]

His disposition had little chance to improve, for on January 11 the ship's engine broke down, and though the sea was quite calm (at least for the time being), sails would be the source of propulsion. He noted piously that it was "just three Months since I took a drop of wine or liquor" "Don't see," he remarked, "that it makes any difference in my health, but it does, somewhat to my pocket." He also lamented, "I find that I spent too much money in Rio and will look out in the future."[28]

However, over the next several days, with her engine repaired, the *Maumee* chugged along at a fair speed against strong headwinds to make 190 miles on January 13. Cushing took a southward course to align his ship with "the strong westerly wind that blows below trade winds and shores latitudes."[29]

On January 21 Cushing wrote that he had succumbed to a severe fever: "For four days I have been confined to my bed with fever, the first attack that I can remember." "I was out of my head a portion of the time," he recorded, "and felt very sick all through it." He concluded by saying, "I have often said that I would like a fever just for variety — to know how it feels — I am satisfied — No more experiments if you please." Moreover, Cushing had encountered the unforgiving torment of a debilitating illness. "To come out of the fictitious infinity of delirium, marred by brain contact with its extravagances," he confessed, only to survey the hard landscape of a utilitarian cabin with no hope of loving consolation — "that is misery indeed." There was modest cheer, nevertheless, in the report that the *Maumee*, under sail, had made 180 miles, even without anticipated encouragement from westerly winds.[30]

On this same day, Cushing recorded a singular tale in his diary:

This evening passed the group of islands that lie so cut off from the rest of the world, in the very center of the Atlantic Ocean. "Trista da Cunha" is 8300 feet in elevation above the water and is settled by a small English colony that voluntarily remained there one time. An English Army Sergeant with two or three companions first left a ship then and lived in "Robinson Crusoe" style among wild birds, wild pigs and goats that had sprung from some left by an exploring ship early in the century. Once in the while ships would touch there — whalers and others — and furnished supplies in exchange for these animals. Then one would go off on a ship and get a wife or his family down there — then another, until quite a prosperous colony was formed, with the Sergeant as Governor. Once a year now, the English Gov't sends out a ship to them with supplies — and this is the only time that they can be sure of seeing any of the outside world. Now the old soldier is dead, and his son-in law, a Connecticut Yankee, holds the reins of this stupendous Government.[31]

Nine days later after narrating his tale of a primitive Shangri-La encircled by the mists and waters of the Atlantic, Cushing's ship anchored in the harbor of Cape Town. The long haul across the Atlantic had taken twenty days and thirteen hours. Cushing promptly left his ship for the comfort and pleasures of the Royal Hotel in order to speed his recovery "by exercise and change of life." He was given a stateroom that had been last occupied by Prince Alfred, a son of Queen Victoria who was serving in the Royal Navy.[32]

After a splendid dinner, Cushing went to the Civil Service Club, where he took "tiffin" (tea) with Judge Pringle and Mr. Lerates, American consular officials. Later in the evening he was introduced to some of the society ladies of Cape Town. The next morning, he rode out before breakfast and then made several protocol visits, including one to the governor of the colony in full dress uniform. In turn, he received several calls from British army and navy officers, a social event that included a lengthy dinner marked by "great jollity."[33]

On February 1 Cushing was again up early for a gallop before breakfast. Later in the day he arranged a dinner party on the ship for a number of his new acquaintances, serving chicken salad accompanied by a selection of wines. After the departure of his male guests, Judge Pringle escorted a troop of female guests to visit the *Maumee*. Both gentlemen and ladies were entertained by music provided by the ensemble for which Cushing had bought instruments. When these daytime ventures concluded, Cushing went ashore to enjoy "a merry evening."[34] Obviously, Cushing had abandoned his temperance pledge to Kate, and he also had reasoned that loyalty to his beloved did not prevent him from enjoying the charms of feminine society in the Cape Colony. At any rate, such occasions were undoubtedly well chaperoned.

On February 2 Cushing and three companions were taken by a handsome barouche pulled by an impressive team of horses to Constantia, a large estate twelve miles from Cape Town, where they were greeted by the proprietor, Mr. Clutie, and his family. The principal industry of this estate, which had been owned by this family for some 150 years, was the production of wine. Sheltered from the rays of the sun by a grove of gigantic oak trees, the great house offered a sweeping vista of orchards and vineyards extending to the edge of a blue ocean. It was, Cushing proclaimed, "one of the finest that it has been my fortune to see."[35]

As one entered the great hall of the mansion, a ferocious leopard with flashing eyes and white fangs challenged further passage; the elder Mr. Clutie had shot this formidable adversary thirty years earlier on the estate. The walls of the great hall were decorated with the trophies of the hunt, "so different from what we see in these days of furs and feathers." Although he may not have realized it, Cushing was introduced to the baronial country house that was still a dominant feature of the English landscape. The image of these stately structures had been installed on the South African terrain of tropical vegetation and threatening beasts that had long vanished from European view. Yet a jarring juxtaposition of the well-ordered panorama of Europe against the raw outline of a land that continued to exhibit vestiges of its primitive nature had, at least superficially, been reconciled. "The whole drive to and from Cape Town was very picturesque," Cushing observed, "[s]ometimes leading for miles through rows of great trees that formed a complete arch over our heads — since the prevailing south east winds caused one row to lean as they grew, and thus completed the leafy screen."[36]

Although Cushing's social adventures kept to a steady drum beat, he did interrupt their rhythm to attend Anglican service according to the liturgy of the "high church," and he "heard a good, sensible sermon." He then went to the Club for some "tiffin." "I observe here," he commented, "that the people manage to get two hearty dinners a day, by calling one of them (at 1 P.M.) 'tiffin' and the other at 7 P.M. dinner." Cushing further warned that "'tiffin' or lunch here, is a spread such as would pass, anywhere as a first class dinner." The next day, he had a jolly good time with officers from a French line of battleship at his hotel, took a sober excursion to the library and museum, and then dined in his full dress uniform with the officers of the 99th Artillery Regiment at their mess. He emerged from this latter event triumphant. "By 3 A.M.," he recalled, he had "laid out most of the 20 red coats drunk as lords."[37] He was sufficiently revived the following day to undertake an excursion into the countryside to visit Clairmont, another country house, where he did not hesitate to give his hosts "my candid opinion about the final settlement of the Alabama claims." Apparently, his frank commentary caused no ill feeling, for he "met several pretty young ladies — gave them some Brazilian bugs [Brazilian women's jewelry] but no carte de visite, as requested — but did leave my autograph."[38]

The birthday of the sultan of Turkey provided Cushing with an introduction to a faith that then had scant presence in Europe and no demonstrable appearance in the United States. The Mohammedan population, mostly from

Malay, celebrated the birthday of the most prominent political figure of the Islamic universe with considerable jubilation. Within the Mohammedan community, "streets were hung with flowers and banners, as was the Chief Mosque," Cushing reported, and, moreover, "Arabic inscriptions were written on all shades of silk — and the whole appearance was decidedly oriental." "In the evening," he noted further, "the Mosque was illuminated; in front was the name of the Sultan in golden letters — surrounded by variegated lamps."[39]

Before leaving Cape Town, Cushing indulged in a shopping spree, during which he purchased some books and acquired several exotic articles, including a robe fabricated from tiger skins, which was called a "Karoos," and another, which had been sewn together from the coats of golden jackals.[40] Shortly before departing, Cushing gave a magnificent reception on the *Maumee* for his hosts. "The popularity of the officers of the United States Navy has become proverbial here, and certainly that reputation was ably supported by the elegant reception of the other evening," a newspaper article announced. This account stated that "the whole ship was decorated with flags and bunting," and then provided a laudatory narration of the "performance of the '*Maumee* Christys,' who had prepared an excellent program of 'troubles,' in the carrying out of which several very clever performances took place, creating a good deal of hearty merriment." This event was the grand and successful opening of a theatrical spectacle that would be staged in a number of ports along the South China Sea and on the coast of Japan. It is to Cushing's credit that he had recognized sufficient talent among his crew for such a venture and had seized an early opportunity to furnish the necessary musical instruments to make it a worthy enterprise. Two members of the crew, Dunmore and Rush, were the acclaimed leaders of this minstrel production. The former actor did a hilarious interpretation of a plantation clog dancer, while the latter delivered an amusing satire of the successful Negro entrepreneur. The Negro minstrel show was considered to be a genuine American theatrical experience by both North Americans and Europeans. Today, it can be viewed as a relic of a discredited past.[41]

After the end of the minstrel show, the guests went to the quarterdeck, now transformed into an elegant dining room, where a lavish supply of drink and food readily sustained them for a litany of toasts. The American consul, a Mr. Gerard, toasted Captain Cushing, who in turn acknowledged those among his guests who came from the ranks of the British military establishment, as well as from the government and mercantile community of the Cape Colony.[42]

Upon the conclusion of evening supper and the requisite toasts, "the decks having been cleared, dancing was commenced and was kept up with great spirit until the small hours were well advanced, when the ship's boats returned with the guests, who universally expressed themselves thoroughly gratified with their evening's entertainment."[43]

Cushing's festivities for the establishment of Cape Town did not prevent him from participating in a fracas brought on by an alleged slight to the reputation of the U.S. Navy. At an entertainment in Cape Town, an English officer made some remark in the presence of the paymaster reflecting upon the Navy. Cushing was consulted the following morning as to what had better be done about it. His reply was immediate and to the point: "Make him apologize or challenge him. I was intending to sail today but will not leave until this affair is settled." An apology was made and the ship sailed the following day.

In timing, this account differs from the version briefly recorded in Cushing's diary, in which Cushing wrote that he had carried a challenge from the paymaster to an English captain, who apologized. This incident occurred on February 11, the day on which he purchased his tiger and jackal robes. His grand shipboard reception was held on February 15, five days before his departure. Regardless of the date, this ancient ritual of chivalry did not cast a cloud on the brilliance of the farewell salute to the worthies of Cape Town from the deck of the USS *Maumee*.[44]

As he prepared to sail, Cushing was reunited joyfully with his terrier, which had been stolen. Cushing had offered a ten-dollar reward for the return of his dog. Five days later Cushing jotted a hasty note in his diary: "My dog brought back by a pious cab-man, who had probably stolen him for the reward." On February 20 the *Maumee* steamed out of Cape Town. On the following day Cushing shut down the steam engines and unfurled his sails. Unfortunately, the much-anticipated west winds failed to appear, and in their place were constantly shifting winds from the southeast and northwest. During much of this fickle weather, Cushing was ill from his second onslaught of fever. Happily, he recorded on March 7 that he was almost recovered.[45]

This dreary tedium of navigating through inhospitable weather took on a grimmer complexion when a member of the crew fell from his perch on the rigging into the ocean. Although the man had served on ships for some thirty years, he had never learned to swim. The *Maumee* was moving at a modest eight knots, and she was quickly turned into the wind, and a boat was lowered, but the exhausted man gave up his struggle. Cushing, who had experienced the rampages and slaughter of war, nevertheless succumbed to melancholic reflection on the quixotic nature of life: "A very death! Terrible, I think to see a strong man, in full enjoyment of heath and vigor — without time for prayer or repentance, and all the time the bright Sun shining down upon the dancing, rippling waves that engulf him. On we go! The poor sailor is tossed to and fro miles behind us in the depths of old Ocean; already stared at by cold eyes of the sharks and fishes as he slides down — down to his cold, sad resting place. It is thy fate — poor Jack! Tomorrow thou wilt be forgotten. And the laugh and song will not cease because thou art not with thy shipmates. God grant that no wife or child — no old Mother or loving sister may bury their broken hearts with thee — poor sailor!"[46]

Quickly, Cushing roused himself from his sad musing, reaffirming his allegiance to the code of those who guard their country. The reaction of the crew and officers to the unexpected loss of a comrade was not the response of "cold-hearted wretches." On the contrary, "It is the stern discipline of the Service that controls us: the discipline of men who learn that death is no stranger to be wondered at — and that life must often be a forfeit to duty. It is this bronzing of men's Souls in the fire of hard experience that fits them for great deeds. When man can bring tears and regrets for what is past, he learns a lesson of wisdom. Why mourn the inevitable?"[47]

On March 13 Cushing recorded that his ship was about one hundred and fifty miles from the island of St. Paul, where he intended to stay for several days. The last sheep had been slaughtered, and although this small volcanic outcrop situated midway between Australia and Java in the Indian Ocean was uninhabited, it had a sufficient supply of fresh fruit and vegetables to replenish shrunken stores. There was also ample opportunity to enjoy a bountiful harvest of fresh fish.[48] On the next day Cushing guided his ship through the narrow entrance to a natural harbor formed by an extinct volcanic crater that was two hundred feet deep with a surface that resembled the glass found in a mirror. The diameter of this virtually land-locked sea was approximately two-thirds of a mile. Surrounding this still lagoon were 800-foot-high towers of stone.

There was an overwhelming supply of different varieties of fish, including a "crawfish that resembled a lobster," and there were several boiling springs in which these lobster-like crustaceans could be quickly boiled. On the shores there was an impressive population of seals and penguins, and the rocky cliffs above the shores were home to a generous colony of wild goats that had a taste somewhat sweeter than mutton. However, the *Maumee* was not alone in this strange tropical outpost, for a French schooner with a cargo of salted fish sought a brief respite on her voyage to the Isle de Bourbon.[49]

Cushing did send a party to hunt wild goats, and he shot 47 penguins and caught 187 fish on the same day. He also walked several hundred feet toward the crater, but became quite tired from his exertions. He found the view was rewarding and observed "several thousand penguins" on his trek. They were "drawn up by brigades in bare spots — regular tribes — not associating in the slightest degree." He noted further that "if a penguin of one tribe got into the midst of a neighboring lot, all attacked him at once and he had regularly to run the gauntlet."[50]

As in the course of his trip across the South Atlantic from Rio de Janeiro to Cape Town, Cushing had suffered from a recurring fever, which contributed much to his mood of depression, in spite of his genuine pleasure in the skills required to navigate surely through ever-changing waters and winds. The euphoria provided by St. Paul cured his body and spirit. He basked in the warm and benign setting offered by this idyllic retreat far removed from the customary noise and confusion of the human race.

After a six-day sojourn in this remote tropical island, a rejuvenated Cushing ordered the anchor pulled, and the *Maumee* commenced her last lap on the voyage to Batavia. She had scarcely got under way when she encountered a New England whaling ship from New Bedford, which had been at sea for nine months. Cushing recorded that this vessel was "full of oil — bound for the Isle of Bourbon." However, he wrote that "we are now bound to Hong Kong — touching at Singapore."[51]

He also jotted in his diary the fact that "this is the second time that we have sailed from a port on a Friday — which frees me from all charges of Sailor Superstition." "Old Jack, Tars," he lamented, "can't get it out of their heads that the day is a fatal or, at least, an unfortunate one."[52] Perhaps there was some truth in the old axiom still revered by ordinary seamen, for the *Maumee* was plagued with very calm seas without the desired push of strong winds. On March 29, after nine days at sea, Cushing woefully commented that he was off course. "This is a bad streak of luck," he complained, for "in nine days we have made but 500 miles on one course where we should have gone fifteen or eighteen hundred. All for sailing on a Friday!"[53]

On the following day he could write that the *Maumee* was on course again; yet the next day, the end of March, he noted gloomily, "We have made but eight hundred miles in eleven days." However, good fortune returned, for on April 5 he recorded that "four days past have been charming weather, including fair wind and bright sky."[54]

The following day Cushing cheerfully reported that the Australian coast was four hundred miles over the horizon and, in obvious good humor, he contentedly observed that "we have been out of Cape Town 49 days and have some miles yet before reaching port, but I am in no hurry and not impatient in the least." Then he proudly proclaimed that "I was born to go to Sea," and "I could live here a year, and not see land if I had plenty of good food and cigars."[55]

On April 10 Cushing wrote that the distance to the Australian coast had shrunk to 200 miles, and ten days later he was anchored in the harbor at Batavia, where he received a hero's welcome. "I am well known here, and a great 'lion,'" he jotted happily. Then he recorded undoubtedly the grandest compliment bestowed upon him thus far in his youthful career: "They call me 'the second Nelson.'" This accolade was proclaimed in a newspaper article in which an account of the destruction of the *Albemarle* appeared.[56]

Unlike his previous stop in Cape Town, however, Cushing did not linger at Batavia. Forsaking adulation and extraordinary dinners, pleasing conversation with fashionable women, concerts, and champagne and billiards at the club for the military and civil establishment, he was resolved to make a quick departure for Hong Kong. He did take a short excursion to inspect a parade of elephants and to gaze upon an assortment of Bengal tigers, leopards, kangaroos, and sundry exotic birds.[57]

On April 22 Cushing pulled up anchor to start the last leg of his long voyage from the Navy Yard of Washington to Hong Kong, the crown jewel of the British presence in China. As he left, he was given a handsome farewell from the admiral in charge of the Dutch fleet in the islands of the East Indies. "He had just come in from the Dutch Governor General's," Cushing wrote, "in the country. He expressed great regret at not having had the opportunity to entertain me.... And congratulated me on my successes."[58] This final salute echoed the warmth of Cushing's reception at Batavia. "I am overcome with the hospitality and the Newspapers," he acknowledged, "and people proposed a public feast in my honor—but I must sail tomorrow!"[59]

It should be observed that Cushing had decided there would be little advantage in sailing to Singapore. The most direct route was to proceed directly along the coast of Indochina to Hong Kong. On April 26 he noted in his diary that "for two days have made 204 miles, on 10 tons of coal and at noon today we are 1000 miles from Hong Kong."[60] On the following day he wrote that "in the past twenty four hours made 207 miles under steam with 10 tons of coal." He added, "We are 140 miles from the coast of Cochin China and eight hundred miles from Hong Kong."[61]

By April 29 the *Maumee* was 400 miles from Hong Kong, which was a hopeful event, because the supply of pineapples was exhausted, although there were plenty of bananas still available. On the other hand, drinking water had proved to be not very refreshing and, as a result, Cushing had been reduced to the expedient of mixing claret with his water. "As I near port," Cushing confessed, "I become more and more anxious about my letters," for "I do long for them."[64]

When Cushing was but a hundred miles from Hong Kong, he could scarcely restrain his feverish anticipation for long accumulated letters from his beloved Kate that surely waited for his careful and repeated reading: "I confess that I am a little excited and I shall think this night a very long one, I am sure, but how I shall be tantalized tomorrow! Imagine the *Maumee* dashing saucily into port, with signals at the mast-head, colors flying, and everything taut and trim. Splash! Goes the anchor taking hold on Chinese mud, and then is heard the shrill whistle of the sailor 'calls,' and the hoarse voice of the Boatswain— 'Awa-a-a-y there! Gig-g-g-s aways!!' Down goes the white boat; in jumps the gig's crew—my flag and pennant goes up—and I shoot off to the Senior Officer's vessel to report my arrival."[63]

Cushing explained in this letter to Kate that his social obligations did not end with his formal call on the British admiral, for Hong Kong was a port that attracted capital ships from many countries. French, German, Russian, Dutch, and American vessels cluttered the harbor. Consequently, there was much ferrying among the ships as officers paid and reciprocated visits prescribed by naval etiquette. On this occasion such pleasant courtesies were sorry exercises that heightened the excitement of seeing the ship that brought those letters that would spark the smoldering memory of a woman and a place that had gradually receded into the shadowy landscape of the past. "The sensation," Cushing informed Kate, "can only be compared to the Christmas eve excitement of childhood; when the stocking was hung up, and sleep banished by eager and restless speculation about that wonderful fur-clad Santa Claus; and what he would bring me."[64]

Cushing finished his letter on a song of hope: "How my longing to see you will rise up in my soul at each word of remembrance and affection." "Ah, Kate! I can hardly wait til tomorrow. Every minute is a long year, until I hold fast your letters," he declared. And then came his invocation: "Good night—darling! May you be always as happy as I shall be tomorrow! As you will make me tomorrow!!"[65]

On May 1 Cushing dropped anchor in the Hong Kong harbor. The great trail across far-stretching avenues of water had been accomplished. But instead of receiving a much-anticipated bundle of tender letters from an adoring Kate, repeating constant love, Cushing collected only two letters. The contents of the second one chilled him to the core, for it strongly hinted that Kate was contemplating the dissolution of their romance. Long dreams of reading fresh declarations of undying love and restless sighs of wishing to touch her gallant swain again were rudely shattered. "How shall I commence! What shall I say!" Such were the cries of shocked disbelief, as Cushing wrote sorrowfully that "my heart is like lead in my bosom—and I am sick with disappointment. Oh! Kate—my own precious girl—I do not know what to think or what to write to you."[66]

Cushing reminded his sweetheart that when she wrote these two letters, she had not yet received those that he had sent to her from Rio de Janeiro. The gist of her first letter, which had been written in December, was a caring and loving missive, but the next one, composed in January, contained equivocal expressions advising that she now hesitated to remain steadfast in her alliance with her far-removed fiancé. "Kate," Cushing reacted in anguish, "it seemed just like the time when you cared so little for me—and as if (as you said) you forced yourself to the task of writing." He then concluded sadly that "I could not help thinking that you grudge the little time that you gave to me amidst the daily gaiety you mention—and I know that my heart tells me that the favor of love was not there."[67]

In rebuttal, Cushing clearly pronounced his bitter disappointment:

You say, at the very first, that it may pain me to know that you force yourself to write to me. My darling if you had dreamed of the true, real pain that the confession did give me — after all these long months in which every thought has been yours — truly and loyally yours — and when day after day my love forced me to pen my thoughts and heart-felt love for you. If you had thought of all this Kate I would not, I am sure, be so sad tonight. I feel so lonely. I cannot express it — for it seems as if I had lost or were to lose all that I care to live for. You half break my heart, Kate, when you say that "if you think that we may be uncongenial you will never marry me." What bad influence has been around you; that you would substitute such terrible suggestions for the old tender, true thoughts. Do you not, indeed, love me? Oh, My darling! Say that you do! I cannot bear to lose you.[68]

Such a profusion of lamentations underscores Cushing's stunned reaction to the very real possibility that Kate was entertaining second thoughts on her alliance with a naval officer, even if he possessed the allure of a youthful Civil War hero. However much he might be applauded at home and on distant shores, he provided no cheer or excitement to a young woman at the apex of youthful charm and beauty. Kate undoubtedly felt that she may well have taken a premature exit. Thus Cushing was prompted to wonder that "perhaps you did not even realize it when you felt that reluctance to give me those few moments in your months of pleasure, when you wrote, calmly, of the possibility of our parting, and jestingly of the attentions you received from others."[69]

In the heat of his passionate entreaties to sway the conscience of his true love, Cushing retained a degree of cool appraisal. He firmly repudiated any association with former feminine attractions in Fredonia, especially Sally Wheelock. He noted that he had long since ceased his visits to her house. In regard to Kate's praise for one of her admirers, a civil engineer, "because he is a good churchman," Cushing asked resolutely, "will you help me to be one too?" "I will try," he pledged, "for your sake and for my own to become worthy to be a member of your Church, dearest, and if I can with a true heart, I will promise to become a member where we are married."[70]

In promising to abandon his family's traditional loyalty to the Baptist Church, Cushing advanced a strong offensive to check Kate's misgivings and restrain her wandering eye. His protestations of ceaseless devotion to her throughout lonely months of separation, which could be proved by his steady flow of letters (now numbering 43), would also provoke somber reflections on an honorable recognition of a binding obligation to her trusting and loving fiancé, a man serving his country in alien climes that might well conceal hazardous challenges. Cushing had proved to be a worthy and responsible candidate for her affections. It was Kate's turn to demonstrate that she could nurture the courage and fortitude of a grown woman. The arrival of the USS *Maumee* in Hong Kong had not marked a joyful reunion between Kate Forbes, the country belle, and William Barker Cushing, the dashing naval hero. Instead, it had revealed the hasty acceptance of a proposal encouraged by the passions of the moment and prompted by a summons to duty that had yet to be acknowledged and ratified.

Chapter 4

Cruising on the Troubled Waters of the Far East

On May 2, after having been sadly disappointed by the paucity of his mail and stunned by the contents of the two letters from Kate, Cushing climbed to the high ground of perspective and sought to restore his customary optimistic spirit. He informed Kate that "I have read, again and again, until I am inclined to tear up what I wrote last evening — and confess, to myself, that I am a foolish fellow." "They are good letters, Kate," he acknowledged, "if they did cost you an effort — and you say more kind things to me than I deserve — and I was foolish not to see that I send too many and that they 'bore' you." He admitted that he was unable to change his natural manner of writing or his preferences on suitable topics of discussion, although he acknowledged that "dull letters must, in time, tire the most serene patience."[1]

Cushing, however, had received another important letter. Admiral Rowan, the new commander of the naval squadron in the Far East, was at Singapore, where he had dispatched notice that he intended to sail shortly for Hong Kong. Cushing predicted that he would arrive sometime during the coming week. He remained ignorant of his immediate orders, but he had picked up a rumor that he might be sent to the capital of Siam. In the morning Cushing put on his formal, or full dress, uniform and then, with cocked hat in hand, boarded his launch to return the courtesy calls of the English commodore and a visiting French captain. After that, he put on a cool white uniform and "pulled into the landing and made my first foot-print upon the soil of China."[2]

Cushing found that "at the pier head were any number of 'pig tails' with bamboo chair — the substitute here for carriages — and the New York hackmen do not compare with them in noisy persistence." "Each one" of these predecessors of the modern taxi driver, Cushing reported, was "eager to carry the 'Melican Man,' and rattled in my ears the praises of his particular conveyance, and filled the air with a mixture of Chinese and pigeon English that leads me to think that another tower of Babel has been attempted here, with the same results as in Ancient times." "I looked them over," he explained, "as I would a lot of horses or cattle and soon selecting a couple of big, muscular fellows, I accepted their invitation to 'Walkee-up-a-top-side-makee-look-see!' and entered the palanquin and was immediately whisked away, up hill and down dale, a walk that was as fast as a horse's trot, but so smooth and easy that the novel ride was far from unpleasant."[3]

The harbor of Hong Kong presented an impressive façade to those aboard ships mooring at the end of their long voyage. In 1841 Britain had taken formal possession of several sandy and rocky islands that in a quick succession of years became a marvel of mercantile enterprise. After some 25 years of construction, rude huts of wood and mud had been displaced by handsome edifices that resembled the splendor of Venetian *loggias* with their colonnades supported by round arches marching in endless procession. This re-creation of the magnificent spectacle of Venetian palaces and piazzas crowned the islands that formed the citadel of a great mercantile empire; however, it had a modern touch, for its main boulevards were lit by gas lamps hanging from a succession of ornate iron poles.[4]

The city, however, was strung like a necklace along the shore that encircled the inner harbor. On one end of this urban strand was the great emporium of Jardine-Matheson, and somewhat behind at a higher elevation was the racetrack. At the other end sprawled the Chinese quarter, Taiping Shan. In the center between these two outposts stood the ceremonial gateway, which was dominated by an imposing clock tower. From this site the great commercial avenue, Queen's Road, could be reached easily, and its course wound into the maze that constituted the Chinese colony. Above this principal artery were two parallel streets that provided access to majestic government buildings and impressive mercantile structures, as well as handsome residences that advertised the opulence of their denizens. Above these ribbons of urban industry was the formidable barrier of steep terrain leading to the summits of mountains that provided the breathtaking backdrop of Hong Kong, then a city of some 1,250,000 inhabitants.[5]

Such was Cushing's initial impression. He remarked that "Hong Kong is not an extensive City, but is very European in its streets and buildings — and American in its large and complete hotels." He quickly observed:

> Most of the stores, and all the trades, are in the hands of the natives — with whom twenty cents a day is very high for labor. One entire street is filled with shops containing ornate articles of Chinese workmanship, such multitudes of curiosities that one gets bewildered in looking at them. Carved ivories; gold and silver filigree work — silks, fans, carved sandal wood, Chinese crockery ware — gorgeous silk suits of pajamas, and suits of crepe; that look like rich creams — all so cheap, compared to our notions of such things — that one is sorely tempted at

every moment to buy, buy, buy. Another street is one long line of tailor shops — another of shoe stores — another of markets — and so on to the end of the chapter. My tailor is the proprietor of an exclusive establishment; and rejoices in the cognomen of "A-King." He makes one an entire uniform of the finest broad cloth for twenty-five dollars — and I probably got cheated at that.[6]

Despite the luxurious display of materials and ornamental objects not readily available at home and, if discovered, would probably command a hefty price, Cushing resolved not to be tempted, because he had learned that the market at Canton offered even a greater range of commodities, many of which could be purchased more reasonably than at Hong Kong. "I do not intend to be swindled as most people are, who first come to China," he argued prudently.[7]

Meanwhile, he did not neglect an opportunity to press forward his campaign to reassure a wavering Kate that he was steadfast in his devotion to her, and at the same time not let her slip off his hook. To that end Cushing announced, "I want you to let me know your favorite colors of silk — or will you trust my taste!" Having thrown out the bait, he quickly drew the line in by advising that "you had better not; for, as I am here, you might as well be entirely suited in your taste; and leave nothing to chance." To further his ploy, he recalled that "I owe Miss Leila [Kate's sister] a dress for that one so patriotically ruined on last July 4th." Cushing then solicited Kate's support: "You must give me a hint as to color &, and if there is anything peculiar to this part of Earth that you or your Mother or Father — or any friend of yours desires — you must not fail to let me know."[8]

An additional flourish to Cushing's argument was his report on the skill of Chinese artists in copying with great accuracy portraits from ambrotype and collodion photographs. "The artist," Cushing had discovered, "will make such a painting in three days; and charges for it — framed — but six dollars."[9] He sought, accordingly, to persuade Kate to send him a better picture of her, which he would have transformed into a handsome oil portrait, which could be installed appropriately in an ornate frame.

Cushing had been compelled by Kate's letter to recognize the wide gulf between them. Not only did an insurmountable distance physically separate them, but their respective opportunities and focuses were also disrupted momentarily. Only the flame of enduring love could preserve their bond. Spiritual union must prevail in the absence of temporal interaction. He was immersed in the duty of sailing a naval ship into strange foreign territory, where he encountered the experience of learning about and becoming reconciled to strange cultures. Kate, on the other hand, remained fixed in the daily routine of life in a small rural village. Her primary pursuits were practicing culinary arts, such as making chocolate candy, making salads, and baking biscuits, as well as mastering the piano keyboard and attempting to acquire the skill of singing those songs that provided the mainstay of entertainment in the Victorian household. In addition to these conventional exercises, Kate enjoyed the attentions of young men who were quite pleased to escort her to various social events throughout any given week. Indeed, she informed Cushing that she had only one free evening in a week to write letters. Sternly, Cushing upbraided his wandering love: "I assure you that while your time is challenged by such eminent rivals, I can hardly comprehend how you found that one evening to spare upon so insignificant a personage as myself." "Am I, then," he asked, "less to you than everything else in the routine of daily life?" Finally, he inquired, "And will you sacrifice my happiness during these two years for such petty reasons as those?"[10]

While Cushing was orchestrating his remonstrance to Kate, he did not neglect to recruit attendants to minister to his creature comforts and at the same time to underscore his status as the captain of a ship of the United States Navy. He wrote confidently that "my 'Comprador'—or man who furnishes my daily marketing—a very oily seeming, handsomely dressed native—whose business cards record the superlative merits of one 'Apee'—brings off ice, meats, fruits & every morning—all the best—and so exceedingly cheap that I am in danger of losing my health in trying to carry out my duty, and eat as much as possible for so little money."[11] He also made arrangements for a private carriage—a bamboo chair to be on call at his discretion. "All around the *Maumee*," he reported, "are hundreds of 'Junks,' 'San Pans' [sampans]." Cushing explained then that "these small boats with an awning aft, for a few feet—of coarse canvas contain whole families—who have no other house—want none." Cushing observed, moreover, "the women seem to do more work than the men—and give good evidence of muscle and endurance in pulling all day long, heavy oars." One of these family sampans performed menial chores and provided a ferry service to shore. He contemplated, furthermore, replacing his steward with a Chinese cook, because the Chinese, he had been told, were quite accomplished in culinary arts.[12]

W. B. Cushing from a photograph taken in China when he commanded the *Maumee*.

On May 4 Cushing invited the doctor and the paymaster on

the *Maumee* to accompany him to a performance of a Chinese opera. Hiring three bamboo chairs, they pushed their way three abreast through the crowd of pedestrians on Queen Regent Street, which had acquired an amber tone as its gas lamps replaced the rays from the sun. Shops were lit by lanterns, which turned each shop "into a gorgeous headquarters for a thousand Christmases."[13] As Cushing and his companions drew closer to their destination, they left the broad streets of central Hong Kong to pass through narrow lanes that traversed the densely populated area where the majority of the Chinese population lived. "In many houses," Cushing heard, "bands of music were playing — wild barbaric airs, to be sure — but with much more harmony than I had imagined them capable of producing." When they reached the theater, Cushing and his friends were engulfed by "a dense crowd of natives, who made a lane for us to the place where a fat fellow was seated; with some assistants — weighing in scales the money tendered, and serving out tickets." Cushing readily recognized that they were being charged "three times the regulation, first-class price — but I had no business to be an American, if I didn't want to pay — and I felt that we had no right to growl."[14]

The Americans, as the only Westerners present, were escorted to seats of honor, which were located in the highest balcony. Cushing found that

> the theater was similar to our own in construction; but was not neat or finished — and the stage was hung full of lights — and suspended in air, instead of footlights. The orchestra sat on the stage, just in rear of the performers — and kept up a continual uproar — in which gongs and bells, and a kind of bugle — very shrill — were the most prominent instruments. The gong seems to mark each tragic point in the play.[15]

It was a romantic drama, in which a stern father, a Mandarin, sells his attractive daughter to an alien suitor. In the opening episode the heroine "was on her knees, before her 'Josh lights' — chin-chin-ing the God 'Josh' for her love in a high shrill chant, ten minutes long." At the conclusion of this lengthy soliloquy her stern father, "in full Mandarin costume" and supporting a long beard, stood before his lamenting daughter. He "approache[d] the Josh sticks, and commence[d] a curse upon his daughter," which was frustrated by a series of outraged rebukes from his daughter's mother and aunt. In rebuttal the Mandarin father, as he stroked his long beard, "announce[d] that he has sold the lovelorn damsel" to someone else. Then followed "High tragedy! — tears! lamentations! High-pitched quartette! Gong!! Bells! Bugle! Tender pleading of daughter! No use!!! Enter old man, with long white beard — fixes things up in some mysterious manner. All go on their knees and salute each other by repeated dips — the forehead touching the floor grand — closing quartette — We may be happy yet — you bet!"[16] In his diary Cushing tersely summed up his reaction by noting that the performers were "very funny in their peculiar costumes and shrill drawling," and the "Orchestra very noisy — Too much gong and bell."[17]

During the latter part of the opera, Cushing and his friends were escorted backstage to "the green room," where they were able to watch the actors and actresses dress and apply their stage make-up, and they were also permitted to examine the costumes worn during the performance. "Some of the robes," Cushing noted, "were richer than anything I ever have seen — worth hundreds of dollars each — and with gold and flowers — No tinsel about them."[18]

After leaving the green room, Cushing and his companions were taken to another chamber, where they were introduced to the spectacle of an opium den. Cushing described the scene:

> Curtains were drawn around platforms of board, large enough for two men to stretch out upon. And on these the smokers reclined — with a light between them and a pot of tea — puffing away at the vile drug that has long since reduced them to an object of dependence upon it. There they live — and there they die — absolute slaves to its influence.[19]

Although all three took several samples of opium, only the doctor felt any sensation, reacting as if he had swallowed several glasses of whiskey. Even if Cushing did not sense any stimulus from his several puffs of opium, he promised solemnly that "I shall never try it again.— it is dangerous." However, this sad panorama remained implanted in his memory:

> I shall never forget the scene — the long room — the curtained recesses — the silent recesses — the silent smokers — the wild, dreamy look of their staring eyes — as they drifted, in couples, off on their road to certain ruin and death — all impresses me with its weird novelty — and when we came out again into the fresh air, and under the starry sky, I felt as if I had come from another World.[20]

The three naval musketeers polished off their survey of evening entertainment in Hong Kong with a visit to a gambling establishment that was crowded with a fascinating throng of Europeans, half-castes, Chinese, and Malaysians. Though Cushing swore that "I never bet," he accepted the challenge of the doctor, who offered a silver dollar if Cushing would try his luck as an accomplice. "Won twelve times out of fifteen; and the doctor raked in a pocket full of silver," he reported.[21] Nevertheless, Cushing assured Kate that he resolutely refused the solicitations of those eager companions who sought to tempt him to try his luck in the plentiful supply of gaming houses that dotted the harbors of the world: "I am principled against it — and would not bet a dollar to win a million."[22]

After narrating to Kate the chronicle of his night out on the town, Cushing renewed his request for a better picture in order to acquire an oil portrait of her. "The Chinese painters," he explained, "have sketched and painted my ship — and have done it to perfection." He described it as "an oil painting, quite large — and represents the beauty at anchor in this harbor."[23] He also wrote that several of his officers had their portraits painted and that several of their friends had likewise taken advantage of this novel opportunity. However, Cushing told Kate that "I only want you — but I would like a larger and clearer picture to take it from." Again he repeated that "an ambrotype or tin-type would answer," pleading, "will you send it?" On that note, he promised that "I'll have one taken of myself also — to match it."[24]

Cushing was pleased greatly to read that Kate had made a dressing gown for him, but he asked her to keep it until he returned. "You say that your love for me is not without solicitude.... What troubles you, my love," he pleaded, "my precious darling?" He argued that "you surely can not doubt me now — and only your own word can make me think you fickle." He then affirmed that "I know that you loved me once — and I am anchored to that delicious certainty."[25] He vowed firmly, "I intend to remain in the United States" for several years after the conclusion of his current stint of two years abroad. He also tempted her with the exciting prospect that "the next time that I go abroad, it will be to the Mediterranean, and we can be together in Europe."[26] The country belle could look forward to a romantic excursion that few young maidens in her arena could anticipate at any stage of their lives.

Over a week later, Cushing complained to Kate that constant official calls and receptions demanded by protocol were sapping his energy. Besides, the heat during the day was almost unbearable, especially when his head was encased in the cocked hat that was an indispensable article of his formal dress uniform. Yet he was surviving and waiting patiently for "the appearance of our Flag Ship, which has touched at Cochin China on her way up here from India, and may not be in for a week yet."[27]

He had, however, some measure of cheer to report: "A week ago I got a letter from Mother, mailed on the 7th of March, and giving me six weeks later news than I had from you." Its long journey had been routed through London and Marseilles.[28] Mary Barker Cushing told her son that she had received his gift of $97 from Gayle. She had enjoyed residing at her boarding houses, but when her daughter Mary Gayle and Mary's husband had decided to establish their own home, they had invited her to live with them. Mary Barker had accepted, but she still retained some doubts. On the other hand, Mary Gayle was now assured of help in household chores, and, more particularly, relief in the nursery, when needed. "I was delighted to hear," Cushing told Kate, "that you and Mary correspond." Moreover, "Mother mentioned you with expressions of the warmest affection." He underscored the comfort that he received from the maternal commentary, but he could not resist a barbed note: "It did me good to read how much she loves and respects you. I want everyone to love you, excepting the men. I think I can give you that entire article that is due to a young lady, from my sex, or at least, all that you could take care of."[29]

"I am delighted to hear of your good resolution," Mary Barker congratulated her son regarding his decision to give up some of his less edifying habits "for the love of Kitty [Kate]." Moreover, Mary Barker affirmed that "she is a girl whose influence is good," and "such a wife will prove a treasure." "Mary and Kitty," his mother commented further, "keep up a brisk correspondence," and "she writes very lively, pleasant letters." Then Mary Barker provided an account of the recent behavior of the rejected Nellie: "Nellie Grosvenor has been all winter in New York and Washington and does not answer Mary's letters, and Milt writes he has not heard from her of late." Mary Barker could not resist the query, "Perhaps she is trying to do better — Could She?"[30]

Cushing, though fortified by his mother's cheerful letter, especially the encouraging news that Kate corresponded regularly with Mary Gayle and also Mary Barker, succumbed once again to a woebegone melancholy. He announced:

> For the first time in life I must confess myself home sick. Sometimes I feel as if I can not wait here until my cruise is over — as though I must in some way, get ordered home. This love for you is a bottomless pit, down which I am sinking deeper and deeper every day and hour. Distance, society, variety — all have no affect upon me. I can't forget you for an instant, and I feel as if bound in chains. Oh, for my old light heartedness — to make time pass more swiftly! Not that I am truly unhappy without you. Dear darling Kate — comfort me and encourage me by your letters — they are next to you in my heart — and I can not do without them — every word is precious.[31]

After his doleful recital of his current state of mind, which certainly was far from his former paeans of robust joy on the challenge of confronting the surging waves of stormy seas, Cushing returned to the obligations of duty in Asian waters. He had received a note from J. R. Goddard, an American missionary who had just arrived at Hong Kong on the American clipper *Windward* from New York. Goddard wrote, "In looking over the shipping list, my wife recognized your name as that of an intimate acquaintance of her brother Lieut. Com'd Albert S. Barker and desired me to inform you of our arrival." He inquired, accordingly, if it would be possible for Cushing to meet them and said, "We shall remain in port about two weeks on board the *Windward*."[32] Cushing went on board the New York clipper, which had just completed a 140-day trip without stopping at any port for either rest or supplies, for a rendezvous with the Goddards, both of whom were missionaries. Reporting that Mrs. Goddard had spent most of her long journey to the Far East battered by seasickness in her cabin, Cushing added, "What she wanted to marry a Missionary, and come out here for — is more then I can explain, but it is all a sort of Puritan stock, and I am not much surprised."[33] Possibly, he recollected the saga of his mother and her sisters seeking husbands and the opportunity to participate in taming a raw frontier.

Cushing performed the obligation of a relative and a naval officer to escort the Goddards on a tour of Hong Kong, and he also put a launch at their disposal whenever they chose to conduct further explorations of the imperial colony. Having noticed that the Reverend Goddard had brought a small selection of books on theological subjects, he also sent a package of books covering a broader range of literature to Mrs. Goddard. Nonetheless, Cushing did not neglect to expand his knowledge of sacred matters, for he also took them to a Buddhist shrine. His narrative of this visit reveals that Cushing's understanding of religions beyond the pale of Christianity was quite limited. He identified the temples as a "Josh" structure, and he could not name the sculptures of the principal gods that were honored. After observing carefully the devotional exercises of the worshipers, especially their system of prayers and lighting sticks of incense, Cushing commented shrewdly that "their religion is a gambling game," because after having selected a particular prayer from a list of those that were favored by one of the gods, they went to a board filled with holes that might accept a lighted incense stick that would represent their prayer. Having located an appropriate slot, "they then throw up into the air, two crooked blocks of wood, and decided, from their relative positions, whether the prayer was granted or not." To this commentary, Cushing added, "They hardly ever pray for anything but money and sensual enjoyments — and are strictly material in all their religious ideas." He concluded with the thought that "it must be hard to convert them."[34]

Returning to mundane pleasures, Cushing took his executive officer, paymaster, and secretary to a Chinese restaurant, where they managed to survive a meal that had a roster of some twenty or thirty dishes, among which were dog, owl and chicken heads. Cushing did manage to digest "Chin dogee!" However, he did not succumb to owl and chicken heads, though he found litchi a pleasant dessert.[35]

Sometime during the first two weeks of May, Rear Admiral S.C. Rowan arrived in Hong Kong on the USS *Piscataqua*, a new steam frigate, to take active command of the Asiatic Squadron. His predecessor, Rear Admiral Bell, had drowned when his launch capsized in the harbor at Osaka during a passage of extraordinary rough weather in January. Unfortunately, Bell had delayed his departure for the United States to ensure the safety of the American envoy to Japan, Robert Van Valkenburgh, who sought to ratify a treaty with Japan that would secure orderly and peaceful commerce between American and Japanese commercial interests. Rowan's squadron consisted of nine ships, the largest of which was the *Piscataqua*, his flagship, which carried 23 guns. The other eight ships were armed with batteries of five to ten guns. Of this number (including the *Maumee*, with nine guns), three were described as shallow draft ships that were suitable for navigating shores and rivers that could shield pirates, seemingly the perennial challenge in Asian waters. Meanwhile, Commodore Goldsborough sailed Bell's flagship, the *Hartford*, which had earned well-deserved recognition as the flagship of Admiral Farragut during the Civil War, to Singapore, where he formally turned over the Far Eastern command to Rowan. It should be noted that the Far Eastern Squadron and the North Pacific Squadron, each with nine ships, were the largest concentrations in the cruising ranks of the United States Navy.[36]

The location of Hong Kong was the response of the British government to the unfavorable circumstances that confronted their merchants at Canton, the great Chinese emporium. Canton was a well-protected city on the Pearl River, which flows through some of the richest provinces of southern China. The distance between Hong Kong and Canton is some 70 miles. To reach Canton, ships had to cross two bars that offered perilous passage. Approximately 30 miles from Hong Kong, the Pearl River contracts into a narrow channel called the Tiger's Mouth, which was guarded by two forts. From that spot to the second bar, a ship had to traverse a tight course barely removed from the confines of opposing banks. At the second bar a ship had to wait for a favorable tide to lift it over the shallows. The first bar, situated seven miles from Canton, was an impossible obstacle to ships of more than 600 tons.[37]

At first, British trade with Canton was in the hands of the East India Company, which had extended its monopoly of trade and governance in India to goods shipped between India and Canton. The primary product that China contributed to this traffic was tea. In the latter years of the eighteenth century, gin ceased to be the favorite drink of mass consumption. Taking its place was tea, which became a mania at the debut of the nineteenth century. The British government made a considerable profit from import duties on Chinese tea. Approximately 20 percent of revenue collected by the government came from the levy on imported tea from China. Although merchants at Canton gained comfortable wealth from their commerce with Chinese exporters, they failed to gain the handsome rewards that they had anticipated.

In London, government officials in the Treasury and bankers were alarmed by the steady flow of bullion that went to China to compensate for the lack of interest in British imports. This inverse ratio of exchange was anathema to conventional economic wisdom. As a consequence, in 1833 the British government ended the East India Company's mandate at Canton, an action prompted particularly by the exertions of two private British merchants, William Jardine and James Matheson, both of whom became legends in the early years of Hong Kong. Until this time, opium had not figured notably in the ledgers of Asian trade. In India it was drunk as a medicinal remedy and also as a beverage promoting a sense of tranquility. Although opium was known in China, it did not have widespread notoriety. In the second decade of the nineteenth century, however, an ever-mounting craving for opium, as a hallucinogen when smoked in conjunction with tobacco, attracted the unscrupulous attention of merchants at Canton.[38]

After 1830 there was no uncertainty about the profits to be gained from opium imports into China. There has been and continues to be a battery of finger-pointing as to the real culprits in this nefarious commerce. The Maoist-Communist regime consistently condemns the perfidious British merchants and their political supervisors for the moral and economic havoc that the drug wrought on Chinese society. On the other hand, a supine Manchu dynasty at Peking was unable or perhaps unwilling to enforce its sanctions against importing opium. It was not until 1841 that the British government abandoned its denunciation of the commerce. Casting aside their moral scruples, Ministers of the Crown argued that if the Chinese bureaucracy lacked the will to enforce its edicts, or was not genuinely interested in doing so, then it was not an obligation of the British authorities to assume such responsibility.

Recent research and commentary demonstrates that knavery and exploitation was by no means limited to Western governments and their merchants. Chinese authorities, even those residing within the sacred precincts of the imperial household, dealt in merchandising opium. Throughout China, members of the bureaucracy used opium as currency to finance (sometimes with profit) their transactions. In the mercantile community, wholesalers, retail distributors, and local purveyors actively promoted the narcotic to reinforce their legitimate commerce. Customers for opium could be found in all walks of life, from the elevated station of the imperial court through the intertwining ranks of the fashionable and powerful senior government officials, to the comfortable residences of wealthy merchants, and to the barracks and households of the imperial army. Such widespread usage savaged all elements of Chinese society, including generous swaths of rural peasantry.[39]

Such arguments recall current debates on the responsibility for drug traffic into the United States and Western Europe. If there were no demand for drugs, then narcotic production should become unprofitable, and growers and distributors would shrink into insignificant numbers. Unfortunately, demand for narcotics remains at levels today in Western countries that are reminiscent of those that persisted in China during the nineteenth century. There are, alas, ruthless rogues, such as Jardine and Matheson (along with their rivals, Lancelot and Wilkinson Dent), who display a bland disregard for morality as they pursue their craft with unrivaled skill. There is a major difference, of course, between past and present. Contemporary authorities in Western nations uniformly attempt to suppress drug traffic, although their strategies vary widely.

It can be argued, however, that the conflict between China and Great Britain was in reality a contest between two cultures. China was an insular society that believed it was the primary sovereign realm on the planet under the just and omnipotent rule of a divine emperor. Economically, the Chinese had developed a self-sufficient society that grew from reasonably comfortable agricultural harvests. Imperial edicts had shut down prospects that could be realized from regular trade by ships plying the seas between China and the East

Indian islands and India. China closed the door on her neighbors and adventurers from distant shores. All those who dwelt beyond the territory governed by the Heavenly Emperor were denounced as barbarians who would be prohibited from contact with the divine sovereign and his privileged subjects.[40]

However, the immediate response to the expansion of the opium trade into China was to provoke an armed conflict between China and Great Britain, which has earned the dubious sobriquet of the "Opium War" (1840–1842). The Chinese viceroy, Commissioner Lin, was determined to put an immediate end to the traffic in opium. If he had been successful, trade between China and foreign merchants would have collapsed. Great Britain would have been deprived of its most favored beverage and its national economy would have suffered a severe blow. The Royal Navy very quickly bottled up leading Chinese ports, such as Canton and Nanking, and the emperor at Peking, who did not wish to submit to the humiliation of recognizing that the British fleet, which had also seized control of the Bay of Chihli, now governed the passage from the sea to his sacred capital, had no choice but to capitulate. He was made to open Canton and four additional ports, Amoy, Shanghai, Ningpo, and Foochow, to the unrestricted entry of British goods and to ensure that Chinese commodities could be purchased readily at those ports. In short, five strategically situated ports on the Chinese coast had been transformed into free trade zones under British supervision.

Moreover, the islands at the mouth of the Pearl estuary had been ceded to Great Britain. On January 26, 1841, the Crown Colony of Hong Kong was proclaimed. The Union Jack now flew on the heights overlooking the waters surrounding the new territorial possession of the British Crown.[41]

By the end of the American Revolution, tea consumption had become an impressive part of the European economy. As a beverage, tea had usurped the privileged niches long occupied by domestic products such beer, wine, and hard spirits. Hardheaded Yankee merchants could not overlook this phenomenal success. In 1783 the *American Express* left New York to explore the Chinese tea market. This venture was under the watchful guidance of the celebrated financier of the American Revolution, Robert Morris. During the first half of the nineteenth century, tea from China was the third most important import after commodities from Britain and Cuba.[42]

There were two main varieties of tea in China: black tea was favored by British consumers, but green tea was preferred by Americans. By decree of Chinese authorities, Canton was the only port open to intercourse with foreign traders. As a consequence, lead containers holding dried leaves ready for marketing had to be transported four or seven hundred miles on various river routes by laborious hauling over the mountain passes that separated these routes.[43]

There was considerable purchasing of silk, but marketing of that material did not measure up to the strong and ever-growing demand for tea. Silk remained a luxury item, as did jade, woodcarving, incense, and bronzes. Along with other Chinese artifacts, such as paper goods and lacquer work, such articles could not sustain the dynamic traffic that would produce profits that made the expense of a lengthy and uncertain passage worthwhile.[44]

Americans were attracted to the opium trade as they explored various strategies of trade with China. The Perkins brothers, for instance, who entered into a venture with the British Northwest Fur Company to sell their pelts to Chinese distributors, possessed a comfortable business from 1816 to 1820. Unfortunately, the supply of skins faded and they had to seek a more profitable commodity to sustain their Chinese trade. In the late 1820s the Perkins brothers were established at Smyrna (Izmir), where in 1804 American traffic in opium began to prosper.[45]

In 1800 Chinese authorities, alarmed by the increasing supply of opium, issued an edict prohibiting its importation. This was a response to the reliance of the East India Company on opium sales to provide silver for the purchase of tea. Specie from London sources had become decidedly limited, and reliance on Spanish sources, particularly those that were obtained through American shipping channels, had become uncertain and expensive. Though American merchants had ready-at-hand access to the Spanish mines on the Pacific coast, revolutionary conflict made the dwindling resources of Spanish mines unreliable.[46]

Consequently, American merchants, who had gained a monopoly of the opium trade in Turkey, looked to the Chinese market as the solution to their need to introduce an alternative to the costly and precarious importation of silver. In 1817–1818 Perkins & Co., the dominant American presence in the Turkey opium business, along with John Cushing and John Sturgis & Co., became the principal pioneers of the American involvement in the sale of opium at Canton, where Russell & Co. (which by 1827 had become the most important American dealer in opium at Canton) joined them. Originally, the two founders of this latter firm, Philip Ammedon and Samuel Russell, in 1808 had entered the opium trade in India. Since the East India Company had a monopoly of British trade in opium in the Far East, Russell & Co. entered the commission business. The East India Company auctioned opium to native Indian speculators, who would then ship it to Canton. Russell & Co. would act as their agent. The opium would be sold clandestinely at Canton to undercover Chinese dealers. The silver received from opium sales would be used to purchase tea or be converted into bills of exchange to cover the expense of acquiring it in India. Of course, some of these bills of exchange represented profit that could be realized in London to provide money for investment.[47]

In 1830 Russell & Co. and Perkins & Co. merged to form the largest American firm at Canton, and soon thereafter it abandoned the opium trade with Turkey to concentrate on the more lucrative supply from India. When

Chinese Commissioner Lin strove to enforce the abolition of opium trade in China, Russell & Co. announced in 1839 that they had ceased trading in the outlawed commerce. At the time it ranked in prestige and wealth behind the great trading houses of Jardine, Matheson, and Dent. The Americans had engaged successfully and prominently in opium traffic at Canton.[48]

Although the American community did not condone the brutality of the British reaction to Commissioner Lin's forthright efforts to implement the imperial strictures against foreign importation of opium into China, it did not wish to practice segregation. On the contrary, members of the American enclave readily resumed their close-knit intercourse with British merchants. Russell & Co. likewise resumed their cordial exchange of financial and shipping assistance with their British colleagues. Receiving little support from their government, American merchants looked to the British for protection. Whatever qualms they may have entertained on the morality of the opium commerce and the havoc it inflicted on Chinese society, they cast them aside to reap the rich dividends from marketing the illicit and destructive drug.[49]

Despite the violence and confusion of the Opium War, Russell & Co. continued to flourish, particularly after the successful mission of Caleb Cushing, who executed the first major diplomatic initiative of the American government with Chinese authorities. The Treaty of Wanghia in 1844 gave Russell & Co. a blank check to engage in opium commerce. American law did not apply to a purely Chinese territorial problem. The essential issue for the American government was to obtain for American merchants the same extraterritorial rights that British firms had received in the Treaty of Nanking. The treaty also confirmed that American missionaries could install missionary establishments, including schools and churches, without fear of retaliation.[50]

American trade with China assumed a global character that is similar in design to that which is implemented today (albeit in a more sophisticated fashion) through modern communications. In the United States a closely interlocking association of families knitted together by family ties, common financial and political interests, and harmonious religious concepts, called the Boston concern, became the nucleus of an international market. Although it did not have the corporate structure of today, the absence of contemporary legal and contractual restraints did not prevent this cohesive assembly in eastern Massachusetts from functioning in a far-flung global system.[51]

Cotton grown in the American South was shipped to Liverpool to provide raw material for the Manchester cotton textile factories. Baring Brothers, a great London merchant bank closely allied with Russell & Co., would issue bills of exchange on the sale of American cotton. These notes would be employed to buy opium in Bengal. The Indian drug would then be distributed in Canton in exchange for tea and other products, while Chinese tea and silks, as well as luxury items, would be purchased in the United States. Revenue from these commodities would be invested in cotton from southern plantations. Americans drank tea; Chinese smoked opium. Two drugs — one a pleasant stimulant, the other a destructive intoxicant — were the fundamental cogs in a global trade cycle that perpetrated the degradation of Negro slavery in the United States and launched the destruction of society in China.

Unfortunately, the Chinese stubbornly refused to implement the treaties of Nanking and Wanghia. British and American merchants expected that their legal systems would have exclusive jurisdiction within their port enclaves, but Chinese officials invariably insisted that their conventional procedures, including the use of torture and, to Western minds, other savage methods of punishment, should prevail. Above all, British and American officials argued that the Anglo-American definition of contract would be practiced exclusively in commercial arrangements with Chinese merchants.

As a result, a bitter series of disputes between Western shippers and Chinese merchants, tax collectors, and regulators dissolved into armed warfare between British military and naval forces and the soldiers of the emperor. Peking was captured and the fabled Summer Palace north of the Forbidden City was sacked.[52] In 1860 the illusion of a Celestial Empire ruled by a divinely empowered sovereign was wrecked beyond repair. China had disintegrated into an amorphous mess, the economy of which was controlled by rapacious Western commercial interests for their own devices. Civil and military officials, whose primary loyalty was to whatever authority might hold sway over them, supplied law and order.[53]

The only bright note in this tragic drama was the triumphant entry of a legion of Christian missionaries of various descriptions, who sought with evangelical fervor to convert the heathen Chinese to the brilliant and everlasting sunshine of the Western creed. However, their sincerity and drive to promote spiritual welfare was an annoyance, if not an outright insult, to the inhabitants of a land that possessed a religious and cultural legacy that, by some definitions, exceeded those cherished by the peoples of the West.[54]

When William Barker Cushing arrived in Hong Kong, Western merchants had penetrated throughout the vast interior of China by establishing trading enclaves or ports on the shores of the great rivers that provided access to remote regions. A network of some 90 of these privileged establishments had replaced the rudimentary collection of five at the formative period of Hong Kong's existence. From Shanghai, steam ships could make their passage up the broad waters of the Yangtze as far as Hankow, a distance of some 582 miles. In 1870 William H. Seward, the secretary of state in Lincoln's administration, surveyed the Yangtze at Hankow after a trip upstream from its estuary.[55]

How much Cushing comprehended of the momentous events that had reached their climax five years before his arrival is difficult to assess. Because of his youth, his knowledge of the recent past was limited. Certainly, his experiences in the horrendous American Civil War remained the focus of his memory. His first encounter with foreign climes and their inhabitants had been shaped by customary tourist activities, such as purchasing photographs and acquiring souvenirs, especially those that might bring pleasure to Kate. The serious business of naval patrolling and guarding the security of American merchants and implementing the policy of the United States had yet to command his attention and execution. For the moment, however, his reaction to the sights and sounds of a strange and perplexing land were undoubtedly shaped by the xenophobic outlook mixed with tinges of racism that prevailed in an isolated community perched on the edge of the vast expanse of the Far East.

However, Cushing, despite his youth, had proved to be an able ship's captain. He had maintained strict discipline in the ranks of his crew and earned the respect of his officers, most of whom were senior in age. Cushing had pursued regular exercises and drills in gunnery and firearms during the long weeks between distant ports. When the *Maumee* reached Hong Kong, she was in sound shape and her complement was well prepared for any engagement that might confront them.

Since his ship might be deployed in the estuary of Hong Kong or even in the lower reach of the Pearl River, he did, indeed, practice a raid against Chinese pirate ships. "I find," he commented, "that piracies upon European vessels are very rare, now'days — but junks often attack and plunder other Junks." He then reported that, "since we have been in here a Merchant junk called the 'Shun-tack-lee'— bound to Canton from this port, has been attacked and captured by two smaller junks only four miles away."[56] The pirates grappled with the side of the merchant ship, and then they dropped several "stink pots" on the deck of their victim; after killing two of the crew, they seized several bags of silver and a sizeable shipment of opium. "I see," Cushing recalled, "that all junks of any size carry cannon, but I learn that there is an order passed for them all to disarm within a month from now." He explained that "the consequence will be that we can determine hereafter, by search, if a junk is a Pirate — since a single weapon will be enough to convict them — I do not know how soon I shall be let loose to lock up these amiable beings."[57]

With such an event in mind, Cushing organized an exercise for the *Maumee*'s crew:

> This forenoon I have had my five boats "called away," and off, maneuvering in the harbor; with armed crews; by signals from the ship. At length, after forming in "line abreast," line ahead & to my satisfaction, I thought I would try them in boarding some ship. Just astern of us was a junk, at anchor with a crew of some twenty men and loaded with marketing. I got the boats formed in "in order of attack" some hundred yards from the junk — and there made signal "Board the enemy." In dashed the boats like lightning — two at his bow and two on the junk's starboard quarter — and in an instant, my men were on the high sides with a rousing cheer — and with drawn cutlasses and pistols.[58]

Cushing's exercise was a resounding success, but one must have some pity for the luckless culprits, the unsuspecting vendors of provisions, who in their panic jumped overboard. Probably not wishing to offend their merry clients, they made the best of their situation.

Despite considerable innocence on the whole panorama of Western penetration on Asian soil, Cushing had sufficient background to comprehend the responsibilities expected of him in the exercise of his position. It is at first glance strange that he would stumble inexcusably upon his arrival at Hong Kong, obviously a dynamic international port and a major citadel of the British military establishment. However limited his understanding may have been regarding the policies and objectives of American policy in the Far East, certainly his knowledge of naval protocol should have rescued him from a disastrous breach of etiquette. Commander Z.L. Tanner, who served on the *Maumee* on her voyage to the Far East, recalled that although Cushing "understood thoroughly the etiquette of the service and usually conformed to it when entering a foreign port, at times, however, he would ignore it entirely; would not make or receive the usual visits of ceremony."[59] On his arrival in Hong Kong, Cushing "had neglected to call upon Admiral Keppel, commanding the British fleet in Chinese waters, as it was his duty to have done."[60] British and American officers had made the appropriate exchange of visits, but Cushing had permitted an ensign, an officer of junior rank, to send his card to Admiral Keppel, who was not on board his ship when the officers from the *Maumee* made their visit. To have assigned a lowly ensign to assume an obligation of the captain of the *Maumee* was a churlish snub for which there was no excuse.

Admiral Keppel did not allow this affront to be disregarded. "The following day," Tanner reminisced, "Admiral Keppel came on board the *Maumee*, where he "was rec'd at the gangway by Cushing, the Executive Officer & Officer of the deck." "After the usual greetings," Tanner stated that "the Admiral enquired for Ensign Emory, saying that he had come on board to return his call," and "he declined Cushing's invitation to go into the cabin and was escorted to the wardroom where he made an unusually long call."[61]

Although "Cushing was considerably upset" by this incident, he ultimately admitted that Keppel's rebuke was well deserved. Such was also the verdict of Cushing's superior, who censored him severely for his incomprehensible behavior.[62] Possibly an explanation for Cushing's puzzling conduct, especially in light of his usually strict allegiance to the Navy's regulations and rules of acceptable behavior, is that he was overwhelmed with anxiety and disappointment by his beloved Kate's unexpectedly chilly prose, when he finally reached Hong Kong after six months without the comfort of any message from her. In his agony Cushing could readily reject naval courtesies as trivial ceremonies that were subordinate to the prospect of losing Kate. Despite Cushing's resumption of preparing his crew for possible combat against pirates and clandestine trade, and his obvious pride in his ship, Cushing could not escape remorse and sorrow in his relations with Kate.

In one moment of sorrowful pleading he cried, "God knows how gladly I would leave my Ship, the Navy — anything — to be at your side, and to plead my own cause to you." He vowed further that "I can not remain away thus, when all my hopes of happiness are endangered: if I have to resign to get home I will do it, rather than lose you — or risk your love."[63] Within a few weeks of entering Hong Kong as the proud proprietor of a sparkling ship and with the proved record of successful navigation of a long and exacting passage through seas that were frequently threatening, Cushing had allowed himself to be driven by his love for a young woman of twenty years to contemplate abandoning an illustrious past and a promising future. Such a precipitous action might not guarantee success in capturing the sure affection of Kate, for a civilian career would not come easily for a man whose entire professional life had been fashioned as a naval officer. Cushing had formulated a perilous course that could well wreck his hopes for both love and fortune.

There was another sobering cause for Cushing to sink into a melancholy mood. As he revealed to Kate, his secretary, Charles Higgins, had to be sent home to Fredonia:

> Mr. Higgins has been troubled for three Months with a cough — which has now become very bad; and is on his lungs. The Surgeon tells me that he has examined him, and fears that he has consumption — thinks he has detected a cavity in the right lung, but says that in a week or two more of observation he can decide. He fears that we must send Mr. Higgins home. The cough is certainly bad — and he has run down a great deal — but he does not know his danger — and I would not let it get to his parents for anything. If he comes home it will be soon enough for them to know it. It is too bad for he is a very nice fellow. I don't let him do any duty, and quietly manage that he shall enjoy himself ashore, as much as pleases.[64]

Higgins did return to Fredonia, where the *Fredonia Censor* announced in its issue of July 29, 1868, that after a long and exhausting trip from Yokohama to San Francisco and then to Panama to reach the United States, he had arrived home. Higgins brought encouraging news on the good health of Cushing and reported, furthermore, that the *Maumee* was the swiftest ship in the Asiatic Squadron. As a consequence, the *Maumee* "has been designated by the Admiral as his tender, and will be used for making excursions between the various ports and up the river into the interior of the country, so that a capital opportunity will be afforded them for sight seeing and adventure." The *Fredonia Censor* reminded its readers of the articles that Higgins had sent from Rio de Janeiro and Cape Town. It reported, "Mr. H. wrote another letter after leaving Cape Town to which he intended making additions at Hong Kong, but was unable to do so during his short stay." Nevertheless, the *Fredonia Censor* promised "it is an interesting description, racily written; we shall print it next week hoping that the writer may soon recover and hereafter furnish us with a continuation of the narrative."⁶⁵ Sadly, Higgins died on September 11, 1868.⁶⁶

It can be argued with reasonable confidence that Cushing's anguish in confronting the very possible conclusion that Kate was in earnest in her hints that she sought to end her alliance with him had momentarily overturned a sober observance of his duty as an officer of the United States Navy. However, there may also have been a strong undercurrent of animosity within the inner crevices of his mind about being exposed to the power of the British military and naval establishment at Hong Kong. Possibly Cushing nursed an antipathy toward the English. He had been reared in a small village close to Lake Erie, where the rural setting still resonated with the echo of the War of 1812. He likewise felt ambivalent about the conduct of the British during the Civil War; in his naval skirmishes, he had encountered the effort of the Royal Navy to implement clandestine trade with Confederate ports.

However, time marches on. The Civil War was rapidly dissolving into a chronicle of tragic proportions linked to a legend of heroic bravery. It was a legacy that held out a promise of a better tomorrow that had yet to be hammered into moral and constitutional reality. Meanwhile, neglected challenges and issues in the Far East had now moved to the forefront. Commodore Perry had opened Japan to Western trade, and Anglo-American cooperation in China assumed increasing importance as French, German, and Russian governments sought commerce and real estate in seas and territory formerly under British and American hegemony. Cushing had yet to learn that the Navy of the United States was not concerned with the conceits of the American hinterland.

Admiral Henry Keppel, the subject of Cushing's unfortunate snub, had entered the ranks of the Royal Navy in 1822 at the age of twelve. In 1867 he was forty-three years older than Cushing. His family had come to England in the entourage of William of Orange in 1688. His ancestors had performed valuable service to William and Mary and also to their successor, Queen Anne, the last of the Stuart monarchs. Under the Hanoverian sovereigns they continued to achieve noteworthy military and naval records. The head of the family had been awarded a peerage and received the title of the Earl of Albemarle. Keppel was a younger son of the fourth earl. He became involved in the Opium War, and later, in 1843–1844, he participated in a campaign against pirates operating from the shores of Borneo. Keppel also served in the Crimean campaign against the Russians in 1856. The French government had recognized his merit by awarding him the Cross of the Legion of Honour. For his accomplishments in China, in 1858 he had been admitted into a historic institution of medieval chivalry, the Order of Bath, now used frequently by the British sovereign to honor men who have accomplished a distinguished record in the service of their country. In his later years Keppel was an intimate friend of the Prince of Wales and his wife Alexandra, and his association with the royal family was underscored by his appointment to be a groom in waiting to Queen Victoria. In 1866 he had been appointed as the commanding officer of the British squadron at its China station, Hong Kong. From this post he visited the treaty ports on the coast of China, and he also implemented relations with the newly installed Mikado at Yeddo (Tokyo), Japan.[67]

Clearly, Keppel was an officer of real mettle. Cushing, the American hero, on the other hand, had damaged his reputation and embarrassed his Navy. His indiscreet behavior, however, did not prevent him from declaring to Kate that "I am a gentleman, Kate, a man of honor and integrity, of fine professional, and first-class social standing, wherever I go — with the means, and the will, to make you happy in every indulgence."[68] In underscoring his stature in society and as a naval officer of recognized accomplishment, Cushing may have remembered his mother's account of the Cushing family's illustrious roots in Massachusetts, and her discovery that the family possessed a coat of arms. His pedigree was rooted in the elite of the Bay Colony and in the leaders of the Revolution.[69]

"I half believe," he agonized, "that you wrote me the story of Mr. Oakley to make me jealous — inventing part of it — and that your yarn about the sleigh ride and under the lap robes."[70] Cushing was treading on uncertain terrain in hinting that Kate would be tempted to tarnish a solemn pledge for the transient pleasure of a snuggle under a Buffalo lap robe. Obviously, Cushing was thoroughly distraught by the absence of complete command over Kate's attention. He was truly the jealous lover. He deplored the news that his rival's company had fostered a fading love for her betrothed. "Do you think," he questioned, "It [is] right to accept so many favors from a gentleman, when you are engaged to me?" "And am I not injured by it," he demanded, "in thus having a rival taking my place, while I am far away, and trusting to your honor?"[71]

Yet Cushing reassured himself that Kate remained true to her promise to become his wife, because "I do not doubt that your noble nature will respond to mine; and that your gentle woman's heart will forgive the doubts that would be injurious to you, were it not that you have tortured my very soul with fear of losing you — while at the same time you speak words of love to me that how very happy we can be, when I return — when I can clasp you in my arms, and be repaid, in one kiss for all that I now suffer."[72] He then envisioned that "we can reproduce the delicious days of last Summer — and in our rides and drives, and rambling walks, can enjoy the certainty of love that has been proven by time and distance and temptation, but which has triumphed over all, as it must, through a life-time."[73]

In a letter to Kate written the day after his impassioned entreaties and sharp-edged remonstrations, accompanied by firm proclamations of enduring faith and love, Cushing resolved not to direct such an overwhelming barrage in the future. His promise must have pleased his twenty-year-old fiancée, who probably did not anticipate such a rousing lecture on true faith beyond the Sunday service pulpit. Cushing did not completely break away from his offensive, although he did ask to be remembered to her sister Leila and their mother, and for the first time he addressed her father as "General," a title accorded to him in courteous recognition of his being head of a volunteer regiment, even though it was never ordered into active service. In an effort to block any parental pressure to have second thoughts about a wandering and, perhaps, straying sailor, Cushing advised Kate to "tell the General that I do not think his remark—'Cushing is at the bottom of the Sea,' very encouraging to you. Tell him that I am not one of the drowning kind, but would be sure to turn up safe, on a whale's back, if the ship were lost."[74]

Two days later Cushing had regained his self-composure and he began to reflect soberly on the emotion-filled salvo that he had hurled against his hapless love. Kate's only real misdemeanor had been to give vent to high-spirited shenanigans that her role as a polished and grown-up woman should not encompass. She had chosen to leave the joyful ranks of feckless young women freshly liberated from their tiresome schooling to be the fiancée of a lieutenant commander in the United States Navy. Both Kate and Cushing had rushed into an overcharged romantic alliance in too short a time; the reality of their long separation could only aggravate doubts and temptations growing from their limited knowledge of each other's true character.

"May I write to you tonight," Cushing asked Kate, "to tell you what a foolish fellow I find myself to be, now that my head is cool and my jealous fit is gone by." He queried, "Will you forgive me, and not be angry at my doubts of you." He assured her that "I have none tonight, and think you just perfect, and if I should get twenty pages from you now, filled with descriptions of the attractions you received, and accepted from gentlemen, I would not flush up a bit or frown even once."

Cushing did not hesitate to acknowledge that he had urged Kate to participate in the customary social activities that were open to her. "Did I not tell you," he reminded her, "when I went away that I <u>wish</u> you to enjoy yourself—and that I had perfect confidence that you would never compromise my honor or your own?" He concluded his song of contrition and prayer for forgiveness with a joyful affirmation of devoted allegiance. "My Kate <u>couldn't</u> wrong me," because "she is nobility itself," was the comforting hymn of the penitent.[75] Cushing continued his evangelical liturgy.

> Kate, <u>darling</u>, help me to be a Christian—it seems to me as if my very Soul leaned on your care and guidance—I couldn't believe in anything good if you fail me. I shudder to think how black and unbelieving my heart would become. I have fixed all my faith on you—and with your aid, I can be truly good—without it how can I ever again believe? I should doubt all things. I feel it, and know it. Will you not always be my guardian—the one living person who shall be my

ideal of true womanhood? You cannot realize, from what you have seen of me, how purely and solemnly I love you now; not human passion — it is refined love, purified by constant thought and prayer — and love that can only be expressed by that one word — <u>devotion</u> but oh, Kate — <u>my love</u> — <u>my life</u>! — it craves love in return — reaches <u>out</u> with a painful longing for your warm woman's heart — not selfishly, but with an intense desire to make you happy — and to honor you above all things. I feel now that my happiness is dependent upon yours — and that my highest earthly wish is to be the medium through which it shall flow to you.[76]

Having confessed his errors and (he hoped) received absolution, a born-again Cushing could reveal his practice of strict economy so that Kate would be comfortably provided with the necessities and amenities of the home, and a husband firmly adhering to the path of righteous behavior. On the other hand, he did not seek to submit to an absolute standard of unflinching conduct. He announced that his mustache and hair were sporting a luxuriant growth and that overall he was "in fine flirting condition." Indeed, he reported that "I had a most bewitching bid for such an entertainment this afternoon — and I wonder if you would care." "Perhaps if I try hard," he teased, "and give my time to it, I may be the gainer of a dressing gown and smoking cap in the end." However, he quickly added, "she is such a perfect lady, and you can not, therefore, object." Cushing could not forego observing, "It seems to me that I've heard that remark before — or — read it some where <u>it couldn't have been in your letter</u>. I must have dreamed it."[77]

Apparently, Cushing failed to recognize that it is not appropriate to proceed directly from making a fervent protestation of enduring love to a woman to dropping a casual hint that you might succumb to a romantic interlude with another of the same species. Possibly Cushing was demonstrating that he functioned in a compartmental regimen — the logical course was to move from one issue to the next. He had been involved all day in a court-martial proceeding he had launched against two officers on his staff, both of whom were volunteers. They had exercised their authority with indifferent respect toward their responsibilities. As a result, they were dismissed from the Navy. Their replacements were two promising graduates from the Naval Academy.

Unfortunately, Cushing encountered considerable difficulty in dismissing his anxiety over the behavior of his fiancée. He wavered from accepting that Kate was enjoying an innocent and transient relationship without any motive but the pleasure of the moment. Certainly, she had no intention of abandoning her true love, a man of real distinction who was serving his country in a distant land that provided little relief from the ever-present dangers of his mission. But Cushing remained haunted by suspicion that Kate sought to rid herself of a remote and overly serious lover who had, in effect, deserted her at a time when the passions of her youth challenged her to explore fresh opportunities.

His fears that the latter explanation was the actual fact could even make their way into his dreams. He wrote to Kate:

> My darling, I dream about you every night — such vivid dreams! — that I feel sad or happy the whole day after. Last night I thought that I was back and met your Father at the store — I noticed something strange about his greeting — and, when he took me aside — saying that he had something to tell me — I saw it all — and I awoke exclaiming aloud, "<u>Don't</u> tell me that!" For God's sake do not say it! And I am not ashamed that tears were on my cheek, that the dream had called forth: for I never felt, waking, such mental agony — and I could scarcely realize that it was a dream. But when I heard the Ship's bell toll out the hour; and the tramp of men and the whistling of the wind above me — I rose from my berth and knelt down, and thanked God that in his mercy, it was but a dream.[78]

After having narrated his dream, which had a hallucinatory character, Cushing returned to his customary recital of current activities or else those that were forthcoming. He announced that the next morning he would navigate his ship toward Canton with Admiral Rowan on board. Obviously, Canton would supply plenty of exciting detail to capture Kate's attention; moreover, he reported that the admiral was contemplating dispatching Cushing to the capital of Siam, where he would present some gifts from the government of the United States to the king. "If I go we will have a grand time," he explained, "in entertaining his majesty on board — and being entertained in turn with fearful tiger fights, Elephant hunts and I shall expect some magnificent presents, also." The reason for such lavishness was that "Men o' War seldom go there — and there will be a big Time." Cushing promised that "if he gives me a big diamond, you shall have it."[79]

Alas, Kate did not have the chance to be the recipient of a handsome sparkling gem from Siam, for her hero received instructions to convey Admiral Rowan to Canton. Rowan sought to persuade the Chinese viceroy for that city and the surrounding territories to accept an Anglo-American request to cooperate in an attempt to halt piracy on the Pearl River. Proudly, Cushing conveyed Rowan on the *Maumee* through the broad waters of the estuary into which flowed the Pearl River. He wrote:

> We left Hong Kong this morning with a dozen guests on board: amongst whom was our jolly and gallant Admiral; and I landed them this afternoon, right side up, and in good order, after a remarkably pleasant nine hours of social pastime — and curious observation. The Canton River is, for fifty miles, one of the widest and most majestic in the world — too wide, indeed, to see clearly from a ship, in its channel, the scenery upon its flanks, but it narrows and each moment becomes filled with interest.[80]

Cushing proceeded to describe the narrow straits delineated by Tiger Island and the first and second bars. He saw hillsides that were dotted by endless rows of tombstones, many of which were arranged in horseshoe configurations. The vast expanse of rice fields eventually gave way to higher ground on which ranged terraced rows of tea-bearing shrubs. The most impressive ornaments of this landscape were "mighty pagodas, standing sentinel like on the crests of the mountains — and the swarm of human life over all — kept me in a state of perpetual wonder and admiration."[81]

"Some of the pagodas," he remarked, "were a thousand feet high, and have stood for nearly as many years." He then commented that "they are not churches, but monuments built to the Gods; and supposed to bring commerce and prosperity to the community in which they stand." These majestic guardians of a sprawling landscape of land and water watched over a mass of "busy, toiling thousands." Cushing had quickly perceived that "a Chinaman is never idle — he works because he must; since the dense population keeps up constant competition in his struggle for life."[82]

Cushing elaborated his reaction to the panorama of multitudes of industrious men and women who seemed never to pause the ceaseless routine of their labor:

> Indeed, the people could not all subsist upon the land. Millions inhabit the water as fish, women and boatmen — living always there — and not permitted to step foot ashore for an instant. In a boat not larger than the small fishing craft you see at Dunkirk, a Chinaman will commence his independent life — assisted by his wife: and in that boat his children are born — his meals eaten; his work, rest, worship accomplished — in fact, his whole life passed. And this goes on, generation after generation — each man leaving his particular calling to his children — and they, in turn, to theirs. A shoemaker, for instance, is probably the descendant of a thousand years of peg drivers. Here at Canton, spread out before me is an immense city of boats — moored in regular streets — each containing as many people as can find room in them to lie down — and, the whole, probably numbering one hundred thousand who are not there for some hours of daily labor merely; but for all their life.[83]

Cushing was interrupted in writing his impressions of Canton and its inhabitants by a message that the American consul was ready to board the ship. Cushing explained that since the admiral's pennant had been hoisted, the *Maumee* had become an official instrument of the diplomacy of the American government. As a result, there would be a number of formal visits to the ship, and "we will [also] be banging away with our great guns for two days to impress the Celestials with the importance of their visitors."[84]

The calm reception that Cushing and his entourage encountered in the channel that flowed past the main harbor of Canton was a far cry from the angry resistance of the Cantonese and their viceroy to the presence of Harry Parkes, the previous British consul. In 1857 Parkes had to summon gunboats and marines from Hong Kong to storm through the walls of Canton in order to gain an audience with the viceroy, with the goal of persuading him to implement the Treaty of Nanking, which had stipulated that Canton was to be open to British merchants and their goods. The obstinacy of the viceroy quickly turned into outright resistance. Negotiations were scuttled and the viceroy seized and dispatched to exile in India, whereupon Parkes assumed the role of governor of Canton and its immediate vicinity. Fortunately, Parkes had a sound knowledge of Chinese, including an understanding of the meandering Cantonese dialect. Although Canton had been pacified and compelled to accept representatives of foreign nations and their traders, China was far from restored to civil peace, and her relations with foreign powers were subject to quixotic change.[85]

The site of foreign shipping and financial interests had been destroyed during the conflict. As a result, Parkes had to negotiate with Chinese authorities for a new location, one where European and American traders and shippers could conduct their operations with reasonable security. Since 1833, the East India Company had lost its monopoly of trade, with the single exception of tea, as far as commerce between Great Britain and the Far East was concerned. However, independent traders — or country shippers, as they were conventionally described — such as Jardine and Dent now held a dominant position in British commerce with China. Parkes decided that a small island named Shaimen would provide adequate protection. However, it had little real terrain. Consequently, its size had to be enlarged by dredging. This island, which was close to the shore of Canton, would be guarded by water, which would make surprise raids difficult and still be convenient to Canton for business and official exchange. Therefore, the prospect that Cushing gazed upon in 1868 as he anchored his ship presented a comfortable façade of prosperous commercial bustle. This harmonious and cheerful landscape was far removed from the stage on which Parkes and his small garrison had been pinned down by a mob of angry Cantonese determined once and for all to rid themselves of interfering foreigners. Cushing probably anchored the *Maumee* on the Bund of Shaimen, which faced the open waters of the Pearl River.[86]

Two years after Cushing made his trip from Hong Kong to Canton, he was followed by William H. Seward, Lincoln's secretary of state, who discovered that the British concession on the island of Shaimen contained thirty or forty foreign *hongs* of generous dimensions. Originally, in the eighteenth century these mercantile establishments had been described as factories, a name that remained in use during the early part of the nineteenth century. Seward caught sight of an Anglican church constructed with white marble, "and a club-house with a good library and billiard room; on the bank, a promenade, handsomely ornamented with gardens, which rejoices in the name of Cha-min (Sand-face)." The American houses, Russell & Co. and Smith and Arthur & Co., had questioned the legal footing that they were required to accept on Shaimen and, therefore, they rebuilt their pavilions in the Chinese quarter on the outskirts of the British concession.[87]

On Sunday morning Cushing awakened to the greeting of a heavy downpour, a common occurrence during the summer months, and although he had been welcomed by Archdeacon Gray, the Anglican cleric who had been with Parkes in the treacherous days a decade earlier, he decided to forego the customary obligation of Sunday service to wait until the sun improved the atmosphere. (Gray, who escorted Cushing on a tour of the principal sights of old Canton, would likewise welcome Seward.)[88] After the drenching rain had ceased and the sun provided a bright dry spell, Cushing searched for the house of a Mr. Oliphant (undoubtedly a partner in Oliphant & Co., which had old roots in Canton and represented New York mercantile interests), where Admiral Rowan was staying. "There amidst books and Pictures — flowers, fruit, cigars, conversation and boundless hospitality, I passed my first day in this ancient City," Cushing wrote in an obvious mellow mood.[89] He recalled:

> We sat out on the wide and cool veranda, watching the river; and looking across it at the immense City — so odd to us — destitute as it is of the tall spires and domes and undulations of our western land. Then we counted the boats that passed by us, in the narrow stream — and you can form some idea of the floating populace, when I tell you that three thousand twenty went by in a single hour, at the rate, estimating fairly, of thirty six thousand boats in twelve hours, while, in none of these are less than eight people living always.[90]

Cushing could not resist telling Kate that "these craft are all worked by women — and it is quite a novel sensation, I can assure you, to sit cozily under the bamboo awning, lolling back upon the mat, while five or six young ladies, with most elaborate headdresses, and exceedingly pretty feet and hands, tug and strain at the heavy oars. In the broiling Sun, for whole hours in one's service."[91]

Despite the fair tableau, Cushing resisted an impulse to display any concern for their tedious and tiring labor. He even shouted, "Chop, Chop," to signal that he wished his crew to quicken their pace. "This," he wondered, "from a man who has often surrendered his seat on a car, to the most unromantic and coarse Irish bag-women, and even female Africans, because they wore crinoline!" He speculated that "perhaps the secret is in the fact that women don't wear crinoline here — but boldly don the breeches!" He concluded his observations with a stern warning that American women should exercise caution. Undoubtedly, "voting will be the next step," he admonished, "to a mania for trousers, and I may, yet, row around in Lake Erie, as I do in the Canton River, propelled by their fair arms and urging them on with a 'Chop! Chop' of impatience."[92]

The following day Cushing and his party were escorted, in a thunderous downpour of rain, through narrow streets to visit a tea shop, where they were invited to taste twenty varieties of tea. From that establishment they moved on to an atelier that was devoted to carving in ivory, where they examined an enormous elephant tusk that was seven feet in length and at its base a foot

4. Cruising on the Troubled Waters of the Far East 75

Cushing in a palanquin — the mode of travel in Hong Kong. No horses were allowed.

wide. This imposing piece was being carved into representations of scenic landscapes for the current Chinese viceroy. Their next stop was at a gallery for painting. Once again, Cushing was attracted to portraits. "One picture in particular," he remarked, "struck me as quite handsome." He explained that "the original was the young wife of a Chinese gentleman living in Hong Kong — I asked ... if she had small feet — and was informed that they were number four." "It seems," Cushing calculated, "that No. 1 is the smallest and most aristocratic, and that the ladies' chances of a high or even respectable marriage depend upon this deformity." He provided a reason: "no decent Chinaman will marry a woman whose feet do not have evidence that she has had them compressed in bandages from earliest infancy."[93]

Cushing and his friends traveled on to an "immense establishment filled with samples of all descriptions of Crockery ware." Although he did not know Kate's preferences, he took a plunge and ordered one hundred and twenty-four pieces of the same pattern chosen by General Grant. "It will be four months before they are done, but they are perfectly elegant — and I know you will like them," he predicted hopefully. He reassured her that Admiral Rowan had ordered the same pattern, without Cushing's prior knowledge. Cushing then added, "I supposed that I must get off a set of silver made to match it." He outlined the structure of the Chinese system of pricing silver objects, explaining, "The Chinese silver workers will make all kinds of ware — charging only thirty-percent over the actual weight in dollars." He gave an illustration of this method: "for instance, I can get five dozen of forks and spoons or heavy fish knife and fork — soup ladle — sugar spoons — pickle fork &&— by giving the worker 175 Mexican dollars to melt down — and he will charge me thirty per cent for the work." He asked, "Shall I do it?"[94] Kate was in a trap. Whatever doubts she may have entertained about her alliance with a distant love, she was now bought by china and silver. Without sacrificing common sense, she could scarcely reject such gifts and retain the respect of her friends and parents.

In his expedition through the maze of twisting lanes that composed the market of Canton, Cushing discovered that the houses were brick and the streets were paved. Over the shops were hung large painted and gilded signs, and the open fronts of the shops revealed a dazzling array of enticing wares and goods. "Miles of jewelry shops pass in review — each shining like Aladdin's Cave — Miles of curiosity stores; miles of silk and tea houses — street upon street in endless succession — of all the trade and manufactures you can conceive of," he pronounced with a touch of awe and even a dash of ecstasy.[95]

In an equivocal mode, Cushing recounted his gastronomic experience in surveying the products of the Chinese market. He observed "whole bundles of rats dressed and dried — ready for cooking," and he also witnessed a number of dogs and a dozen cats that were ready for boiling or frying. In regard to the latter, he had been informed that their eyes were judged "to be the greatest of delicacies." Meditating on this strange delicatessen, Cushing argued that the consumption of cats and rats by the Chinese "is highly creditable to them if looked upon in the right light — for it demonstrates how anxious they are that justice shall be done to all things — since they show no partiality to cats and rats alike."[96]

Cushing continued his excursions though the alleys and streets of Canton, as well as enjoying the amenities of hospitable merchants. All these pleasantries were pursued, despite constant showers and dull skies. "All here is so novel," he acknowledged happily, "that I enjoy it mightily; and only wish that our stay might be prolonged."[97] He provided an outline of his daily routine:

> I go off to breakfast at the house of some opulent merchant in company with the Admiral and his staff— such pleasant social breakfasts! There are never less than a dozen at the table, and are men, all of them. *Men* I say — yes! — for alas! There are no European or American Women in Canton — and our social gatherings are not illuminated by the smiles of beauty. Every evening, at half after eight, I sit down to a princely dinner at some hospitable house — and not smothered in dress coat — but clad in cool white from top to toe — and the refreshing "punkeer" waving overhead banishing both heat and insects. Each afternoon in our rove about — (sometimes in our chairs — sometimes walking — with those handy articles following us) through temples, floating streets and palace grounds — or up on the old City walls to the famous pagoda, from which the entire city can be seen, stretching out miles and miles until dim in the hazy distance.[98]

When through with his comfortable repast, Cushing frequently would stroll down to the river to gaze upon the lush profusion of boats, during which times he paid particular attention to "flower junks." These highly ornamented ships had two stories, and their elaborately carved and gilded exteriors were complemented by their equally plush interiors, which featured rows of ornate chandeliers and tables loaded with flowers and fruit. The flower junks were a focal point for social entertainment for Chinese men in the evening, where they could join in convivial conversation with their friends as numerous girls with elaborate painted faces balancing "helmet-like head dresses" sat behind them.

Cushing was particularly fascinated by the make-up and hairstyle of these girls. He told Kate:

> The amiable damsels had each a box of paint in front of them which they plastered on tight at the table, until their prominent cheek bones glowed to the bloom of roses. I wish that I could give you some idea of the way in which the hair is dressed. It is the most elaborate piece of work that I have ever seen. The most complicated thing of the kind in the United States or Europe is simplicity itself compared to it.[99]

At the end of the meal the girls left the men to sit in space reserved for musicians and performers. Each girl sang in sequence, displaying a "shrill and (to us) discordant voice — accompanied by a string band of six or eight pieces." He announced, moreover, "the combination of sounds would put to shame a hundred excited tom cats." "These fair maidens," he decided, "are not strictly speaking 'comme il faut'; but many are taken as wives, nevertheless, by wealthy Chinese who sometimes pay as high as five hundred dollars to buy her of the people who own her." Cushing observed that "the girls had no smiles for the 'barbarians'; and seemed not to see us." However, they enjoyed frolicking with the "young bloods," who took considerable delight in fondling them publicly as they indulged in a whiff of opium.[100]

Cushing had been particularly intrigued during his exploration of the streets and byways of the sprawling market of Canton by the fact that every shop had a "Josh or Joshn" (Buddha) prominently surrounded by flowers, decorations, and lighted tapers and candles, which burned day and night. This phenomenon prompted him to declare, "I should go into the idol department if I wanted to do business and make money in China." Images of Buddha appeared to Cushing to be an indispensable necessity to the Chinese, whether they lived on the water or on land. He asserted that "this people beat the Roman Catholics, beyond comparison, in their outward show of devotion and worship."[101] On the other hand, despite his initial impression of the character of Chinese worship (formed when he had visited a temple in Hong Kong with the Goddards), Cushing sought to improve his fragmentary knowledge of Chinese Buddhism by visiting a prominent temple not too far removed from the core of the Canton. He wrote a thorough review of this trip, which obviously had provoked reflection on the whole spectrum of religious thought and practice. His Baptist background anchored the evangelical fervor of the raw concepts of righteousness and salvation that prevailed in the frontier, but could not readily prompt appreciation of a religion far removed from the tenets found in the worship of his boyhood. He recorded that "at five o'clock, one evening, we all went in company with a Missionary who speaks the language, to an immense Buddhist temple in Ho-Nam." He quickly surmised that "the Josh houses that I saw at Hong Kong might have been bodily placed on the altar." He proceeded to give a lengthy description of the edifice:

> The building was huge in extent; covering fifty acres of ground — and inhabited by three hundred priests. There were numerous walls, archways, and paved court-yards intervening between the inner temple of worship and the outside world — and at each of the gates, as we advanced, were horrible-looking figures, twenty feet high — standing as guardians — clad in gorgeous robes and twined about with serpents and dragons. The God of Mirth and the God of Anger are the only two that I can name.[102]

Cushing felt some sense of awe in the colorful and stately pageantry that he then watched, for he acknowledged that "the worship in the temple was quite impressive; and if I had not known where I was I should have thought myself amongst the Roman Catholics." He then provided a descriptive tapestry of the ceremony and liturgy:

> Three hundred priests, with heads shaved bare, chanted before the altars — clad in long robes of mouse colored cloth draped with yellow — folding their hands in prayer — prostrating themselves before the idols — and marching around with solemn chant. The idols seemed to be of bronze — and numbered about fifty — all being about twelve feet high, excepting "Josh [Buddha]," who must have been twenty. There were three figures of him. They also have a "Trinity" — representing the past, present and future — and these figures illustrated the idea. Is it not singular that these pagans recognized "three persons in one God" — and that the forms of worship used by them for thousands of years, are so similar to those of the Catholic Church![103]

When on June 2 a messenger from the imperial viceroy summoned Admiral Rowan and his staff to an official audience, the climax and real purpose of the trip occurred. Cushing recorded that the journey from the ship to the vice-regal palace took an hour and a half and the deployment of a squadron of coolie-borne and -propelled bamboo chairs. Cries of "Stand back! Big Mandarins! Mandarins!!" kept curious crowds at a respectful distance, allowing the clumsy caravan to proceed at a steady pace. After parading through several courtyards, Admiral Rowan, his officers, a missionary serving as an interpreter, and the American consul arrived before "the door of reception," where they were greeted by "the great Mandarin of the red button — 'Ching Su-lo' — Mighty ruler of two broad provinces." His Eminence was a man of some 60 years. He had thin gray hair, a mustache, and sagging shoulders, but also sharp eyes. He wore long black robes, which were adorned with "the blue shield of his rank." Cushing observed that "on his head was a conical hat, with the blood red button — and plume of peacock feathers — and around his neck were two strings of beads — one of jade-stone (the Chinese diamond) and the other of peach stones."[104]

The viceroy conducted his guests along series of corridors, which led to the hall in which formal audiences were conducted. "It was a large and handsome room," Cushing wrote, "with a raised dais or throne at the upper end — upon which the Admiral was seated — we being in red-draped chairs at his right and left — while the Viceroy, according to his notions of politeness, took a stool near the door — surrounded by his interpreters and suite." Before discussing the topic at hand, the viceroy served each of his guests a cup of tea.[105]

In his conversation, Rowan requested that the Chinese assist the foreign navies stationed at Hong Kong in their proposal to disarm all junks, including those employed in fishing. "I was much amused," Cushing recalled, "to see the wily old Statesman made an immediate answer by motioning us to the 'chow chow' table — which was placed in the middle of the room, and loaded with sweetmeats and confections." Each guest had a fork and knife and a small plate. The viceroy served each man a bit of whatever delicacy was directly in front of his plate.

The same etiquette was expected of Rowan. Cushing joked that "it did look funny to see our gallant old Admiral taking up a preserved plum, carefully, on his fork, and gravely passing it across the table to the Viceroy." The beverage served was a concoction resembling sherry. Cushing and his companions were required to take a sip at two-minute intervals, when the viceroy "would take his little cup in both hands — look earnestly, all 'round the table, and drink — a challenge that we were bound to accept." However, the quality of the drink did not hinder Cushing from amply consuming the various condiments adorning the table.[106]

At 2:00 P.M. on the following Thursday, the viceroy made a return visit to the *Maumee*. Cushing, with some amusement, described the spectacle to Kate:

> Our visitor came in great state — attended to the landing by a large body of troops; and escorted off to our vessel by several Chinese Men o' War — Such noise of gunpowder gongs and bells I never heard before. He came in a large carved frescoed junk — pulled by two hundred oars — preceded by a smaller boat; in which was his "card bearer," who presented cards to the Admiral, myself, and the Consul. I enclose the card. It is quite a curiosity — being the card of the highest dignitary of the Empire, next to the Emperor himself. He was formerly the Prime Minister of China. My ship was dressed off in flags and looked very gay — and my officers were all in full dress. We received him with great ceremony and fired a salute of twenty-one guns, both on his arrival and at his departure. The old fellow got quite jolly, especially after the first ten minutes at the table;

where he stowed away a quantity of Chicken Salad, Fredonia Strawberries, Champagne, Sherry tea and where he did me the honor to drink a bumper with me — holding up his glass with a grin to show that it was empty — and also paid me the compliment to enquire my name, age — a thing that is looked upon as a marked courtesy.[107]

The reception concluded with a thorough inspection of the ship and its equipment. The viceroy was permitted to fire off the primer of one of the cannons; the loud bang pleased him very much. While he remained on the *Maumee*, a crowd of armed junks surrounded it. Cushing speculated that the "wary old Celestial" might have feared being abducted and carried off to exile in a distant land, as had been the fate of a predecessor during the regime of Harry Parkes.[108]

Such was the conclusion of Admiral Rowan's foray into the turbulent waters of diplomatic navigation with Chinese authorities. Having a long history of trade with China, British merchants had become skeptical about the trading ethics of their Chinese counterparts. A late eighteenth-century account asserted trenchantly that "the Chinese in general have been represented as the most dishonest, low, thieving set in the world; employing their natural quickness only to improve the arts of cheating the nations they deal with, especially the Europeans, whom they cheat with great ease, particularly the English: but they observe that none but a Chinese can cheat a Chinese."[109] The author of this scathing commentary, however, tempered his denunciation by admitting that such disparaging reports came from the traders and sailors who frequented the ports and harbors of China, which undoubtedly attracted the usual swarm of disreputable men who practiced any number of illicit pursuits. He acknowledged, "But it seems not just to attempt to characterize a great nation by a few instances of this kind, though well attested," and he suggested further that "we appear not to be sufficiently acquainted with the interior parts of China to form an accurate judgment of the manners and characters of the inhabitants."[110]

The Second Opium War started at Canton, but eventually reached its climax at Peking, which was occupied by an Anglo-French expeditionary force that finished its triumphant sweep by sacking the fabled Summer Palace in the heart of imperial China. In 1860 the emperor and his entourage were compelled to accede to the full roster of treaty ports that had been demanded by the British, who were joined in this stipulation by the French and Americans. The nearly four years' worth of internecine conflict that had engulfed the American nation had obviously diverted attention from the mounting international rivalry for power and trade in the Far East.

The immediate task of Admiral Rowan in 1868 was to assist the British in rooting out piracy on the Pearl River. There were, however, other arenas where pirates were able to execute their daring attacks with impunity. On June

8 Cushing informed Kate that his preparations for sailing to Nagasaki had been suspended temporarily to permit him to assist the British naval forces in crimping the extent and ferocity of piratical onslaughts. An English gunboat had entered the harbor from the Gulf of Tonkin, where a dozen ships well armed with cannon had attacked it. The English gunboat sank one adversary and captured another, but had been compelled to break off the engagement. "So the British Commodore has proposed to Admiral Rowan a joint expedition to attack the pirates," Cushing explained, "and I am the one selected to take charge of the movement."[111]

"Of course I am pleased," Cushing reassured Kate, "and the more as I am to start for Japan as soon as I see fit." He announced that "if the pirates are lively, I shall remain amongst them for some time — and try to make a little money — and to rub off the enervating rust of idleness — but the moment it gets dull — off I will go to a cooler climate." He mentioned that he was receiving a Mandarin from Canton to provide instruction on the terrain and inhabitants, and repeated his intention to make a profit on this excursion: "I do not intend to reap less than half the honors of the expedition." He warned, therefore, that "if John Bull gets 'to wind'ard' of me he will have to get up very early." He had been cautioned, "from the Englishman, that the pirates 'fight like blazes'— and that we may safely anticipate sharp work."[112]

Cushing did confess that "sometimes when I think of what you wrote about losing your love for me in that first four months — I feel a little reckless — and, as if I would try to get 'used up' in some fight." However, speaking on an introspective note, he added, "I will see how I happen to look at it when the time comes — but it is probable that I shall continue to look out for 'Number One' as usual."[113]

Cushing's orders from Admiral Rowan stated that fourteen well-armed junks had engaged the British gunboat. "You will put yourself in communication with Commodore Jones," the orders ran, "and say that you are ready to leave with his gunboats at any time he may order her Majesty's vessels to depart on this service." Rowan, furthermore, stipulated that "you will have a frank understanding with the Commander of the *Algerine* and get from him all the important information, which his long experience in chasing pirates, will enable him to give you — and above all let nothing be done by either party that might disturb the harmony and good feeling that exists in the two squadrons."[114]

Rowan also advised Cushing to "arrange with the Commander of the English gun boat signals for danger and one for depth of water, and permit him to lead over doubtful bottoms, where your vessel, drawing twice the water of the *Algerine* might be hazarded upon rocks or shoals. It may be that you can get [a] reliable pilot; the Commodore may be able to name [someone]." In conclusion, Rowan stated that Cushing should reach Yokohama on July 1. He left a store ship, the *Onward*, to provide additional supplies and, finally, advised that Cushing should anticipate an allowance of ten days to cover the distance from the Gulf of Tonkin to Japan.[115]

On the eve of his departure, Cushing received a notice from Ellis King, the American consul at Canton, that, in reply to Cushing's request for a Chinese officer to assist in negotiations with local officials, Major Wong Ting Yeo of the Lung-Mum Regiment had been detailed to serve under Cushing's command.[116] Cushing had requested that the viceroy, who had been well pleased with his reception on the *Maumee* at Canton, be asked if he might provide "a Mandarin to assist me in detecting the pirates, amidst the thousands of vessels on the Coast." Consequently, Cushing wrote that "yesterday a Chinese Man o' War came down — and soon the desired Official came over the side, with his suite — in considerable state — and preceded, as usual, by his card bearer, who handed me his card marked with the usual goose tracks, and a letter of introduction from the consul — from the latter of which I became informed that my visitor was the blue button Mandarin General 'Wong-Ting-Yeo' — commanding the 'Lung-Mum' forces."[117] Cushing's Mandarin guest was accompanied by an interpreter, "who spoke very good English — and I was enabled to converse with the blue-button as freely as desired." Yet Cushing was careful to avoid too familiar relations with Wong Ting Yeo and his staff, for he put them into quarters reserved for ward room officers, "not being willing to take even so important a fellow into my Cabin — as it is best to stand very much upon 'dignity' with this people in order to keep them impressed with our importance."[118]

Thus, Cushing was prepared to sail to the Gulf of Tonkin to swipe happily at any brazen pirates that might drop onto his horizon. In this way, he had a chance to renew his reputation for bold action on the sea, and at the same time seize the opportunity to garner lucrative prize money.

In the short interlude between making arrangements for his tour duty and actually departing, Cushing admitted to Kate that he was enjoying a spell of conviviality. He attended a ball at the Portuguese Club, where he spent a pleasant evening dancing with several Portuguese belles and managed to employ his meager Spanish and French with some success. Perhaps he may have reflected that his reluctance to pursue his Spanish lessons at Annapolis, which had occasioned his abrupt dismissal, had been truly a mistaken protest. His social life took on formality with a dinner given by the British commodore, and the arrival of both a Russian and a Prussian ship provided a round of visitations among officers of ships anchored in the harbor.[119]

On the evening before leaving Hong Kong, Cushing gave a gala reception for the official and social establishment of the British colony, enlarging and embellishing the minstrel performance that he had inaugurated successfully at Cape Town. A newspaper account of this event reveals that this purely American musical phenomenon struck the largely English audience as a curious novelty that provided a rare glimpse into a purely American form of music and comedy. "The 'Amateur Minstrels' on board the USS *Maumee*," the correspondent reported, "entertained a large number of their friends last evening with a performance which, to say the least, was highly gratifying to their guests and deserves at present more than a mere passing notice." He elaborated: "The program consists entirely of 'Minstrely,' that is the delineation of what in The United States is termed the 'Essence of ol' Virginia.' The 'awkward nigger' with his plantation shoes clog dances into the 'respectable colored gen'man,' who sports a gold watch and chain, all of whom took their turn in keeping the audience in a continued laugh."[120]

The author of this article was particularly impressed by the performances of two of the cast, Dunmore and Rush. Dunmore "as a jig dancer ... is far ahead of many professionals we have seen, while the stump speech of Rush was as funny as it was original."[121] Undoubtedly, Rush is the sailor to whom Cushing referred on December 21, 1867, when, shortly before landing in Rio de Janeiro, he wrote in his diary, "[I] have given the men permission to organize a troop of 'Nigger Minstrels' for the entertainment of the guests &c." "The leader of them," Cushing noted, "was 'middle man' in a company of them ashore." Cushing, nevertheless, was perplexed about the background of this man, who enlisted for the lowly position of a coal heaver: "I don't know how he came to ship as coal heaver."[122]

On the day that Cushing had granted permission to form a musical ensemble, he overheard the petitioner talking about his employment: "Now that I am down to this; and am a coal bearer for this engine, I hope that if I die you'll burn my body up in the furnaces." When his auditors asked why he wished this end to his life, he replied, "Because I wish my ashes to mingle with the grate [great]." Rush was the performer who delivered a "Ten Minutes in Congress 'Stump speech,'" which the newspaper report described as being "as funny as it was original."[123]

In a quick note to Kate before sailing, Cushing said that "last night our entertainment was given and attended by the best people in Hong Kong." The program had been a stunning triumph. "I laughed as did everyone, until my sides ached," he cheerfully declared.[124] To confirm his stunning reception, Cushing sent Kate a clipping from a newspaper describing the glittering event staged on the decks of the *Maumee*. "Oh! By the Way! I must enclose in this letter," he wrote, "the newspaper notice of our entertainment at Hong Kong, and an article from an English paper about our visit to Canton." He then proclaimed the capstone of his sojourn at Hong Kong: "The English are mad that our Admiral was honored by a visit; while their's never have been. It was a remarkable thing for the Governor General to visit us — and the writer is mistaken in asserting that he has twice visited American Ships. The *Maumee* is the first foreign Man o' War that has ever had that honor."[125]

In pouring tropical rain and sweltering heat, the *Maumee* slowly slipped away from the harbor of Hong Kong toward the Gulf of Tonkin to track Chinese pirates. In his cabin, Cushing, drenched by perspiration and fatigued by stifling heat, pondered whether he would find his prey and whether the ensuing struggle would inflict irreparable injury on his crew and himself. Possibly the impending typhoon season would dash the *Maumee* upon hidden shoals and rocks in uncharted currents. He had not heard from his beloved Kate, except for the heartbreaking letters that he had received in Hong Kong. He had written to Kate that "they who fight for Country — bravely and victoriously — may leave a legacy of honor to their children. They who are true to love elevate their humanity, in the sight of heaven and Earth."[126] This message could point to the realization of a cherished dream, or it could stand as the final testament of a man who fought for his country and in the memory of the woman he loved. As Hong Kong faded in rain and mist, a new entry would be made in the log of Lieutenant Commander Cushing.

Chapter 5

From Tropical Heat to Northern Turbulence

As Cushing sailed southward toward the Gulf of Tonkin, he discovered that his journey was more complex than he had originally envisioned. On June 15 he informed Kate that in "the two days since I last wrote I have steamed three hundred miles and visited five cities." Moreover, he wrote that "I have pulled through indescribable channels — got tangled up in non navigable straits — and needed, and had a whole corps of interpreters to understand the people I have seen, and to make them comprehend me." He was now anchored at Wong Pao (Huangpu), a town on the shore of Hainan, a sizeable island on the edge of the Gulf of Tonkin.[1]

However, Cushing was now conducting a solitary mission. The British had discovered that their gunboat had attacked a convoy of well-armed merchant ships. Instead of encountering a flock of pirate junks, the British gunboat had attacked, and damaged, peaceful Chinese vessels plying their normal trade. Obviously, the British Navy was sorely embarrassed by this wayward event, and it had decided not to proceed in a search for the ferocious (and nonexistent) pirate armada. Nevertheless, there was still an ample supply of pirates in waters between Hong Kong and the Gulf of Tonkin. Deprived of a rare opportunity to lead an Anglo-American squadron in a joint operation, Cushing boldly resolved to venture out on his own initiative. He yearned to return to the challenging opportunities of naval engagement that had given him fame and recognition. Besides, there was a chance to gain some prize money. Ambition, fortune, and glory beckoned.[2]

His orders from Admiral Rowan, of course, had been written on the assumption of a joint Anglo-American operation, not a solo adventure undertaken by Cushing. However, Rowan had also stipulated that Cushing should meet him at Yokohama on July 1. There was plenty of time for a quick survey of the island of Hainan, where considerable bands of pirates flourished. Since telegraph communication did not yet exist in China and Japan, messages were sent and received by steamer service. Presumably, Rowan would order Cushing to sail promptly to Japan; therefore, Cushing could either wait in Hong Kong for his new orders or he could sail directly to Japan to receive the orders in person. The challenge of pirates was naturally the more enticing choice for an ambitious young officer. Cushing must have been aware that the *Maumee*, along with several other ships of her design, had been dispatched to the China station because their light draft permitted them to navigate shallow coastal waters and penetrate a considerable distance up rivers. Such attributes would enable these ships to search out and destroy raiding flotillas of pirates. In the light of his Civil War exploits, Cushing was an admirable candidate to engage in such a mission.[3]

Not having the services of a knowledgeable pilot from the British Navy, Cushing shrewdly sought aid from the viceroy at Canton. American diplomats had always told Chinese authorities that they preferred peaceful and cooperative relations to the gunboat coercion of British and other European initiatives. As a result, the viceroy dispatched a leading officer from a prize regiment in his jurisdiction. With this Mandarin, Cushing acquired an entrée into Chinese society that few Westerners were granted. He also had a sure guide in the treacherous shores and inlets of Hainan.

Cushing revealed, nevertheless, that he entertained some misgivings about his bold decision to undertake a courageous but perilous adventure, which might be interpreted as a self-centered exploit that carelessly pushed aside far more important obligations. He had admonished Kate over and over again regarding her responsibility to him, but in turn he could now be denounced as having disregarded his pledge to her. Although piracy remained a constant challenge for Western naval commanders in the Far East, chasing pirates was not at that time the most pressing concern of the Asiatic Squadron. Cushing could be accused of undertaking an unnecessary and irresponsible sideshow.

"I must confess," he confided to his beloved, "that I should dread to meet it [death] down here, amongst these islands — where no seamanship can avail to save us from wreck." As he explained, "In an open Sea I would brave anything — out here there is so much land, and so many shoals, there would be a slim chance for the *Maumee*." He reverted quickly to his former declaration: "But, as I have said before, I don't believe that I <u>could</u> sink, knowing that you are waiting for me — or, if I ever do go down, I want you to know, and always remember, that your name was the last on my lips — and mingled in my heart with my last prayer to God."[4]

Cushing then lapsed once again into an offensive mode. "Do you think it strange," he demanded, "that I should write this, after you confessed to me that when everyone thought me lost, you were giving me no thought, not one regret — but accepting the marked attentions of another." He further reminded her that "when your own Father and Mother believed my Ship had gone down, on its voyage to Rio — you were 'trying to fan the faint flame — which burned so dimly' — that little dying spark of love — and were gayer than ever before."⁵

"I never mentioned this view of the case before," Cushing reminded Kate, "but I must ask you, now ... if I ought not to feel badly over your letter." He then declared, "But, notwithstanding this acknowledgement of yours that my death would not trouble you, or interfere with your amusements — even while it cuts me to the Soul — and mortifies my pride and dignity — I can still say, and truly — that I love you, and bless you above all things on Earth."⁶

Cushing pronounced, finally, an affirmation of faith and love. He began by acknowledging that "I know that I <u>should</u> be indignant — and that wounded pride would stifle love; but when you promised to be my wife, I threw away all safeguard, all defense, and gave you my life and happiness to your keeping." "I can never be untrue," he vowed, "to the woman I love, even if she is untrue to herself." For that reason, he confessed, "If you cease to care for me I must bear the blow like a man — but I will have no other image in my heart — no other than yours — to the very grave." Then Cushing concluded his testament with a benediction: "And so, with tenderest wishes for your happiness — with prayers for you and true <u>love</u> kisses — I bid you good night!"⁷

Before proceeding to chronicle Cushing's foray along the coast of Hainan, it is appropriate to place his experiences in Hong Kong and Canton in the context of American diplomacy in the Far East. The extension of commerce and finance from the shores of New York City and the ports of New England had evolved into a global industry that exercised considerable influence over the economy of the United States and contributed significantly to the structure of American society and its moral order. Commodore Perry's successful attempt to pry open the tightly capped lid that prohibited interaction between Japan and foreign countries opened the prospect of extending the thriving trade and investment at Canton and the rapidly expanding treaty ports along the Chinese coast and along the lower reaches of the Yangtze River to Japan.

Although the Civil War had diverted resources and focused attention on the titanic struggle to preserve the Union, American interest in the Pacific did not erode. During this time, Seward, as secretary of state, engineered the acquisition of Alaska. Derided as an "icebox" and purchased to remove Russia from the North American continent, Alaska connected North America, through a long chain of islands that trailed from the mainland westward across the Pacific, to Japan. Thus, the still raw environment of the newly minted American economy and society collided with an ancient and long-burnished culture. Despite their skeptical appraisal of the cultural attributes of a society that still bore the imprint of its frontier antecedents, the Japanese resolved to emulate the military and manufacturing technology of Western countries. Thus, Japan would preserve its political independence along with its cultural heritage. The ignominious fate of China, an ancient civilization reduced to tatters and compelled to allow considerable stretches of its territory to be recognized as colonial enclaves, would be avoided.

The primary task of the United States Navy was to protect the shores of the republic from hostile incursions, but it had acquired another role that was becoming equally important in light of the growth of American commerce in the Far East: protecting American mercantile interests and implementing the goals of its foreign policy. From the establishment of the American republic until the Civil War, the major concern of the Navy had been guarding the shores and territorial waters of the United States. The War of 1812 demonstrated that this was an assignment beyond the reach of a small cruising fleet; the overwhelming might of the Royal Navy had effectively controlled the American coast on the Atlantic. There was, however, a significant exception to British naval supremacy in North America, for American squadrons on Lake Erie and Lake Ontario were able to temper British naval ambitions. As a result, shortly after the end of hostilities, British and American negotiators agreed to restrict the number of their ships on the Great Lakes, and in 1832 the British withdrew their last ship from service on the lakes that separated British Canada from the United States. Finally, the settlement of the boundary between the United States and Canada permitted a peaceful, if guarded, understanding between a British colony and an independent country. American attention, furthermore, was diverted by the disastrous performance of the Spanish empire in South and Central America and the ensuing war with Mexico.[8]

Although Britain kept a wary eye on the infant American nation, her main focus remained her long-standing conflict with revolutionary and Napoleonic France. From 1793 until 1815, a span of 22 years (with a brief break from 1801 until 1803), Britain and France slugged it out in a conflict that gradually discarded any ideological trappings as it dissolved into a power struggle. After the Treaty of Vienna in 1815, France, under whatever regime, remained the constant antagonist of Great Britain. As a result, the principal task of the Royal Navy was to control the Dover Channel and the waters immediately connected to it. The major battle fleet of the Royal Navy was stationed at ports along the Channel. Mastery of the Channel essentially gave Britain the key to sea lanes into the Mediterranean and to those that flowed down the African coast and across to the Americas. Therefore, Britain effectively controlled the routes that led to India and the Far East.[9]

Paradoxically, the great British Empire of the nineteenth century, like its predecessor in the eighteenth century, was not the creation of naval intervention or strategy. Both empires were essentially the products of mercantile ventures that expanded enough to require the protection of the Royal Navy not only to maintain their current prosperity but also, and more importantly, to hold at bay those hostile to their enterprises, whether unfriendly neighbors or avaricious rivals from the European continent. Accordingly, British naval forces beyond the Channel were mainly frigates designed to move swiftly from one point of contention to the next as gunboats that could master the shores and inlets of colonial settlements. There were a few major sea battles that involved the majestic ships of the line that restored memories of Nelson's era: at Navarino the British Navy inadvertently sank the Turkish fleet, and in Algeria it bombarded the fortifications of a recalcitrant bey. Of course, its major deployment was in the Crimean War, where it shelled Russian forts and troops.[10]

Despite the adventurism of a bumptiously patriotic prime minister, Viscount Palmerston, and the British misguided project of constructing a Confederate commerce raider, the *Alabama*, Great Britain and the United States slipped easily into a comfortable relationship. Trade and a common cultural heritage made the bonding a natural occurrence. As observed in the preceding chapter, American merchants at Hong Kong and Canton initially relied on protection from British military and naval forces. The modest number of American naval ships and army regiments were occupied with engagements in Mexico and on the North American continent during the first half of the nineteenth century. Sending ships and men on expeditions to lands far removed from the United States was a novel idea that received scant attention in a society then fixed on a vision of the splendid bounty to be garnered from the riches of the frontier, much of which still remained an untamed wilderness.

The Civil War confirmed the political union of the United States, and in 1869 a completed transcontinental railroad linked the Atlantic and Pacific Oceans of North America. San Francisco quickly became the truly great gateway for Americans to explore the lucrative opportunities that might be discovered in the mysterious seas and lands of the Orient. Within several years after Appomattox, an American naval squadron appeared in the Far East on a permanent basis to advance the commerce of American business and to reinforce the diplomatic initiatives of representatives of the American government. It was a small squadron of only nine or ten ships. However, since the United States did not seek to acquire colonies, a small cruising fleet was, in most instances, satisfactory.

The change in the responsibility of the Navy from the exigencies of the Civil War to the challenges presented by the expansion of American mercantile interests in Asia was recognized by Gideon Welles in his annual report as secretary of the Navy Department to Congress in December 1867. Welles emphasized the number of ships committed to the Asiatic Squadron, and he pointed out that the USS *Hartford*, the flagship, had been selected by the commander of the American fleet to escort Robert Van Valkenburgh, the recently assigned American minister to Japan, to his formal introduction to the shogun at Yokohama. The immediate purpose of Van Valkenburgh's visit to the shogun was to arrange for additional ports to be made available to American traders, for at that time, American merchant ships were only permitted to enter at Nagasaki and Yokohama. The ports of Hakodadi, Neegata, Nanou, Mikuni, Tsuruga, and Miyatsu were duly surveyed, and all of these ports eventually received American ships. Welles underscored his narrative by asserting that the Pacific Mail Steamship Company was opening regular service from San Francisco to Japan, and then to Hong Kong. Its steamship *Colorado* had arrived at the latter destination in January 1867 after a rapid trip of 29½ days.[11] Welles warned forthrightly:

> American commerce in the East suffered some detriment during our civil war, and others have profited by our misfortune. Prussia has, within a few years, become conspicuous as a mercantile power in the east. Sailing vessels under her flag are seen in every port, receiving freights at lower rates than are offered by either American or British ships, and German merchants are securing a thriving business in that quarter. Apprehensions are expressed that we are not destined to recover the prestige of our former successful mercantile marine in the China seas, unless it be by means of steam vessels built for that trade.[12]

The British Navy, obviously, maintained a sizeable force in the Far East. It had a well-protected anchorage at Hong Kong from whence it could slip up and down the coast of China, and also could readily sail into the seas adjacent to Japan. At the time of the bombardment of Canton, it consisted of thirteen steamers, twenty gunboats, three sloops and three frigates, the largest of which carried sixty-four guns. There were also three hospital ships. In sum, the British naval force consisted of 42 ships, the majority of which were primarily employed in riverine and shore operations. Some indication of the viewpoint of the Royal Navy on the nature of its fleet in the Far East can be ascertained by noting that the ship on which Keppel proudly sailed to inspect British installations in the various coastal ports in China, and also to make an official visit to the recently seated Mikado at Tokyo, was the *Rodney*, the last wooden sailing ship still in active service. Fitted with steam machinery, she served the flagship of the China station until 1870. Having 92 guns, she was the most formidable ship that the Royal Navy deployed in the Far East. It should be noted, however, that the *Rodney* was the last of a noble lineage that belonged to the halcyon days of Nelson and his captains. She had been replaced by the *Warrior*, the first iron battleship in the Royal Navy. At her inauguration, the *Warrior* was the most powerful ship of her class in the world. She was nine thousand tons in displacement. This impressive vessel and her sisters were constructed to maintain British naval superiority in the Channel; they were not needed in the Far East.[13]

George Robeson, who became the U.S. naval secretary during the Grant administration, recognized the importance of the Far East to American commerce. He remarked astutely: "The completion of the Pacific railroad must largely increase our intercourse with the East, and as the presence of a strong naval force constitutes our most powerful appeal to Asian respect, it is deemed advisable to keep on this station as large a squadron as possible not only for the protection of our citizens, but to increase the prestige of our representatives in that quarter."[14]

Robeson pointed out that the United States was insulated by a large expanse of water from the immediate threat of an attack, but it had also provided the peace and stability that permitted the rapid development of an industrial economy. Lucrative markets for American products could be discovered by following the natural passages of the oceans. Emphasizing the importance of the coast-to-coast rail link, Robeson asserted:

> We have already opened steam communication between Europe and the East across our continent and through our ports on either ocean. In this age time is an essential element of wealth, and we may reasonably expect that the route which connects the trade of the East with the markets of Europe in forty days will, if fairly fostered and protected, practically supersede that which consumes twice that period. The nation controlling the trade of the East has always been the leading one in the commerce of the world, looking to this as the source of national wealth and maintaining a powerful navy for its protection.[15]

In light of his commentary on the importance of commerce with the Far East and the vital role of the Navy in ensuring the safety of American ventures, Robeson lamented the fact that a single ironclad warship of the French or British navy could wipe out any of the wooden ships that still comprised the cruising squadrons of the United States. Thus, the *Warrior* had rendered the American Navy obsolete. Robeson argued that the Navy should be authorized to commence building, as soon as possible, at least ten ironclad ships that could rival those of France and Britain. Robeson in 1868 advocated a Navy building program similar to that which the British had inaugurated with the *Warrior* in 1861, but that would not be implemented in the United States until almost a quarter of a century later. Meanwhile, American mercantile interests, now expanding at a rapid rate, would depend on the limited security offered by an increasingly fragile fleet.[16]

The history of Western intervention into the Far East and, more immediately, the effort of the United States to renew its foothold as a leading contender for commerce with China and Japan had already formed the background for the activities of Cushing at Hong Kong. His venture to Hainan, a large island perched on the edge of the Gulf of Tonkin, gave him ample opportunity to display his skill not only as a naval officer but more particularly as a representative of the American government. He had a splendid occasion to demonstrate, in performing a task with the cooperation of Chinese authorities, that the United States was not seeking territorial aggrandizement as an instrument of trade, but instead to maintain friendly and cooperative intercourse with the peoples of Asia. His success in conveying this policy became evident quickly.

Cushing wrote that he had taken an excursion into the interior of Hainan, which, according to his calculations, had brought him some hundred miles from where the *Maumee* had been anchored. Because of the considerable distance that separated Cushing from his ship, he had "spent last night at the Capital of the province." He described "Hoi-Hon" (perhaps Haikou?) as "quite a lively place, and very picturesque. I took a formal dinner ashore with my blue button friend 'Hong'—who has a large and fine house there—and was formally called upon by half a dozen Mandarins—who dined with us."[17] Cushing reported cheerfully to Kate:

> I gained great credit in the Celestial eyes by a dexterous use of chop-sticks; and did violence to my stomach by drinking down cups of splendid tea to wash down a tit-bit of chicken's head—eyes and all—that a glass-button dignitary put on my plate with his fingers as a special piece of politeness. The truth is they are all a very jolly and hospitable set—and Wong Luig Lo is the prince of good fellows. What's the use of standing in dignity with a man who sends on board—as he did—twelve dozen chickens—two thousand eggs—one hundred melons—and a bushel of oranges and lychees?[18]

Cushing had discovered that Wong was a man of considerable distinction. "He turns out," he informed Kate, "to be a bigger gun than I took him for, and is received at every port with much formality." In Cushing's words, "Salutes are fired from forts and junks—and Officials, of all kinds, hasten onboard to pay their respects to the distinguished caller." "It seems that 'Wong' (I am familiar you see) is famous as a Military Man and a hero—and wears a badge of Merit which belongs to but fifteen in the whole Empire." Cushing was told by Wong that the viceroy at Canton had been so pleased with his reception on the *Maumee* that he dispatched Wong, a truly illustrious senior officer, rather than a conventional escort, as a special favor.[19]

Cushing then proceeded to provide a description of the uncharted terrain he was exploring with the indispensable assistance of his distinguished Mandarin companion and his entourage:

> Hainan is a large island—province of China—one hundred miles in diameter— and with numerous cities on its coast. The Country is very flat; and only here and there a mountain rises—crowned by its tall pagoda—more majestic in its loneliness than if surrounded by fellows. The most curious thing is that the people speak an entirely different language from that used at Canton and Hong Kong—not understanding a word of those dialects. Not only is this true—but, in a run of one hundred miles around a portion of its coast, I find a people who speak neither the one nor the other—and whose habits differ essentially.[20]

Cushing supplied an additional comment on the social habits of the residents of Hainan, observing that "the women just here, look like men and do all the usual work of men; while the latter stay at home and play the part of women."[21] Toward the end of his odyssey, Cushing, again the recipient of an extraordinary gesture from Wong, was permitted to make an unprecedented exploration of a large city "from which foreigners are entirely excluded — but whose gates opened to us at the magical name of Wong Luig Yo." In a lyrical mood, Cushing described his journey as follows:

> The country through which we passed in going was charming — the road winding through delicious foliage — shading us from the burning Sun: and past many fine Country houses belonging to Chinese gentlemen. We passed one fine pagoda — and any number of "Joss houses" on the way and saw some very pretty China girls too — who peeped out from behind the screens, that front all doorways here — smiling and chattering in innocent wonder as the long line of chairs passed — with their queer load of "barbarians" or "foreign devils" — as their kindler [sic] call us. The head-dresses were quite as elaborate, but entirely different from those at Hong Kong and Canton but the paint is put on the face in just as liberal a manner. The girls [sic] lips were painted in a bright scarlet — and contrasting with brilliantly white teeth, looked quite tempting. I didn't taste however.[22]

Cushing discovered that he was the central attraction not only for the fair maidens of Hainan, but likewise for large throngs of spectators who gathered to study the features of the strange visitor from a distant and unknown clime. "In the City," Cushing reported, "we were treated with courtesy wherever we went — but had hard work to get through the curious crowd that turned out to see us — though we had a guard of Chinese soldiers with us to clear the way." When Cushing sought to inspect an assortment of local souvenirs, "a mob collected that blocked up the entire street." "Old and young," he recalled, "pressed and pushed to get a good look at us." Cushing remembered also that the "poor merchant stood for an hour — with big horn spectacles on nose and bamboo umbrella in hand — as much interested in our every movement as if they [the merchants] were a lot of school boys — staring for the first time at a Menagerie of wild beasts."[23]

Cushing, however, was ultimately rescued by Wong, who escorted him to a reception at the residence of another "blue button," whose mansion was as impressive as the one occupied by the viceroy in Canton. Cushing acknowledged readily that "every day I get a better opinion of the higher class of Chinese — and I am much interested in this association with them — I am 'au fait,' already in the ceremonies of a 'chin chin' with any of them." "Having so good an interpreter," he claimed, "I am able to converse about as well as if I know the language — and I find the higher Mandarins sensible and well informed, besides being as courteous and hospitable a set as I ever expect to see."[24]

Cushing concluded his rambles on Hainan with a philosophical commentary on a sweeping panorama dominated by endless rows of graves in precisely marked rows. This awesome sight prompted him to muse on a religious note as he returned to his ship. He remarked, "I now find that they form, in outline, the exact representation of the Greek letter 'Omega.'" "Is it not strange," he wondered, "that the tomb — mans [sic] end — should be fashioned with this symbol?" He reasoned that "it is either a very remarkable coincidence, or else it opens a door to much curious reasoning as to connections of people and languages." "This has been the established shape of tombs in China," he maintained, "for thousands of years — and will be until the Omega of time." He then, with a skillful ploy, suggested that Kate should ask the Episcopal minister at Fredonia, a Mr. Arey, "if the coincidence is not remarkable?"[25] Thus, Cushing exploited an opportunity to hint that his Baptist background could be replaced by the formal liturgy of the Episcopal rite.

Although Cushing had scoured countless bays and inlets for two hundred miles along the coast of Hainan, he turned up not a single lair of pirates nor any flotilla of their junks. On one occasion, Cushing and his men thought that they had finally struck a worthy prey. Unfortunately, after successfully attacking two junks that were sailing in tandem, they discovered that they had overtaken two innocent merchant vessels.[26] However, Cushing and his crew did encounter victims of a particularly outrageous and cruel piratical foray. A German ship from Bremen was captured by pirates, who unloaded the German ship's cargo and then locked the German crew and their Chinese passengers in coal lockers, fastening the hatches securely. The ship was then scuttled. Before it sank, the German crew pushed their hatch free and found one boat that had not been smashed by the pirates. By stuffing blankets into the holes that the pirates had punctured into this boat, eventually the German crew reached the safety of the shore. Tragically, the Chinese passengers failed to pry open their hatch, and perished with the ship.[27]

The discomfort of the German crew was intensified greatly by being compelled to march for two miles in the burning rays of the sun over roasting sand. They were completely exposed, except for trousers. As a result, their skin was seared to the point that it simply peeled off. They were finally rescued by a local Mandarin. A Chinese gunboat was conveying them to Hong Kong, where the pirates were perhaps already celebrating their good fortune. Cushing ended his account of the misfortune of the ship and crew from Bremen by vowing that "next winter I'm coming down here, in good, sober, earnest, and uncrippled by any orders from the Admiral — biding my time, I shall show these fellows some tricks worth two of theirs."[28]

When Cushing returned to Hong Kong, he found that Wong, his Mandarin guide and companion during his excursion to Hainan, was waiting for him. True to his promise, Wong had arranged a grand dinner party for Cushing and the officers of the *Maumee*. Cushing explained cheerfully:

> We were entertained by Chinese music and singing girls — theatricals — and a dinner that I thought would never end. It commenced with eight soups one after the other — the first being "bird's nest" — and by no means bad. We did not rise from the table until three in the morning. Our host had six of his friends to meet us at dinner and all tried to be very jolly. They insisted always upon drinking

"bumpers"—draining their glasses to the last drop—and holding them upside down as a challenge to us—but as, out of politeness to us they had furnished sherry wine instead of the national liquor "Samshie"—they soon got the worst of that game—and were left as "tight as bricks" when we went home in the early morning.[29]

The following day, Cushing entertained his Chinese friend on the *Maumee* with a musical performance, which undoubtedly employed selections from the minstrel shows that had been so successful. Afterward, Cushing and his officers were invited to another festive dinner by their Chinese host. Cushing decided, however, that he had had enough merriment and declined to attend, but he dispatched eight of his officers, who reported happily that this second celebration was "even more fun than the night before." With perhaps a tinge of melancholy, Cushing noted, "Now our Mandarin has gone back to Canton, and I shall not see him again until next winter; but I am sure I am sworn 'brother' with himself and three others—and expect to see China very pleasantly in consequence." Cushing was pleased, moreover, to announce that "it is thought quite singular here how popular I have become with these fellows—who are usually so very reserved and suspicious." He observed that his Chinese friends "hate the English—and Wong predicts a bloody war in the future."[30]

Cushing's introduction to China had proved to be more successful than probably had been anticipated. It is certain that the *Maumee* and her captain had been sent to the Far East to patrol coastal waters, but Cushing's experience in the Civil War also made him an admirable choice for forays against the ceaseless raids of pirates. He had not yet had an opportunity to demonstrate his skill and courage in naval combat in the Far East; unfortunately, the expedition to Hainan had made it clear that trolling for pirates required considerable patience and plenty of time. On the other hand, Cushing had revealed that he had a real talent for diplomacy. Unlike most Western representatives (including Americans), Cushing had displayed natural skills for expanding a perfunctory exercise in diplomatic exchange into a lasting relationship that bridged the customary barriers of language and culture. Cushing was not a conventional naval officer whose training and outlook restricted his service to naval matters, but rather had promoted himself into the ranks of those who advocate the political and economic objectives of their country.

Alas, in his private diplomacy, Cushing still lacked sure proof that his campaign to retain Kate's affections had achieved at least a degree of success. "It is four Months now since your last [letter] was dated," he lamented, "and it frightens me so that I half dread for the next—even while I long for it, and count the hours until it shall come." "Be good," he pleaded, "to me, darling!" He added, "Be true and constant to me!" and vowed that "I will make you very happy sometime, if you will trust me—and will try never again to leave you like this." He ended his letter with an affectionate salute: "Good bye—My—

My own precious Kate." Cushing had entered Hong Kong hoping for comforting and even exhilarating words of love. Instead, he had been the recipient of messages of doubt and second thoughts. He left Hong Kong still uncertain as to whether Kate had accepted his critique of her conduct and, above all, if she had responded affirmatively to his passionate declarations of enduring love.[31]

Cushing arrived at Yokohama on July 3, two days later than the date advised by Admiral Rowan. Nevertheless, Cushing could participate in the celebration of July 4th held by the American colony at that port, which he described joyfully to Kate. He had also received the long-awaited response to his epistles written at Hong Kong. On a ringing declaration of unrestrained elation, Cushing announced, "I am just in from Sea to-day, and am very busy — as I am at anchor near the Flag Ship and am constantly required to go and come Officially — and to receive and return calls from and to various National Ships."[32]

Despite the pressure of a constant swirl of official receptions, Cushing managed to write a hasty note to Kate in which he explained jubilantly that he had read her message, and that she "had just rendered me so happy by a charming letter — full of love and Sunshine — such a one as no one but her can write, and which has driven away all my 'blues' in one half hour." He then proceeded to offer a paean of heartfelt gratitude for the glad tidings that Kate had sent him:

> Thank you! Bless you! My love — my own dear sweetheart — the whole World, life — all things — seem brighter and better since I have read it. To be sure I had hoped for at least two — one for March and one for April, but there is more in quality than in quantity — after all — and you are so good in these sixteen pages that my heart is content — and the clouds are all blown away. You do love me — I am not forgotten — that is enough for me. Oh how I love you for your trust and constancy![33]

Cushing reported to Kate that he had additional pleasure in receiving a fresh slate of officers. His original staff had been volunteers — that is, men who had accepted appointments on a temporary basis, mostly during the Civil War. They were now being replaced by regular officers who sought a professional career in the Navy. One of them, Lieutenant Commander Mullan, had been at Annapolis with Cushing; he would serve as executive officer on the *Maumee*. Cushing would remain for two weeks at Yokohama, and then would sail to Osaka to assist in opening the port to American shipping. However, in three days he intended to visit Yeddo (Tokyo), now the capital city of Japan, which he had been told was the largest city in the world in terms of population.[34]

Undoubtedly to Cushing's surprise, Kate mounted a lively counterattack. He had to face the stark reality that his romantic life was still facing the perils of separation and misunderstanding introduced by irregular correspondence. He launched a spirited rebuttal:

> Oh Kate — Kate! You sweet, naughty, charming, tantalizing, darling! How is it that you — so many thousand miles away — seem to influence my whole life — to govern my every moment of thought and action. If I am about to do anything I wonder always "what would Kate think?" If I see anything curious or pretty "shall I get it for Kate?" and if I ride or drive to attend a pleasant party I only wish for your presence with me — and quite lose the pleasure in contrasting my feelings with those experienced during one of the precious moments in your society during the past dear Summer.³⁵

Despite his declaration of unrelenting love for Kate, even to the extent of allowing it to dominate the course of his daily thought, he renewed his claim of being in the humiliating position of an abused suitor. He lectured the fair Kate that she seemed to hearken to the "laws of the Medes and Persians" in her letters to him, because she appeared resolved "never to write me a letter without introducing into it — in part — a something bitter." He elucidated, "Either you have been losing your love for me — or have been flirting — or, as in your last, coolly inform me that I am a great egotist — and once made you very angry, while at the same time you fail to tell me what I said and leave me in danger of offending again in the future."³⁶

Bluntly, Cushing charged ahead to proclaim, "If there is any place on Earth, Kate, where I might turn 'Egotist' — and assume the plumage of the great peacock 'I' — it is in the little town called Fredonia away off in Western New York." He then continued his frontal assault by admitting that "I <u>do</u> feel <u>head</u> and <u>shoulders</u> above most people there — and, probably so express myself — thus provoking your wrath." Cushing reminded Kate that his great and boundless love for her readily prompted him to respect her admonitions and to mend his conduct. Kate, Cushing advised, had the challenge of reforming her arrogant lover and teaching him the gentle manners of civilized society, which is one of the legendary arts of the feminine species.³⁷ Abruptly, Cushing dropped his conciliatory tone to warn Kate:

> If (as I do not suppose) you wish me to show my modesty by pretending to live intellectually or socially with such poor failures in the coinage of human nature as are represented by young men Parker and Putnam of Fredonia — the Stevens boys — dozens of others I might mention — Why then I could only say that I can never do it — and that my Egotism, in <u>such comparisons</u> is <u>incurable</u>. But seriously speaking — I think that you were <u>unjust</u> to me. I've given my time since your letter came to a careful self-examination and I do not think that I am egotistical. I shall try, always, to preserve my <u>self respect</u> — a worthy effort, certainly since it can only be done by leading an honorable and upright life.³⁸

After having produced an optimistic appraisal of his character, Cushing left the subject to relate the celebration of July 4th in the harbor of Yokohama, where the American squadron consisted of four ships. There were some 20 other warships of Western powers in the harbor. At noon the American flagship fired a salvo. Immediately, 24 ships were firing 21-gun salutes. Cushing reported that the noise produced by the roar of cannons was deafening and "in two minutes the whole harbor lost to view — buried in the thick-rolling sulfur smoke that filled the trembling air." Halfway through this ceremony, Cushing observed that he could only see the tops of the masts of the American fleet, from which flew the Stars and Stripes. This martial spectacle brought a lump of patriotic emotion to Cushing's throat. He exclaimed, "I felt my heart swell with pride, to think how all Nations did it honor — that England gave it royal honor. Is it not a singular spectacle to witness — this celebration by England of the successful rebellion of her fairest provinces? A rebellion that took place less than a century ago?"[39] In the evening Cushing attended a formal dinner at the residence of the American minister, Robert Van Valkenburgh. Twenty-four sat at the table, including two ladies from San Francisco. "As they had been but lately come," Cushing wrote, "from the 'Golden State,' I was much interested hearing about all my friends there — and I have seldom found time pass more quickly than it did that evening — dinners are generally, <u>so</u> stupid." At the conclusion of dinner Cushing had the honor of assisting the ladies in lighting "all the combustibles and explosive material, collected for display." He was happy to inform Kate that "I didn't tell them how near I came to burning up Miss Leila but I thought of it — and took great care not to get too near the muslin this time."[40]

Even as Cushing was presiding over the igniting of fireworks to proclaim the date of American independence, his festive display was outshined by a neighboring attraction:

> But there were greater fire-works than these to mark the evening — for only fifteen miles away the great City of Yeddo [Tokyo] was burning — and the whole eastern Sky was red and lurid with the flames. A battle was in progress between the forces of the "Mikado" and the "Tycoon" [Shogun] — right the midst of the City — and the Minister's dispatches said the Southern troops [forces loyal to the Mikado at Kyoto] had fired the houses, and were burning up women and children. No quarter was given upon either side — but results are not yet decisive — and combat still progresses.[41]

Cushing was in the middle of the climactic struggle between the imperial court at Kyoto and those loyal to the long-exercised supremacy of the shogun at Yeddo. For some 200 years the Mikados, or emperors, of Japan had been content to dwell in seclusion in their official palace at Kyoto, where they occupied themselves with the trivial pursuit of elaborate rituals associated with their station as both secular and heavenly governors. In reality, their sovereignty had become the property of families that were nominally ranked as vassals. The heads of these powerful dynasties carried the official title of "shogun." A major policy of the shogun governors had been to exclude Western merchants and missionaries from Japan. Only at the tip of the island, where it came close to

Korea and China, could Westerners reside in Japan at the port of Nagasaki. In 1637 Portuguese and Spanish agents were expelled, but Dutch and Chinese traders were permitted to engage in commerce.[42]

On July 8, 1853, a fleet of four ships commanded by Commodore Perry arrived near Yeddo to persuade the shogunate, at the request of President Fillmore, to open several ports to American shipping. The Americans were dispatched to Nagasaki, where they, along with Russian merchants, soon overturned the Dutch monopoly. Considerable resentment arose over the accommodating reaction of the shogun and his entourage to the blunt solicitations of the Americans and numerous European powers that soon adopted similar proposals. Emperor Komei at Kyoto exploited this popular undercurrent of protest to launch a campaign to resurrect the ancient sovereignty of his predecessors. The power struggle between emperor and shogun quickly assumed an ideological twist: it was a contest between long-hallowed native customs and alien conventions. This conflict received dramatic impact when Komei resolved to restore the Shinto cult to an honored position in the imperial court. To reinforce his allegiance to the traditional religious structure of Japan, he ordered the expulsion of Christian missionaries and the subjection of their converts.[43]

Then this equation became suddenly far more complicated. Komei unexpectedly died at the early age of 36, probably from smallpox, although there is speculation that he may have been the victim of poison, a mishap not unknown within the imperial court. His son, a stripling of sixteen years, ascended to the throne. Immediately, he was confronted with the religious dogmas and policy axioms of his father. Emperor Meiji promptly showed real mettle. He matured rapidly and chose his counselors wisely, persevering with his father's ambition to restore sovereignty to the Mikado. As a result, the shogun surrendered his authority, and the long rule of the shogunate dissolved. The surprise, however, was that Meiji reversed the anti-foreign program of his father. Instead, he adopted the conciliatory policy of the shogun. Meiji did more than approve of an expansion of the number of treaty ports (those ports open to foreign intercourse)—he pursued a course of accepting and implementing Western polity and technology inside Japan. The imperial court symbolized this radical transformation: Western dress was adopted and the customs and protocol of European courts were implemented. In 25 years, Japan became a part of the Western world. For the United States, the indisputable proof of the rise of Japan as a vibrant industrial nation with a modern bureaucracy was the appearance of a navy that defeated a Russian fleet and that could contemplate challenging American naval influence in the Far East.[44]

For the present moment, however, the smoke and flames from a burning Yeddo underscored the final triumph of those loyal to the cause of the Mikado. For the most part, foreign ships and troops had remained neutral. For instance,

Cushing remarked, "The ironclad ram *Stonewall* which is sold to Japan, is at anchor here, under the American flag. Both parties have tried to get her; but we will not give her up until we see how things turn out politically." The *Stonewall* had been built by a French shipyard at Bordeaux for service in the Confederate Navy. She was constructed for use in shallow waters in the Hampton Roads area, in Mobile Bay, or on the Mississippi as a ram. Her design did not encourage sailing on open seas, since she did not ride over the waves but ploughed through them. Initially, the French government prohibited her sale to the Confederacy, and she was sold to Denmark, then engaged in war with Prussia. An abrupt end to this conflict persuaded the Danes to return the vessel to the French shipyard, which then was permitted to complete the original transaction with the Confederacy. When the *Stonewall* arrived at Havana in May 1865, however, the Civil War was over, and Spanish authorities gave her up to the United States. In turn, the American government sold her to Japan. She arrived at Yokohama after giving her American crew an exhilarating passage around Cape Horn and across the rolling waters of the Pacific Ocean. She can be recognized as the first major ship in the newly established imperial fleet under the name of *Kotetsu* and, latterly, *Adzuma*, until she was taken out of active service with the Imperial Navy in 1888. It can thus be argued that Cushing witnessed the inaugural step in the formation of the modern Japanese navy.[45]

Cushing informed Kate that he had been riding in the immediate vicinity of the anchorage, and had encountered a number of wounded soldiers:

> The soldiers are quite formidable looking men — armed with huge swords — and they strut around as if looking for someone to quarrel with. They do not like foreigners — were it not for the English and French regiments quartered here — Japan would soon be too hot for Europeans. As it is great care is exercised not to offend or insult the people. The Japanese nobles are as haughty and proud as any living man — and when they move through the streets in chairs or on horseback — surrounded by their armed suite — they manage to take up the whole of it — and woe to the man who happens to run against even a single retainer.[46]

Cushing's observations were correct. When Admiral Rowen's predecessor, Admiral Bell, had provided a naval ship to convey Robert Van Valkenburgh to Yokohama to negotiate the opening of the ports of Osaka and Hiogo to American traders, a treaty had been ratified successfully with the shogun. On January 1, 1868, British and American warships at Osaka and Hiogo had fired twenty-one salutes in recognition of the new accord, and Japanese vessels had returned the salute with an equal number of salvos. Unfortunately, shortly after this festive event, Admiral Bell drowned when his barge capsized in the bay at Osaka. Further complications developed on January 27 as the forces of the Mikado struck at Osaka, an important citadel of the shogun. The recently negotiated treaty was repudiated, and the shogun sought temporary refuge on

January 31 aboard the USS *Iroquois*. The next day, however, he was transferred to one of his warships.[47]

It is interesting to note that Alfred Thayer Mahan at this time was serving as executive officer on the *Iroquois*. In his memoir of his early years, Mahan recounted the tale of a disheveled and befuddled shogun arriving at and departing from an overnight refuge to escape the victorious forces of the Mikado after their successful onslaught on Osaka. Apparently, Mahan and Cushing had only superficial contact, for neither mentions the other in correspondence or, in Mahan's case, commentaries on naval matters. Possibly, their lack of any social intercourse is largely explained by the circumstances of their respective duties. Cushing arrived in Japan just in time to celebrate July 4th. He left in August to go to Tiensing (Tianjing) and Peking (Beijing), returning in October. Mahan, meanwhile, was dispatched to northern Japan to unravel the strange appearance of an American ship guided by Chinese coolies, who were apparently the crew but did not have officers or official papers or national colors. They did have some furs, and a rumor from an unidentified source stated that she was a ship that had left Peru with twelve thousand dollars in gold. (It is doubtful that this mystery was ever satisfactorily solved). Thereafter, Mahan's travels took him to Shanghai, and then to Hainan to search for a missing French corvette, probably a victim of pirates, and subsequently to Hong Kong and then to Nagasaki, where he fell ill. When he came to his senses, he found himself in Yokohama. Mahan had been appointed to command the *Iroquois* to replace the former officer, who had been assigned to be the captain of the flagship, the *Piscataqua*.[48]

On February 8 an envoy from the Mikado informed the American legation that a change of government had occurred, but a considerable amount of lawlessness still persisted. Foreign nationals were attacked during incidents, which suggested that the Mikado's regime lacked the will to protect the citizens and representatives of Western governments, or perhaps had yet to create a policy and then enforce it. Under such conditions, foreign military and naval forces had occupied Yokohama, which was then pacified.[49]

Unfortunately, fighting continued to cause death and destruction in Yeddo, and a month later Cushing had to tell Kate that though Yeddo was only fifteen miles from Yokohama, it "is now a dangerous place for foreigners since Civil war is raging—and the people are greatly excited."[50] It would not be until November that Meiji formally occupied the shogun's citadel, which would then be transformed into the imperial residence.[51]

Cushing shrewdly introduced some observations on several of the celebrated pastimes of the Japanese, such as kite flying; among other things, he noted the custom of flying fish-shaped kites over the houses where there was a child who had been born during the past year. He likewise examined samples of ornamental horticulture, trees and shrubs that had been pruned meticulously into the shapes of birds and other animals. He especially appreciated the art of fashioning dwarf trees and shrubs from conventional-sized models that could flourish in ordinary flower pots.[52]

His reaction to Japanese women was to express horror at their custom of blackening their teeth. This was a peculiar practice that gave them a bizarre character and also caused their teeth to decay. He also marveled at their habit of bundling their infants in wraps that could be strapped on their backs. There the babies slept with their faces frequently pointed directly into the rays of the sun. After being exposed to such burning sunshine, Cushing figured that his face would be in a raw state. Finally, he reported that he had been exploring Yokohama street by street, a practice that he had inaugurated at Canton. He promised Kate that he would send her an account of houses, theaters, shops, lectures, temples, and schools, as well as descriptions of Japanese wares and silks. Apparently, he had decided to disregard Kate's protest that his narrations could be tedious.[53]

Indeed, Cushing preferred to emphasize the dramatic social and political events that he encountered and to give short notice to elementary preoccupations. Hence, Cushing provided Kate with a bulletin on the political state of Japan at that moment: The Mikado and his ministers were attempting to conciliate foreign representatives and residents. The prime minister, a member of the Satsuma clan, which had been a principal support to the emperor, had decided to promote cordial relations with Western nations. He had "recently issued a proclamation ordering that foreigners should no longer be called barbarians, dogs or sheep and that we may be deemed civilized." Cushing responded with a joyful acclamation: "Hurrah for him!!! Isn't that kind I am no longer a sheep! I have ceased to be a dog! The dog when I was a barbarian has passed away!! Blessed be Satsuma!!!"[54] Whatever may have been Cushing's genuine feelings on the course of Japanese politics, he was apparently unaware of the various factions that had been fighting for power and also that the names of their chiefs should not be confused with the titles given to their clans. Both the clans and feudal daimyos changed from time to time, as did their policies and loyalties.

Kate was informed that, although her fiancé missed her with ever-growing intensity, he nevertheless sought solace in the pleasant society of the foreign colony at Yokohama. He revealed that every evening he attended a dinner engagement. "There are," he warned, "quite a number of very pleasant American ladies — but only two or three unmarried — these wouldn't be single if they were worth having — for wives are at a high premium out in this part of the world — and when it is rumored that a moderately pleasing lady has come in on the Steamer from San Francisco — she generally gets a dozen or so of proposals through speaking trumpets from the shore, as soon as the ship has anchored."[55]

However, Kate had no cause to worry that her heartsick Romeo would succumb to the charms of some available woman wandering discontentedly on a distant shore, for Cushing warned her that he had been ordered to the port of Tianjin. Elements of those forces who had participated in the T'ai P'ing Rebellion were still active, and there was considerable anxiety that property and lives of foreign residents of that port might be in jeopardy. The T'ai P'ing Rebellion had been a popular protest of Han Chinese against Manchu and Mongolian governance. Cushing commented that "the Chinese rebel army is near by, and American interests demand protection — so I am to go there and keep an eye on both parties with a view to making mince meat of the first one who misbehaves." His principal regret was that he had to leave Japan, where the weather was pleasant and sunny. (He had probably been warned that the climate at Beijing could be excessively hot and that there was always the constant threat of dust storms sweeping from the dry plains of northern China beyond the Great Wall.) He likewise regretted that since there was no mail steamer between Hong Kong and Tianjin, he had to arrange for her letters to be, if possible, forwarded to Tianjin by a ship carrying naval and other official papers. As he revived his proclamations of eternal love and his lasting misery at being separated from her, he once again asked if there were any materials that her mother or she would wish to obtain. He suggested that sable furs would be an appropriate acquisition.[56]

Before joining Cushing on the road to the Forbidden City, a review of several letters written to him during his exodus from Hong Kong to Yeddo by his mother, Mary Barker Cushing, will provide some useful insight on family matters. In June Mary Barker informed her son that his sister Mary had safely delivered a son. Now Mary Barker was a grandmother and Cushing had become an uncle. The baby was given the name of Alonzo, in memory of Cushing's brother who had fallen at Gettysburg. She also reported that Howard was leading a contingent of

Mother Mary Barker Cushing came from an illustrious New England family and was related to many prominent families in Boston, including the Adamses and Hancocks.

troops to Fort Union in New Mexico. Milton was in San Francisco, where he anticipated that he would receive orders to sail to Alaska. She had not heard from Kitty Forbes for some two months. Although Mary Barker Cushing had also written to Nellie Grosvenor, she had received no reply. Laconically, Mary Barker wrote that "they are quite friendly with each other," and she hoped that they "will be loving sisters" (a reference to Milton's pursuit of Nellie).[57]

Almost a month later Mary Barker Cushing wrote again to her wandering son. In her letter she lamented that she had not heard from him for three months. Kitty Forbes also had not answered several of her recent letters, nor had Nellie Grosvenor.[58] Finally, on July 20, 1868, Mary Barker Cushing received two letters from her son. The first had been written at St. Paul, the island in the Indian Ocean, and the second at Hong Kong. She acknowledged that Cushing had asked Gayle to look after prize money that he had received from the government. This money, she advised, would be invested in United States bonds, which (she assured Cushing) represented the safest mode of preserving private capital. In an age when government regulators and legislated guarantees were unknown, most securities and even bank deposits could quickly become worthless. "I want to live to see," she vowed, "my boys married and approve highly of your looking ahead and shaping your course for such an auspicious event."[59]

Mary Barker Cushing then delivered a warning shot across her son's bow. She reported that "Mary had just had a good letter from dear Kitty." Then came the stinging revelation: "Kitty loves society, and finds it convenient to accept gentleman's [sic] attentions, but I presume he knows well, that she is engaged to you." She quickly reassured her son that "I shall write you all about it when I go there, and look out for your interests." She further informed Cushing that Milton was not having much luck in wooing Nellie. "I love my children better than myself," she declared, "and grieve that Milton seems doomed to be disappointed." She continued: "I think Nellie intends to break off with, for she will not notice his letters. Or [sic] us, in any way, and I am afraid Milt will lose all he has invested with Mr. Grosvenor but as he keeps close about business matters, cannot positively say."[60]

She revealed both her affection for her sons and her concern for their future happiness, stating that Milton "will see that you do not lose your $1000, never fear about that." She promised to write to Cushing upon the subject very soon. "It was kind," she explained, "in him to make me that generous allotment, without it I should be dependent, and life a burden." She revealed that she was now boarding with Mary and Ned Gayle in order to help Mary in her recovery from childbirth and to assist with the rearing of the first addition to the Cushing ménage. She provided the Gayles with thirty dollars a month for her quarters and food. In this fashion, Mary Barker preserved her independence and at the same time had the comfort and joy of being with her family.[61]

5. From Tropical Heat to Northern Turbulence

At the beginning of August, Mary Barker was able to provide her son with a degree of reassurance on the state of his relationship with his fiancée. "Kitty F is all right," she claimed. On the other hand, as Mary Barker had already discovered, Kate enjoyed the conviviality of the social life pursued by youthful men and women. While Cushing was challenged by the duties of a naval officer in command of a ship sailing in unfamiliar waters and (when anchored) able to explore strange lands filled with wondrous sights and inhabitants whose dress and customs were fascinating, Kate was faced with the bleak task of waiting patiently in solitude for the pleasures that can only be sampled in the buoyancy of youth. She confided to Mary, Cushing's sister, that it was "not nice to have ones [sic] beau so far away." However, Mary Barker commented dryly, "I presume that Mr. O. knows how matters stand and governs himself accordingly."[62]

In other news, Milton's romance, which had appeared to be in a precarious state, now was flourishing. Mary Barker happily announced that "Nellie is true as gold and loves him devotedly as ever." The explanation for this remarkable turn of events was that Milton's ship, the USS *Suwanee*, en route to Alaska, struck a rock on July 9 while being navigated by a pilot through Shadwell Passage and sank, forcing its complement to take refuge on an island not far from Vancouver. No one perished, but clothes, uniforms, and other personal belongings were lost. On reading a report of the accident in newspapers, Nellie displayed considerable consternation. Mary Barker wrote that "Nellie G has nearly been wild with anxiety and has written us many letters of inquiry."[63]

Clarification of Milton's adventures on the Canadian coast is provided by a jaunty letter he wrote to Cushing after being rescued. From Vancouver, British Columbia, Milton saluted his brother with the boyhood nickname "Coons." This sobriquet had been bestowed on Cushing on his recovery from an accident in Chicago at the age of three, when he had been knocked unconscious. Upon regaining his wits, he was asked his family name. Still dazed, he blurted out, "Bill Coons," a nickname given him by a brother.[64]

"Your most highly <u>Esteemed</u> Epistle, of no date, from Hong Kong greeted my famished eye balls yesterday on my return from a somewhat unsuccessful picnic, which I will duly describe hereafter." Milton then defended his reputation as a worthy correspondent:

> You begin your valued communication with the calm assertion of what you believe to be a fact, but which is in reality a fiction, to wit: that I have not written to your nautical excellence for over a year, whereas I have in fact written twice at least within that time, directing once to Rio and again Hong Kong. Still I admit that our style of correspondence has not been of a nature to encourage the manufacturers of stationery; to say nothing of those delightful sentiments that should be kept alive in the breasts of brothers.[65]

Milton proceeded to declare his resolution to write a communiqué that should soothe his brother's ruffled feelings:

> Before I begin upon matters affecting myself I will answer enquires respecting a young lady whose father's name begins with M. and ends well. It is rumored among the gossips who frequent tea parties that the said ornament to society is destined to make happy the home of a wealthy S.F. banker. I know the man — and think him a first rate fellow. Sanders (to whom I gave your love and who returns his) thinks that the lady aforesaid will not marry anyone. I have an impression she has so stated to him.... By the way, old boy, do you think it is quite fair for you to string palpitating female hearts as you would a brochette and carry them about you for the mere fun of the thing? I told S of your affair du cour [*sic*] in the East and suppose that is the cat to which you refer — one which you desire me to stuff into the bag again. All right. I am very glad your vessel is fine. May her shadow never grow less, & may she steal unawares upon many villainous but unsuspecting pirates, thereby giving you great glory and unlimited cash.[66]

It would appear that Cushing's previously mentioned encounter with a handsome and vivacious San Francisco belle was more than a passing dalliance; indeed, it may well have been a truly serious romantic excursion that had floundered on the twin shoals of naval duty and money, after which the dejected suitor had seized a ripening country miss on a rebound to the high ground of self-esteem. On the other hand, if luck prevailed, it was possible that the lady in San Francisco might accept a reconciliation. In the meantime, Milton would undertake a mission to stabilize the wandering attention of Kate (Kitty) on her commitment to Cushing.

Milton also provided an account of the destruction of the *Suwanee*, which had been on a cruise for a year along the Mexican and Central American coasts. After returning to San Francisco for repairs, the *Suwanee* was ordered to sail to Sitka, a large island close to the Alaskan coast, which had a good harbor. Sitka had been an entrepot for the Russians, and now served the same function for Americans. Having deposited its cargo, the *Suwanee* followed its orders to accompany the flagship of the Northern Pacific Squadron to San Francisco. On July 7 it sailed from Victoria, British Columbia, and while traversing the Shadwell Passage, it struck a rock and promptly sank. The crew and officers took refuge on Hope Island, where, surrounded by untamed virgin forest, they remained for five days until rescued by a British warship. Milton advised that this "picnic" had cost the government half a million dollars. He also stated that he was likely to be sent to the East in a few weeks, where presumably he would have an occasion to reconnect with Nellie, who had not written to him for more than two months.[67]

On August 8, 1868, Cushing wrote to his mother that he would shortly leave Japan by the Inland Sea to reach Tientsin (Tianjin), the nearest major port to Peking (Beijing), in order to protect American merchants and missionaries and their property against Chinese insurgents, who were still numerous in that particular area. He expected to remain there for approximately two months before returning to Japan. He had enjoyed the amenities of the foreign colony at Yokohama. "There is a very large fleet of Men O'War," he explained, "here now — including three iron-clads, and society is very gay," confessing that "I dine out every evening." He also announced that he was giving an entertainment on the *Maumee*, where undoubtedly he intended to present another version of his now well-practiced minstrel show. Cushing further informed his mother that he had sent her a hundred silver dollars in care of a fellow officer, who was returning to the United States. He mentioned, moreover, that "I have purchased a hundred dollars worth of beautiful photographs illustrating the people and scenery of Japan — and when I get home I can, with their help give you full idea of every thing."[68] Four days later, he was able to tell his mother that President Grant had awarded Alonzo, posthumously, the rank of colonel. Alonzo had perished heroically as he fired his cannon at the charging Confederate soldiers before the ramparts at Cemetery Ridge at Gettysburg.[69]

When Cushing received his orders from Admiral Rowan, he was given specific instructions on his mission. Cushing was to relieve Lieutenant Commander Yates, the captain of the *Ashuelot*, either at Tako or near the mouth of the Peilo River, and provide him with his orders for his succeeding operations. Cushing was also to interview the American consul at Tientsin. If possible, Cushing should navigate the Pei Ho River to Tientsin, where he should remain until the river became too shallow for safe movement with the coming of winter weather. The principal concern was to survey the current security of American residents in the vicinity of the ports of Tientsin and Chufu, especially the ubiquitous array of missionaries.[70]

Cushing arrived at the Chinese port of Chufu (Yantai), which was a supply and coaling station, to prepare for his trip up the Pei Ho River to Tientsin. Although he found that the city was an ordinary urban landscape of the type that could be seen readily throughout China (with the probable exception of Canton and Peking), he nonetheless welcomed the pleasures of the Chinese marketplace. "What would our Fredonia housekeepers," he asked Kate, "think of buying ten dozen chickens for one dollar — or four dozen doves at the same price?" He proceeded to reveal that "my Steward purchased yesterday two hundred and fifty fresh eggs for fifty cents! The best beef," he continued, "is six cents a pound." He advised Kate that he intended to put on weight, and was thinking that two hundred pounds would be an advisable figure to reach, especially as the chilling temperatures of winter approached.[71]

Before confronting winter's bite, Cushing had to stand guard over his countrymen at Tientsin and then explore the mysteries of Peking. The former might well present a perilous challenge, but the latter surely would offer a rare and intriguing experience. As he faced his latest trip into unknown territory, he wrote a final farewell to Kate: "Be true to me, dear, dear Kate. As true as I am to you. I can ask no more than that. We should know ourselves and each other by this time. I think and trust fully to the future. Remember that there is one far from you who can truly subscribe himself— with his whole heart."[72]

Chapter 6

Wandering Among the Crumbling Remnants of the Celestial Empire

On August 27, 1868, the USS *Maumee* entered the mouth of the Pei Ho River, which was still guarded, if only symbolically, by sturdy forts that commanded the bluffs overlooking the village of Taku nestled along the river's edge. These formidable bastions had once protected the coastal gateway to the hub of imperial China, but in 1858, British forces under Lord Elgin had succeeded in overwhelming these forts. Since Chinese authorities had not abandoned their obstinate tactics in refusing to broaden the scope of prevailing treaty arrangements, in the following year British naval and army units attempted to repeat their previous success, only to be repulsed by a ferocious and well-directed resistance. Ultimately, in 1860, an Anglo-French expeditionary force occupied Beijing and extended its control over the imperial domain of Manchu territory.[1]

Cushing would have been supplied with some background orientation on the dramatic events of a decade earlier, but he had little opportunity to muse on them, let alone speculate on their legacy. He found himself preoccupied with traversing "the narrowest and most crooked stream I ever entered, through a country as flat as the ocean — every inch cultivated; and by towns and villages so numerous that it seemed almost one continuous City." Although Cushing had picked up a pilot at the river's mouth, the Pei Ho proved true to its reputation as a narrow, twisting, meandering stream with a shallow bottom that greatly increased hazardous navigation. Cushing, indeed, experienced "grounding several times on what, fortunately proved to be soft mud banks."[2]

After a trip of approximately sixty miles, the *Maumee* eventually reached Tianjin (then called Tientsin) at eight in the evening. Although the route by road was much shorter, only some thirty-four miles, its wretched state rendered it virtually impassable. Because of frozen ice, the river passage invariably became unusable at the end of November. It remained, nevertheless, a sure link to the Chinese capital, not only for foreign shippers and dignitaries, but also for the Imperial government to its provinces south of the Yellow River needing to communicate with the imperial government. On arriving at Tianjin, Cushing learned happily that the marauding rebel army had disbanded. He at once resolved to visit Beijing (then called Peking).[3]

Tianjin today is a glistening port and commercial arena that still serves as a vital artery providing communication for the government with its various administrative jurisdictions and an all-important highway for mercantile and diplomatic networks beyond China's frontiers. This stunning panorama is a far cry from the primitive landscape of Cushing's time, inhabited by a backward population that still struggled in the gloom of illiteracy and elementary technology. Cushing was overwhelmed by the appalling conditions of the land and its people. Accompanied by his executive officer, Commander Mullen, and Ensign Emory, the son of U.S. Army General Emory, he reported that "the early morning of September 2nd found us inspecting a lot of Chinese carts, drawn up on the warf [sic], and supposed to be intended as means to convey us on the eighty miles of rough road leading to the Capital."

Cushing then went on to exclaim:

> A Chinese cart! Shall I ever forget it! My aching bones answer No!!! And I believe them. Take an American, two wheeled dray, put on it a butcher's cart cover harness it to a slow and stubborn mule — fasten another such animal — with a continual propensity to lie down and rool [sic] over by two pieces of rope to one hub — let the institution be presided over by a very dirty Chinaman — and you have this great Empire's most modern and approved mode of conveyance."

This contraption had no springs, and its passengers sat directly over the axle. In this awkward position they were expected to jerk and jolt over a dirt road with ruts two or three feet deep for eighty miles to Beijing. Cushing and his companions placed mattresses on the bottom of the cart, tucked their valises behind their backs, and installed blankets and robes along the side to guard against sudden thrusts from the cart's sides. This lead cart was accompanied by two others, transported food ("chow-chow") and Chinese porters.[4]

As the three officers passed through Tianjin, they were assaulted by several Chinese men who attempted to push them off the carts. The American naval officers naturally responded by knocking the Chinese invaders to the ground. However, the invaders pursued them, "keeping up a volley of shrieks at the drivers — such as none but an enraged celestial can utter." Cushing admitted that "the three modest and unpretending 'barbarians of the West' came in, too, for their share of native curiosity ... and I, in the leading cart, with cigar in mouth, and purple smoking cap on head and followed by four other conveyances — was instantly looked upon as a big Mandarin attended by his suite."

This armada reached a drawbridge providing a crossing over the Pei Ho River, which flows through Tianjin. Realizing that the drawbridge had been swung closed to permit the passage of a great number of junks and small craft, and that this operation was likely to take several hours, Cushing sent Ensign Emory to tell the undistinguished Mandarin responsible for the bridge that "I was a big Mandarin proceeding with my suite on an official visit to Peking [sic] and that I must have instant passage."[5]

Although the drawbridge was swung to permit traffic to pass over the river, Cushing and his companions found themselves at the center of a roaring debate between the supporters of the mule drivers and their passengers and the angry aggressors who sought to displace them. Presently, Cushing was able to discover the cause of the uproar, which threatened to dissolve into a pitched battle. It turned out that Cushing had engaged carts that had been hired and paid for by several natives to transport them to the Chinese capital. The proprietor of the carts, however, refused to return money that he had received from the original passengers.

Thereupon, Cushing "seized my canton by his long que and giving it a twist, swore by 'Joss,' and all other heathen gods, that I would amputate that sacred article of personal adornment, if he did not instantly disburse his ill gotten 'cash,' and still the troubled waters." The clamorous racket subsided as Cushing's parade crossed the opposite bank of the river. After their unfortunate adversaries had received their money, Cushing observed on departing from Tianjin that it "is a pleasing village of five hundred thousand inhabitants and it took us some time to get out of it — but at length we got clear of all its rocks and shoals — and pushed out into the broad channel of a country road."[6]

Before proceeding, he prudently exchanged three dollars into Chinese currency in order to pay expenses on the road. The rate of exchange was overwhelmingly favorable to the American visitors. He received three thousand copper coins, which he poured into a sack and then slung over the back of a dismayed mule. This beast of burden, however, "took deliberate revenge on the road for he sought out the deepest ruts and largest stones and trundled the chow-chow cart in such a way, that half our plates were broken by the time we had gone eighteen miles and halted at the hospitable town called Lai-Chin for tiffin."

By that time Cushing had become well acquainted with a sprawling landscape that revealed a monotonous prospect with a flat terrain, which, however, was populated by a dense carpet of well-cultivated fields surrounded by a constant succession of comfortable-looking villages. The road, alas, was not a reassuring experience, for the drivers insisted on inserting the wheels of their carts "in the same furrows that had been worn for the last thousand years." Cushing recalled that "I was tossed about like a ball first on one side and then on the other — every moment uttering groans that might have moved stones to tears of sympathy — until, just at dark, we passed a walled and turreted fortress or castle — and came to the 'Yung Loer-Lin inn'— where we were received by the affable landlord 'Chin-Chang.' And where we were shown a room where we might eat, sleep and even wash — a custom foreign to the habits of the people of Northern China." Cushing and his companions dined on beef and eggs, which they accompanied with many cups of tea. After fortifying their aching bodies, they sought the solace of sleep. Cushing had his bed brought in from the cart and installed on a spot set aside in the room for mattresses. As he prepared to sleep, he was attacked by persistent swarms of mosquitoes and fleas. He returned in great haste to the cart, where he remained until midnight, when the party resumed their travels on a road long reduced to a primitive track unworthy of the lofty pretensions of the race they had been constructed to serve. The total cost of the brief stop at the inn, including shelter for the mules and quarters for servants and drivers of the carts, was thirty cents in U.S. currency. At least that modest charge could be counted as compensation for the rigors of the journey.[7]

The motive for attempting to employ the timing of a midnight express on a dirt trail in nineteenth-century China was to arrive in Beijing before the city gates swung shut at nightfall. "For an hour after we had started," Cushing recorded, "I sat out in front, by the driver, with my legs dangling down over the shafts, whistling in the bright moon-light, or learning how to drive mules in a Chinese way but at length I got to romancing about robbers and bandits — imagining or trying to imagine an adventure in every dark grove of trees that we passed through — and ere I knew that I was asleep — and had tumbled back into the cart — where I slept until I was awaken by a tremendous roar of thunder — and some big drops of rain."[8]

In a few minutes a torrential downpour drenched the three naval officers. As they huddled under a blanket at the bottom of the cart, they watched a spectacular show of electrical fireworks, including a sensational display of forked lighting. One bolt struck a large tree that stood no more than twenty yards from their cart. During this melee of natural fury, the Chinese drivers and servants fled to some unknown sanctuary, leaving their mules literally stuck in the mud and their passengers in the meager shelter offered by the carts.

This violent storm soon departed, and Cushing dispatched several servants who had remained with them to discover the hideouts of the fleeing drivers, who were then ordered to proceed or be left to fend for themselves. The journey resumed quickly, and at dawn, although the road had been transformed into an almost impassable bog, Beijing was a scant 20 miles away. Obviously, the spirits of Cushing and his fellow officers were considerably refreshed by the knowledge that the greater part of their formidable trip was behind them and their goal was now within striking distance.[9] Cushing provided Kate with a thorough description of Chinese accommodations for weary travelers. Obviously, he could not resist the dangerous experiment of expanding the cultural horizons of a young woman who delighted in the pleasures of society, but found the challenge of acquiring further instruction on the habits and traditions of distant lands a somewhat trying experience. His narrative is sufficiently novel and merits reproduction:

> The inns in Northern China are constructed around a square acre or so of ground. The sides of the square being a long row of one story shanties. The beds, that I mentioned before, are called "Kangs" and are built entirely of brick forming a platform about two feet above the floor. The whole surface being about the size of two American beds. As this is a cold climate, arrangements are made to keep warm by an oven, formed in this brick work, and a series of brick flues passing under the sleeper. A fire of charcoal or millet stalks is built in this oven and the heat and hot smoke, passing through the bricks give warmth. Chinamen are not infrequently smothered by this use of charcoal. This brick bed is quite an institution, try it.[10]

At about one in the afternoon, Cushing and his companions rode through an imposing gateway in a formidable wall that was one of a series of such barriers erected to prevent invaders from reaching the Imperial City. Plowing its way across a seemingly endless plain in drizzling rain, the little caravan unexpectedly came across a herd of elk. Cushing promptly seized his rifle and shot a stag. His prize possessed a magnificent headdress of antlers, which Cushing announced he intended to ship home. At four in the afternoon the procession of carts passed through the gate of the outer wall to enter the capital. He took care to inform Kate that Beijing was composed of four cities: the Chinese quarter; the Tartar quarter; the Imperial City, the center for administration and governance; and the Forbidden City, residence of the emperor and his court.[11]

Cushing and his companions were carried to the American legation, which was situated in the Tartar quarter next to the wall that encircled the Chinese quarter. Safely ensconced, they had fresh water baths and dressed in clean clothes. They were soon ready to enjoy a truly tasty dinner before retiring for a much-needed peaceful night's rest. Sleeping until ten o'clock the next morning, they awoke to find the courtyard filled with tradesmen peddling their wares with hoarse cries. They offered "every variety of trinket peculiar to Northern China, and stacks of Russian and Corean [sic] sables, ermines, astrakhans, &c." Cushing also reported that "there were old 'red lacquer' boxes, cabinets and 'lucky sticks,' the beautiful and curious inlaid and enameled vases the making of which is now lost — porcelains — vases carved from the horn of the rhinoceros old cracked chinaware — all sorts of gimkracks [sic] that might tempt the curio hunter."[12]

Declining to purchase anything on that morning, the three tourists had ample opportunity to bargain during their stay at the legation, for the swarm of traders came every morning and evening. Cushing nevertheless found that bargaining for a respectable price was a taxing experience. A Chinese merchant would begin by suggesting a far-fetched price, which a prudent customer should reject. In turn, the customer should offer the lowest price that he thought might be accepted. Inevitably, if the calculations of the prospective purchaser were within the range of true value, the Chinese merchant would cry, "Can Do!"[13]

"But before I left the city to return to my ship," Cushing wrote to Kate, "my pocket was much lighter — and I am entirely satisfied with my bargains." He could not resist a good opportunity to tweak Kate's curiosity. "I will not tell you," he slyly cautioned, "what I bought — for if I tell you everything I shall have nothing to surprise you with when I go home — but I'll whisper to you that." Then he laid the bait: "If I did get a large suit of sable — that they were the finest in Peking — had belonged to the Emperor's brother — and are to be worn, in future, if they do not spoil on ship-board, but Ah! But I am breaking my resolution — to my story!"[14]

As the tourists began their first exploration of the Chinese metropolis, they easily decided to forego employing carts. Instead, they chose to employ donkeys. However, they were taken aback by the diminutive stature of the local breed, which were the size of a large sheep and had no saddles, except a small bag attached to their backs. A rope halter was provided in place of a bridle. A club for giving them a nod on either side of their head would direct the animals on their proper course. Being some six feet in height, Cushing thought that he might present a ludicrous picture to the natives. Although anxious to preserve his dignity, he nevertheless undertook an experimental sally, and was pleased to note that the populace took no notice of him except to stare at his naval uniform. Becoming accustomed to this strange locomotion, Cushing reflected, "I enjoyed the novelty, as I once did my Midshipman scrapes, on the same class of animal, in the Azores Islands, when my five feet of jacketed rascality used to fly over their heads and roll in Portuguese dust."[15]

Cushing observed that the streets were wide but dusty and presented a "strange mixture of splendor and decay, in the shape of golden painted stone temples roofed with brilliantly glistening, colored tiles and houses blackened by the dust and storms of ages." Riding through another gate, they passed through a high wall to find that they had entered the Imperial City, where they surveyed a generously sized lake that was covered by an expansive carpet of lotus blossoms. From that pleasing spectacle, they rode to the wall of the Forbidden City, where the emperor and his entourage lived: "No foreigner has ever entered its gates; and the wall is so high and so well guarded that nothing but the pagoda towers can be seen from outside."[16]

Cushing then narrated his account of a truly rare and sensational event:

> Riding around this we came to another walled enclosure in the midst of which rose a hill some two hundred feet high surmounted by a beautiful pavilion. I was informed by the Secretary of the Legation, who was with us, that was called the

"Sacred Garden" & "Sacred Hill," and that no foreigner had ever been permitted to look in; much less to enter as it commanded a near and complete view of the Forbidden City. Just then we came to a door in the inner angle of the buttress of the wall — which I observed to be left up ajar and I instantly flung myself from my donkey: and made for it at a run. The others followed me at once and dashed in at a run passing the surprised guards; and were lost, in an instant, amidst flowers and trees. Now, said I, we are in for it, and might as well go to the hill top and see the sights. And at the hill we dashed right through everything while a wild hub-bub of howls and lamentations arose from our rear, from pursuing Chinamen, whose necks were in danger from our success. Not a little to our dismay we found the hill planted thickly with briers; but through them we went, covered with scratches tripping and tumbling panting and laughing but going up faster I think, than it was ever before ascended until we reached the top and tumbled down exhausted on the pavilion's marble terrace. There, right across one field, was the "Forbidden" City. Two hundred yards away was the Emperor's palace side by side (separated by a wall) with that of his Mother the "Empress Dowager" and the present ruler of China. There was a small lake and some beautiful gardens with ornamental arbors, made of rich-looking green and blue enameled tiles. The houses of the royal Princess and Emperor's guard all in splendid repair and looking truly like a scene dreamed from the Arabian Nights. The houses were all roofed with the imperial yellow enameled tiles — and shone brilliantly in the sun giving a rich golden appearance to all and the tall, many-colored pagodas at the gates and angles added dignity and majesty to the scene. The hill upon which we were is said to be artificial, having been made four hundred years ago, from coal sent from various provinces. The pavilion, in which we were, was richly decorated with a variety of blue, green, and yellow tiles; and contained a bronze idol, some twenty feet high.[17]

A few minutes after their dramatic rush to the pavilion, the American explorers were surrounded by a throng of some hundred guards, who, with cries and moans betraying their fear of a dire fate if their carelessness should be discovered, pled and cajoled with the perpetrators of their shame to quickly depart. Instead, Cushing and his comrades calmly contemplated the splendid tableau for ten or fifteen minutes, until they had absorbed this rare glimpse of China's legendary past. "At length," Cushing wrote, "we went down, and out of the garden jubilant that we were the only foreigners who had ever entered the sacred garden, or seen the Forbidden City." Furthermore, he noted that "our exploit created quite an excitement in diplomatic circles, and is much talked of as if we had visited the Moon, but as no official complaint has been made, I conclude that the Chinamen whose heads we endangered kept our visit to themselves."[18]

To use modern definitions, the Forbidden City was an amalgamation of several distinct compounds or precincts. The separate units are ranged on a south-north axis. The major gateway on the south side looks toward the fertile and hospitable regions of central and southern China. The northern gate points toward the cold chill of the snow-covered plains and mountains of Mongolia.

The Hall of Supreme Harmony is the first and most imposing of the buildings standing in a direct line on the south-north axis. In this structure the emperor held his public audiences and receptions. On occasions of great importance, for example, grand parades of victorious troops accompanied by cheering throngs provided a colorful recognition of the might of the Celestial Sovereign. On other occasions, the emperor received foreign dignitaries as well as petitions from his subjects. It was in this vast hall that he was installed on his throne as the truly divine governor of his empire. As a representative of his country on official business, Lieutenant Commander William Barker Cushing of the United States Navy could be admitted to this chamber for a formal audience.[19]

Beyond the great reception hall, where the emperor conducted much of his ceremony and supervised public business, are two smaller pavilions, again on the axis between the southern and northern gates. These two pavilions were reserved for confidential conversations between the emperor and his government officials and members of the court. In one of these pavilions the emperor greeted the most successful of those who had passed rigorous exams that admitted them into the ranks of the far-flung bureaucracy of the Chinese empire. The principal focus of these exams was to evaluate a candidate's knowledge of the ideas and logic of Confucian thought and how they could be deployed to resolve issues confronting the people of China and their governors.[20]

After these two pavilions came a barrier of gates and walls that separated the emperor's private residence from the rest of the Forbidden City. It was within this sanctuary that the emperors enjoyed the pleasures of family life and the society of their concubines. This was the site of curious phenomena, at least to Western minds, provided by eunuchs who kept a watchful eye on the flock of courtesans attached to the imperial domicile, a charge that easily encouraged constant strife within the imperial household as each eunuch strove to bring his candidate to the emperor's gaze.

Immediately behind the private residences of the emperor and his family was an elaborate network of gardens, which still survives today. Then came the formal gate, which was the principal opening of the wall of the Forbidden City along its northern extremity. In Cushing's time, however, another wall with a gate facing the northern gateway of the Forbidden City encircled a relatively modest enclosure that was dominated by a steep hill. On top of this hill were five temples constructed in 1758. As Cushing noted, the hill is artificial, formed from piles of coal that had been stacked during the reign of a Ming Emperor, Yongle (1402–1424). This ruler may be ranked as the true founder of Beijing as the political center of China and the Forbidden City as the pivotal site of imperial tribal governance, although Kublai Khan (1216–1294), the celebrated Mongol, became emperor of the Chinese empire in 1271 and established the seat of his regime at Beijing. Later on, the piles of coal, which were probably collected to provide heat during periods of winds and gusty squalls of winter snow, became covered by dirt from artificial basins carved out to create pleasure lakes in the parks that provided a pleasing landscape in the area behind the Forbidden City. Coal Hill, as this artificial mound was nicknamed, became a favorite spot for promenading by the residents of the imperial court, particularly women. It was accepted as an extension of the private grounds of the emperor and his entourage. Although Coal Hill had fallen into an unkempt state, with a little bit of luck Cushing and his friends might have encountered some of the emperor's concubines. Such a collision undoubtedly would have prompted a truly elaborate and memorable display of fireworks.[21]

As previously noted, Z. L. Tanner met Cushing in the summer of 1864 in Philadelphia and had followed Cushing's destruction of the *Albemarle* and subsequent exploits until the end of the Civil War. Tanner was dispatched to serve with the Asiatic squadron and had been assigned to the *Maumee* on July 4, 1868, upon the arrival of Cushing from Hong Kong. Tanner remained assigned to the *Maumee* until she was decommissioned. He was detached on November 17, 1869. Since Tanner was not a member of the American excursion to Beijing, his account came from secondhand sources. It would appear that as an officer on the *Maumee*, he had been instructed to remain with the ship. Undoubtedly, his account was derived from casual conversations with his fellow officers. His assertion, therefore, that Cushing pursued this sensational venture solo and paused momentarily to deliver a cry of triumph at the climax of his ascent of Coal Hill must be accepted with considerable skepticism. In his letter to Kate, Cushing describes a spectacle of fairy-tale enchantment in a passage expressing awe and invoking images of the "Arabian Nights." He had caught a rare glimpse of the majesty and dominions of the once magnificent Celestial Empire.[22]

The novelty of the dash of the three American naval officers into the inner sanctum of the Forbidden City is further elucidated when one recalls that this inner sanctum had become the last refuge of the tattered remnants of imperial authority and administration. The central government had been appropriated by Dowager Empress Tz'u Hsi, whose fundamental policy was to monopolize the remaining vestiges of imperial power. Unfortunately, her definition of sovereignty was limited to palace intrigue and comfort. The Forbidden City served as a place of confinement for adolescent emperors, who were kept under her strict observation. Although the dowager empress frequently resided in villas in the pleasant grounds bordering artificial lakes near the northern fringe of the Forbidden City or at the Summer Palace that she had constructed to take the place of the one destroyed by British and French troops, she considered the Forbidden City her ultimate refuge.[23]

When William Henry Seward, secretary of state under Lincoln, visited Beijing in 1870, he was not invited to any formal audience by the court or senior Chinese officials within the walls of the Forbidden City. Instead, Prince

Kung, the brother of the late emperor and the uncle of the present incumbent, now serving as regent, visited Seward at the American legation.[24]

Such was not the sole function of the Forbidden City during the prime of the Ming and Ch'ing dynasties. When the Russian ambassador traveled from St. Petersburg across the vast plains of Siberia to meet with the Ch'ing emperor K'ang-his, he encountered a cultivated and enlightened regime. The rituals of the court and the official affairs, both foreign and domestic, of the empire were conducted regularly within the walls of the Forbidden City. The majority of these activities was held in halls that were open to all participants or even to the general public.[25]

The spectacular panorama of the imperial sanctuary within the closely guarded citadel of the Forbidden City of the nineteenth century contrasted dramatically with the dingy streets and buildings surrounding it. Cushing observed that the city contained many public edifices that "showed abundant traces of days of glory long past" and "everywhere in its limits are ruins of great and beautiful works," but he lamented that "decay seems to go on without check, and unless soon arrested by a rich and willing Emperor, must soon gain complete victory."[26]

Alas, no such emperor marched to lift the siege of his beleaguered empire and a bleak horizon continued to be dominated by an aging dowager empress, whose history was that of a concubine who survived by her astute mastery of the entangling machinations that prompted a never-ending flow of intrigues in the imperial household. Through her rigid control of adolescent emperors, the dowager empress could exercise ascendancy over the chief officers of the court and bureaucracy. Tragically, she was unable to graduate from the petty squabbles of her immediate circle to attain a genuine understanding of domestic issues and diplomacy at the critical moment when China was compelled to come to terms with western economics and foreign colonial expansion on her soil.

As a result, the once awesome authority of the emperor was restricted to Beijing and its immediate environs. The coast and major rivers of China were governed by colonial powers. In the interior, warlords, former ranking military officers and governors of provinces or important districts assumed the sovereign authority once enforced omnipotently from the celestial throne in the Forbidden City.

In 1911 the empire collapsed and was replaced by a Western-style government. However, throughout the twentieth century China continued to be overrun by foreign invaders, principally the Japanese. Finally, a Communist faction evolved into a popular national movement. The People's Republic was proclaimed in 1949 from the Tiananmen Gate of the Forbidden City, the very portal used by a long succession of Ming and Ch'ing emperors on travels to expedite their unlimited suzerainty over their far-flung realms. Today China has little affinity with its illustrious past. The art and literature of centuries of imperial leadership have little relevance to contemporary Chinese society, which is slowly and carefully striving to revive its legacy and integrate it into the mainstream of modern ideas and prevailing conventions.

It is not extravagant to suggest that Cushing sensed that he was witnessing the demise of a once great society that had made significant contributions to the civilizing of the world. Certainly he wrote in that vein when he informed Kate that "during our visit to Peking we went, of course, to see the observatory — where we saw immense bronze instruments used in observations fifteen hundred years ago, in the golden age of China, when science and literature flourished." Cushing marveled to learn that these ancient instruments still functioned as precisely "as when first constructed — though exposed to the open air for so many centuries; and are scientifically correct as astronomical instruments."[27]

A similar relic from the illustrious Chinese past also caught Cushing's attention and respectful admiration. Not too far from the impressive display of artifacts that he described to Kate "is the Jesuit Observatory — five hundred years old — consisting of a solid ton of masonry, a hundred feet high, and fifty yards square at the top. On this elevated platform there are a dozen colossal astronomical instruments, cast in bronze, supported by huge bronze dragons — made under the supervision of Jesuits, who were once strong in China. Amongst these is a globe of the heavens — covered with raised stars and planets illustrating the whole planetary system then understood. It is at least twelve feet in diameter: yet after 500 years of neglect in the open air; it turns readily upon its axis by the pressure of a hand. The graduation of the circles to minutes and seconds and the correctness with which the ecliptic and other great circles were laid down — surprised me very much — and I must always look upon the observatory as the greatest curiosity in China."[28]

Although Cushing deplored the prevalence of decay that was visible in the streets and facades of Beijing, he was pleasantly surprised at the respectable condition of the numerous temples, the chief of which was Yonghe Gong, an elaborate establishment that still stands today as a major attraction. Originally, it served as a palace for the fourth son of the celebrated Ch'ing emperor K'ang Xis. Eventually, this son became emperor, and in turn was succeeded by his own son in 1745, who adhered to the practice of donating his private residence to a religious order. In this case, a Lamaist order from Tibet was granted the privilege of occupying the opulent palace and its grounds. Because of their costume, this group was identified as the "yellow hat" sect.

Cushing wrote an extensive narrative of his exploration of this particular site: "The temple of 'Yung-Ho-King' is the largest in Peking — and was formerly the palace of the heir to the throne. That was three hundred years ago — and it was then customary for the princes when ascending the throne, to present their former houses to some religious sect as temples. The Lamaist religion was then the most popular and powerful (imported into China from Tibet) and to that order this palace was given. The Lamaist sect is now Buddhist, to all intents and purposes. This temple covers about forty square acres of ground — and is surrounded by high walls. It has at least twenty large buildings, besides the quarters of the priests of whom two thousand are officiating there."

As he traversed through a labyrinth of corridors and halls, Cushing succumbed to a common temptation that preys on tourists. After admiring a statue of Buddha, which had been carved from a single large tree, he decided to acquire one of the hundreds of statues that decorated the row of niches and pedestals that filled the interior of the temple: "I tried hard to get one of a lot of brass ones, about a foot high, a beautiful female, tastefully dressed in a necklace and pair of bracelets." When, however, Cushing attempted to purchase it, the elderly priest escorting him turned him down. Even a bribe failed to persuade this ancient monk to relent, as he announced emphatically that his head would be cut off if he should accept such a reward.[29]

Undaunted, Cushing resorted to desperate measures, attempting to purloin a statue when his elderly watchdog's attention was diverted to other chores. His guide did not relax his careful scrutiny, and Cushing was compelled to abandon his strategy. He then adopted a more subtle scheme. On one of the altars or ledges, he surreptitiously removed a statue from its customary position. His watchful companion thought that Cushing had pocketed the statue. The aged caretaker "came rushing down — the very picture of fright and terror — he had actually turned ash color and trembled in every fiber."[30]

Eventually, Cushing had pity on his terrified guardian: "I took him to the altar and showed him the missing article — and while he was replacing it I managed to pocket a very pretty idol of stone — some 300 years old — which he did not miss — and as there were some thousand like it — probably will not." Having accomplished his sly stratagem, Cushing suffered a shock of remorse, and sought to cloak his thieving prank as a defense of Christian principles. "This was a case," he argued, "where stealing was a virtue — I stole an idol — and so aided the cause of Christianity." At the same time, he realized that he was navigating in treacherous waters. He sought reassurance and sympathy from his fiancée: "Ask Mr. Arey if I was not right."[31]

Apparently, his qualms of conscience were not a distracting burden, for Cushing proceeded to the next prominent landmark — the Temple of Confucius and an academy dedicated to the study of the philosophy of Confucius. Today, these structures are known respectively as Kong Miao and Guozijian. Drawing away from his skepticism of Buddha, Cushing saw considerable merit in the rigorous logic of Confucian theorems. Cushing told Kate that he had surveyed

> a handsome temple erected in honor of the great Chinese sage "Confucius"; who died about two hundred years before Christ. No worship is held there and it con-

tains nothing but a simple shrine and tablet with the characters on it denoting his name. Confucius is everything to these people. They believe in his teaching as firmly as Christians do in Christ — and there is no higher honor in the Empire than that paid to a man who passes a thorough examination in the work of Confucius. A tablet of stone, seven feet high is erected to such a man, with an inscription of honor. There were but eleven such tablets in the court yard of the Confucian building of honor at Peking — and all but one seemed to be very old — so you can imagine how rarely any gain the much coveted prize. Confucius works are the Chinese Classics [sic]. And for fear that, if preserved only upon paper or parchment, they may be lost or destroyed, two hundred black marble tablets have been erected in the grounds of a handsome building called "The Emperor's Pavilion" in the City.[32]

Cushing was much entranced with the size and purpose of these impressive marble slabs. He calculated that "each tablet is ten feet high and engraved on both sides — and they stand in the open air, upright, like huge tomb stones." "They are," he concluded, "amongst the most curious things to be seen in China."[33] Beyond the monolithic record of the writings of Confucius stood the emperor's pavilion with a pagoda-shaped roof of yellow tile. Any structure or article tinted with yellow signified an intimate association with the emperor and his activities. The pavilion was situated in a setting that was encircled by a moat, in which an armada of goldfish swam. This moat could be crossed by traversing one of four attractive marble bridges. Standing sentinel before the pavilion was an impressive triumphal arch. Nevertheless, the imposing design and ornamentation of the grounds on which the pavilion stood was not matched by its plain interior, where the only ornament was an elaborately decorated throne of gold. From time to time the emperor visited this pavilion to listen to lectures on the philosophy of Confucius.[34]

Cushing completed his discussion of the temples he surveyed in Beijing by commenting that "one Mohammedan Mosque — built in thoroughly Turkish style, looked odd and interesting amongst all these heathen temples." It appears that Cushing considered the faith of the Prophet Mohammed to have a kindred heritage with Judaism and Christianity. The cults of Asia, including that of Buddha, despite their widespread allegiance, were in his view classified as constituents of a lengthy catalog of idolatrous sects.[35]

Turning from his tour of the buildings and monuments of Beijing, Cushing described the passing parade of humanity, which he claimed was dominated by two major streams, each of which represented an extreme edge of society. The first that he described was the impressive cavalcade of Mandarins of all ranks with servants and retainers. Some were conveyed in ceremonial carts, but others rode majestically on horseback. All of these Mandarins displayed the degree of their importance by showing red, blue, and white glass buttons. Cushing kept carefully in mind the fact that the emperor and those officials who occupied positions of great authority were invariably Tartars or Manchus, who could be readily distinguished from the southern Chinese by their mustaches and beards. The smooth-skinned Chinese, especially those in southern China, Cushing labeled as "effeminate" in appearance. Wishing to be even-handed, he mentioned a popular jibe that "one 'Cantonese' will whip a dozen Northerners."[36]

The second stream was filled with swarms of destitute beggars who shuffled unimpeded through the streets and alleys of the capital. "They are regularly organized," Cushing had discovered, "under 'head men,' and are at perfect liberty to stand in front of a store all day long and trouble the proprietor, unless he pays something." To avoid such a siege, Cushing reported that "sometimes the store men seek an interview with the 'head man' and pay him a large sum to be relieved of all such visits. The 'head man,' in such cases gives the merchant a red slip of paper to paste up in front of his store, with an order inscribed on it, for all beggars to cease to molest him."[37] Cushing was startled to encounter a well-known bridge that was constantly filled with inhabitants of all ages and genders who lived on it throughout the year. Some had been born on that bridge; others would die on it. Despite such a sickening spectacle, Cushing calculated that "half of the professional beggars are hearty, able-bodied men; too lazy to work." Tragically, he observed, "The Chinese have no institutions of charity, and as a result, the truly ill and indigent wander without any solace."[38]

A fitting conclusion to Cushing's narrative of his tour of Beijing is his description of the walls of the city, which gave it the appearance of a fortified city in medieval Europe. The Tartar quarter was sixteen square miles and protected by a ring of walls that were approximately fifty feet high and forty feet thick. These walls were segmented at every seventy yards by a buttress or tower and crowned with a parapet, which was similar to those employed in medieval European fortifications. "The walls of the whole city," Cushing claimed, "are thirty miles in circumference — and are pierced by sixteen gates — huge arches — with iron doors — each surmounted by a wide, four-storied pagoda, which frowns at one approaching through hundreds of portholes."[39]

At the end of six days of exploring the sights and mysteries of Beijing, Cushing and his companions decided to visit the region that was situated on the border of Mongolia and the land of the Tartars. Their main goal, naturally, was to inspect the Great Wall. On this sojourn, they were joined by an American merchant, whom they had probably met at the American legation. On September 7, the travelers left in six carts loaded with supplies and retainers for their first stop, which was nine miles in the distance. They arrived at Ta Chung Ssu, where their escorts prepared breakfast. During this interval, they visited the temple, where an enormous bell hung. This bell had been cast in 1402, and it had been transported to its present site in 1743. Cushing wrote, "We found it truly a curiosity as it is the largest bell hung in the World — and is completely covered with forty thousand characters, cast in the most perfect manner with it — and inside as well as out. It is 18 feet high — 15 in diameter at the rim — and one foot thick there — and weighs two hundred and sixty pounds [*sic*]. I stood in the gallery near the top, and pitched copper 'cash' through the hole in the top of the bronze monster; as there is a superstition that those who succeed on doing so will meet with good fortune. I also told the shaven-headed old 'Bonze,' who acted as our guide, that I desired to strike the bell — but he explained that the attention of the 'Rain God' was called by the noise — and we would get wet. Nevertheless I gave it an awful bang with the big swinging lever of wood in use for that purpose — and curiously enough we were caught in a terrific thunder storm that very night. Wasn't that funny? I suppose that the priests will take the storm as another strong proof of the merits of the 'God Caller.'"[40]

On completing their breakfast, the intrepid explorers proceeded to ride to the park, which until recently had been the site of the world-renowned Summer Palace of the Chinese emperors. Emperor Qianlong (1736–1796) had extended several lakes within the park into a large stretch of water that was constantly kept at a sizeable extent by a steady flow of water from a nearby natural source known as the Jade Spring. At the same time, the emperor had constructed a resplendent palace that was designed after the prevailing tastes in European architecture and décor, but also with a nod to the majestic scale of the royal Chateau at Versailles. Tragically, an Anglo-French expeditionary force burned the palace and looted its priceless contents in 1860, a ruthless and barbaric episode that gave the lie to European claims of superior civilization. Admittedly, Chinese authorities at Beijing, in the confusion of a disintegrating regime, had executed several diplomatic emissaries as spies, and for a time it seemed possible that the flamboyantly aggressive negotiator on behalf of British mercantile interests, the legendary Sir Harry Parks, might suffer the same fate.[41]

After crossing a marble bridge, the undaunted adventurers passed through a granite corridor that was lined with bronze lions: "Here we were positively refused admittance — and even our bribes were absolutely rejected — so after half an hour, spent in efforts to talk over the Chinese guard — we walked around the walls until we found a place that might well be scaled — and over we went."[42] This daring repetition of the bold adventure on Coal Hill is clearly an example of the reckless sporting psychology that prompted the previous challenge. It was an escapade pushed by an impulse of the moment. The solemn responsibilities associated with the uniform of officers of the United States Navy were tossed lightly aside.

Cushing offered a disingenuous defense of their conduct: "It seems that the grounds are closed to foreigners, in consequence of the misconduct of some young men from the English Legation — who went in there and shot two of the Emperor's deer." He then proceeded to describe their initial scouting of the park. "When inside the walls," he reported, "we walked down to the gate to show ourselves to the guard — laughed at their wonder and dismay — and then set out on a tour of the grounds." As Cushing continued his promenade through the park, he spoke of the beauty of the spot. He observed that "the grounds are several miles square — and the country rises in gentle hills and advantage has been taken of the natural features of the ground; so that the whole furnishes every variety of hill and dale — woodland and lawn interspersed with canals, pools, cascades and lakes — while wide granite avenues and fine marble bridges conduct to pagodas, temples and pavilions — and to gardens and groves filled with deer and the choicest birds of China."[43]

Cushing claimed that "the most notable work of art remaining in 'Yung Ming Yung' [round and splendid garden] is a temple of bronze — situated on the side of a romantic artificial hill — built of rocks — with as much art as to resemble nature — and through which a (once) secret path leads, winding in and out through to the temple doors."[44] Having conquered Coal Hill, Cushing was eager to attempt another assault on a prohibited imperial sanctuary. "The Chinese had piled up," Cushing discovered, "briers and brush to prevent an approach to this curious place of worship — and warned me that snakes were numerous — but I managed to get up the marble steps; and went in; scratched — but minus snake bites."[45]

After surveying the pleasant landscape, where there were a number of melancholy prospects of the broken remnants of a once splendid panorama, Cushing and his fellow tourists left the Summer Palace at a quick pace and sought the comforts of their lodging for the night. As twilight commenced, they entered the pass through the mountains to Nan Kon, where they intended to finish their day. This pass had been made by Mother Nature; it was a rocky bed of a river that had disappeared a long time ago. There had, however, been little effort to level and grade the rocks and boulders into a smooth surface that could provide swift and comfortable communication between China and her Mongolian neighbors across the northern frontier.

Despite the extraordinary discomfort the intrepid and bone-weary travelers had to endure, a torture considerably augmented by the rigid construction of Chinese carts that lacked even the most elementary system of springs or mechanics of suspension, they reached their shelter at eight in the evening. In half an hour Cushing recalled that "four foreigners were laughing and joking over our tea — and thinking of the oddity of this traveling with impunity in the most sacred and revered portions of China." He marveled, moreover, that although "we ordered everything with a 'high hand' — and made everyone do as we pleased; but though many leagues from any assistance in case of danger — and surrounded by a hundred thousand Chinamen who were not accustomed to the visits of Europeans — we were treated with courtesy and attention, and our word was law." "I think," Cushing concluded, "that this Empire is one of the safest in the whole World for travelers—provided two or three go in company to deter robbers from attack in the mountain passes."[46]

Cushing and his colleagues had traveled some thirty miles from Beijing, and were now fifteen miles away from the Great Wall. To reach their final destination, they had to abandon transportation by cart and instead resort to the sturdy backs of donkeys. They also acquired a guide. "We started off," Cushing wrote, "under the guidance of as dirty and ragged a Celestial as China can boast." Cushing asserted that "Chang" indeed "was a professional guide, and had two or three letters from travelers whom he had accompanied—he could point out the best path between the stones, and was very amusing as a buffoon, keeping us constantly laughing."[47]

Cushing reported that the Nan Kon pass was fifteen miles of stone rubble over which the little donkeys had to search carefully for a sure footing. In the twelfth century, Cushing had learned, when Kublai Khan invaded China through this pass, a stone road had been built. The surface of this road was sufficiently hard and smooth to permit a steady flow of traffic. Five miles from the village of Nan Kon the weary tourists encountered a truly imposing arch decorated with grandly carved gods playing various musical instruments. It also displayed inscriptions in Tibetan Sanskrit, Mongolian Chinese, and a language now unknown.[48]

As the donkeys stumbled toward the Great Wall, they carried their riders under a series of arches, which were guarded by a number of towers mounted at the top of the high walls of the narrow trail. Suddenly the end of the tunnel was reached, and a long stretch of mountain ranges appeared. On the top of these ranges was anchored a never-ending ribbon of stone wall. As Cushing told Kate, "We came in sight of the veritable 'great wall' of China—a work as old as the Christian Era—yes—older too—but standing today high, strong and defiant as in those 'Bible times'—only now they front no more an enemy in Tartary—for a Tartar is on the throne and Tartars own land and fortunes also."[49]

Cushing then provided a short description of the spectacle: "Well we lunched on 'great wall'—and two of us walked on it for some miles, to where it reaches one of the highest ridges of the mountains—and a view was had that but few ever witnessed. The vast plain was visible for sixty miles—with its winding streams and walled towns—and, on both hands, the wall wound its murky way along, as far as the eye could reach—on the highest mountain ridges and peaks."[50]

Cushing estimated that the wall was fifteen hundred miles in length. Where he stood, he calculated that the wall was about thirty feet high and thirty feet thick. Every hundred yards a tower reinforced the wall, which had a palisade rampart. The wall was constructed from blocks of stone, but its parapets and towers were made of brick. Actual calculations of the total length of the Great Wall vary. The main string of the wall is at least some 1700 miles in length, but if the whole stretch is measured, then it is probably closer to 2500. A more impressive figure is to say that the Great Wall would reach from New York to Denver — that is, from the Atlantic shore to the Rocky Mountains. Cushing's account of the method employed in the construction of the Great Wall should be modified by understanding that its interior mass was composed of tramped, or pressured, dirt. Its foundation is stone block, but its superstructure is brick.[51]

Upon discreetly picking up a brick from the Great Wall as a souvenir, Cushing was ready for the thirty-mile trip to Nan Kon. During this venture Lt. Commander Mullen, Cushing's executive officer, fell off his donkey four times and the other gentlemen tumbled down twice. Cushing himself survived sore, but not bruised. At the inn they welcomed a rest and a good night's sleep in the company of the usual cluster of fleas. At five the following morning, they left the inn to begin a fifteen-mile trip to the fabled arena of the tombs of the Ming emperors. They came to a large plain, which was ringed by mountains, and as they descended they passed through three imposing arches containing gigantic commemorative blocks that were supported on the backs of gigantic marble turtles.[52]

Cushing and his comrades then encountered a series of immense stone animals. Cushing recalled that "there were eight lions, four seated and four standing — four camels in lifelike positions — four elephants — four 'griffins' — four horses — eight kings, and eight priests." Each of these monster effigies had been carved from a single block of stone, "and each was five or six times life size." Beyond this procession of guards was a granite causeway and bridge that led to a marble avenue that ended at the tomb of Chang Ling, who was the founder of Beijing and the first emperor to be buried at this site and in the particular style of tomb that was adapted by his successors.[53]

Cushing recorded, "His tomb covers about six acres of ground — and is surrounded by a high wall. Passing through a pagoda — built and arched gateway — we came to a marble paved court-yard and then to another handsome hall — succeeded by a court-yard and charming garden — upon which fronts the shrine. It is in a building of marble — with imperial yellow tiles on its roof— and in the center of a hall two hundred and fifty feet long by one hundred broad — supported by 32 pillars — (exclusive of many in the wall) each twelve feet in circumference and seventy feet high."[54]

From that imposing regal entry to the imperial mausoleum, Cushing and his companions moved to the actual tomb, which had been enclosed in a large brick mound that could be entered by means of a tunnel. This winding passage functioned as a whispering gallery as it revealed a pagoda that contained an impressive stone tablet proclaiming the emperor's achievements. As the intrepid visitors surveyed the solemn scene, they had their "Tiffin" and celebrated their venture "with a right jolly time singing." Cushing recalled that "the buildings were handsomely frescoed and in good repair; and the marble carvings — terraces — and enameled tiling were rich and durable." Once again, Cushing could not resist the temptation to pocket a tangible souvenir of the occasion, and removed a yellow tile from a corner of the shrine. Suspecting that his impetuous action had not escaped the watchful eye of a custodian, Cushing was careful to leave a generous tip.[55]

Cushing and his comrades decided to end their whirlwind tour of the great monuments of imperial China in order to reach Beijing before the city gates were shut. They paid their guide a bountiful reward, but when he protested that he had not received enough, they resolved to teach him a lesson. They informed their avaricious guide that if he practiced their instructions in negotiating with foreign visitors, he would easily receive double the amount that he initially sought. "The instruction," Cushing described, "was in regard to saluting Englishmen — and we taught him in so doing to place one thumb on the end of the nose, extending the hand, with the thumb of the other hand applied to the little finger of the first — seconded by a wag of the fingers." Cushing speculated cheerfully that "I can imagine him thus saluting some crusty, red-faced Britton — and the consequent knock down that he will get for the seeming insult."[56]

To add a polished postscript to their jocular prank, the three naval officers wrote a requested letter of recommendation in doggerel rhythm:

> This dirty "Cuss" whose name is "Chang,"
> (The filthiest poet ever sang)
> Desires of this Christian gang
> A letter to commend him.
> He'll stick to you what're befall;
> He'll show you China's greatest wall;
> Her rocks and fields — "Ming Tombs" and all —
> And so — The Devil mend him!![57]

Such was the climax of Cushing's tour of the landscape and monuments of the Mongolian dominion in northern China. Cushing and his companions did, however, take a brief break in their hurried trip to Beijing to quickly inspect a shrine dedicated to the Black Dragon. This being, represented by a wooden statue, which was supposed to have the ability to produce rain to refresh parched throats and dusty acres, appeared reluctant to measure up to his reputation. A disgusted emperor thus condemned it to exile. Happily, on the eve of departing through the Great Wall to the stark Mongolian plains, a mighty downpour ended a prolonged drought. A grateful emperor, who had dispatched the wooden effigy into exile with a chain around its neck, now brought him back to his temple, where he was promptly covered with rich robes of imperial yellow. Wishing for a dry journey to the imperial capital,

Cushing gave the wooden statue a friendly wink, and then hurried with his friends to reach the gates before they closed, a task that they accomplished successfully shortly before five o'clock.[58]

Instead of restricting themselves to the formal routine of the American legation, Cushing and company negotiated with a Buddhist monk at his temple for an accommodation that would permit them to enjoy an informal routine conforming to their predilections. Undoubtedly, Cushing departed from Beijing by the Southern Gate, which, along with the accompanying walls, has long since disappeared. Also gone are the Tartar and Chinese quarters. The Gate of the Forbidden City that opened toward the south, which was reserved for the coming and going of the emperor, today serves as a public entrance and displays an immense portrait of Mao Zedung, who on October 1, 1949, proclaimed a socialist republic. In the immediate vicinity of the Forbidden City, there survive some of the Hutongs, where many of the officials who worked in government bureaus inside the Forbidden City, as well as a sizeable number of merchants and laboring families, lived within courtyards encircled by their dwellings and storerooms.

It was along these narrow alleys that Cushing explored the dusty and crowded shops and houses of ordinary inhabitants, and studied the green-tiled palaces of imperial princes and powerful Mandarins. Some of these imposing structures still exist today. Much, however, of the urban landscape that Cushing described has vanished. Tiananmen Square is known now as the stage of a massive and spectacular demonstration in June 1989, demanding the rule of democracy. Today, the square is dominated by the Great Hall of the People, a large arena reserved for functions of the Communist regime, and also by the mausoleum of Mao Zedung.

The Forbidden City is finally being restored as a genuine reminder of the great cultural and artistic legacy of China as it bustles onto the stage as a world power with a modern economic apparatus. Cushing explored the remnants of a fading empire, but long after his generation departed, the Phoenix has reappeared with glowing promise.

On their return trip to their ship, Cushing and his companions rumbled on a thirteen-mile stretch of road that led from Beijing to Fung Chow onto the Pei Ho River, where they boarded a boat to navigate 120 miles of river to reach the USS *Maumee* in two days. As soon as he boarded his ship, Cushing had the duty of entertaining the newly appointed American minister to China, J. Ross Browne, who was accompanied by his family and official entourage. "There are two marriageable daughters," Cushing informed Kate, "with whom I danced all last evening; but they are as homely as hedge fences — and will be 'below par' even out here where women are so scarce." He also revealed that he had called upon and subsequently received on board the viceroy of all the northern provinces, a ritual that demanded "lots of humbug — full dress —

cannon firing etc." Consequently, he was quite eager to follow his fresh orders to sail to Nagasaki, where he would receive further instructions.[59]

Cushing's reception for the newly appointed American minister and his diplomatic gestures to Chinese authorities were not purely ceremonial, because at this time Russell & Co., long a well-recognized competitor against British merchant interests at Hong Kong, had achieved without question a monopoly of trade along the long but lucrative Yangtze River. Although the British governed Shanghai, they had lost their normal ascendancy in trading to their American rival, which had extended its robust competitive operation to the route between Shanghai and Tientsin. Thus, American commerce had secured a predominant position in commerce at Shanghai and on the Yangtze River as well as gaining a firm foothold on the all-important water artery that linked Beijing by sea and river to the central and southern provinces of its empire. As that empire slipped into impotency, Americans were aggressive contenders for the spoils.[61]

Cushing concluded his lengthy narrative of his adventures in Beijing and contiguous territory with a strong declaration of continuing love for Kate. He pled for her to recognize "how true the heart is that you have won — and give me all the warm confidence and affection of an affianced wife." "If I could but feel sure," he agonized, "that you entirely love me I should be the happiest of men — that one great blessing would be enough to live for — or if need be, to die for." Then he prayed, "Let us be <u>all the World</u> to each other, dearest — as man and wife should be — seeking for happiness in the hearts of each other — and looking always to the sunshine Leife [*sic*] is bright before us — and we can gaze into the future with joyous faces — but as we go forward let it be hand in hand Kate — as we were indeed one."[61]

Cushing once more took care to reaffirm his steady devotion and loyalty to Kate. "I feel that I have left behind me," he claimed, "some object as essential to peace and happiness as blood is to life — and I know that it is you, dear Kate, who is so influence [*sic*] my very soul, for whom I am constantly sighing; and of whom my dreams are full." He could not resist once again lecturing Kate on the subject of his faith in her constancy, which he trusted matched his firm attachment to her. "Do you think," he inquired, "that I write such long letters to 23 sweet hearts — And will that little — tailor Philo Stevens — win his bet?" Obviously, Kate still could not resist the temptation of flirting with some of the rustic gallants of village society.

Changing course, Cushing expressed his great joy in learning from a letter he had just received that he had become an uncle to "a boy named after my dearest brother who fought so bravely and died so grandly at Gettysburg!" He promptly informed Kate, as he had his mother, that President Grant had posthumously promoted Alonzo to the rank of colonel. Cushing also revealed his regret that he would not greet his nephew as an infant but rather as a young lad. "I shall be a Commodore just about in time," he mused, "to look out for him as Midshipman Alonzo Cushing Gayle."[62]

In general, Cushing told Kate that he enjoyed cruising Asian waters, where he had the opportunity to explore exotic climes and survey strange sights that relatively few Westerners had witnessed. His health was very much improved, and hopefully the pleasant and refreshing climate of Japan would cure the remaining traces of a cold and he would be able to avoid any bronchitis. On that cheerful note, Cushing and the USS *Maumee* slipped down the Pei Ho River to the Gulf of Chihli, then into the Yellow Sea to the East China Sea and the port of Nagasaki.[63]

Chapter 7

Imperial Japan

Cushing had anticipated that a vital link with his youthful sweetheart would be forged by his arrival at Hong Kong. Unfortunately, the Suez Canal was not fully operational and the transcontinental railroad joining the Pacific and Atlantic shores had not been completed.[1] Mail communication moved at a slow pace, although the Pacific Steamship Company in 1867 commenced regular service from its terminal in San Francisco to Tokyo, Osaka, Nagasaki, and then to Shanghai. This regular circuit was executed on a twice-monthly schedule, which concluded at Hong Kong. But the cumbersome and uncertain network of mail that had produced so much aggravation for Cushing was quickly forgotten when he arrived at Nagasaki in the first week of October to find seven letters that assured him that Kate remained resolute in her affection for him and that she was governed by steadfast loyalty to her commitment. Cushing had won the battle for her abiding love, which had raged since his arrival at Hong Kong.

At once Cushing wrote to his beloved that it was almost impossible to describe "the perfect passion of love that is awakened in my heart by the flood of tender, pure and womanly words that you have sent to comfort and reassure me." Yet he could not resist reminding Kate of her confession that she had taken advantage of his isolated and lonely situation. Consequently, she did "tease me to make me jealous in times past — and that you did not like to write to me." On the other hand, he acknowledged that she must have been puzzled on how to respond to such a torrent of impassioned expressions of unquenchable affection. He speculated that in a state of distraught confusion, he had sought refuge in light and sometimes frivolous commentary. Cushing reassured Kate that "I do not feel cross or sorry for it now, for as you say it is all in the past, and can not be again."[2]

Still, he sought to convey the depth of his anguish as he had contemplated that there was reason to believe that Kate had abandoned her affection for a distant fiancé, who might well never return to her embrace:

> I was miserable — very unhappy — but if it is my forgiveness you want, you know now — how eagerly and fully I can assure you of it. I did not dare dream that there was such tenderness and passion in your nature; or that if so, I could ever call it forth, and then I read page after page of the most beautiful thoughts — words and sentences that actually seem to have to turn into kisses and caresses, so full they are with the very essence of truest love — when I see this, my heart seems full enough to burst — and I thank God, who rules all things — that I am happier than ever before in life. Such sweet, comforting, fascinating letters! They seem too good to be true — and I am afraid to let them leave my sight.[3]

On further reflection, Cushing succumbed to a remorseful mood, and sought to comfort a lonely and impatient young woman:

> You say that you realize how dependant [sic] you are upon gentlemen's society. How selfish it was in me not to fulfill my obligation to make you happy until many long months are past. My darling I did not mean to be ungenerous — but I love you so dearly! And you wrote so coldly that I couldn't help being jealous. It is no longer. I beg your pardon — and I also beg that you will in all things follow the inclinations of your noble heart. See whom you please — go with whom you please — and be just as happy for every atom of attention others can give you while I am gone. I will offer a million fold when I return — for every drop of happiness they give you I will bring Oceans — and if you have sad and lonely moments in this long waiting for your love — think that he will devote all his life to repay you.[4]

Cushing acknowledged that he had given in to unjustified spasms of jealousy, but he understood Kate's passionate nature. In a postscript to his rambling reaction to Kate's letters, in which she had proclaimed her loyalty to her true love and at the same time defended her conduct, he revealed that she had succeeded in reassuring her distraught fiancé, but she had also edged him into a defensive position. Kate had advised him to read a chapter from one of the epistles of St. Paul in the New Testament. Cushing described her as his Christian sweetheart, and he rejoiced to discover that devotion to the Christian message was implanted not only in her heart but also in her mind. "I love you my precious one," he confessed solemnly, "for your loving thoughts of my eternal welfare." However, he concluded his letter on a jocular note, quite possibly seeking to retake some lost ground. He proclaimed that "if I shouldn't come home until 1870 and you dare have that threatened flirtation with the nicest man about town I'll get command of the *Michigan* on Lake Erie and bombard Fredonia!" He asserted also that he "would marry one of Ross Browne's daughters and live in China forever."[5] Probably Kate had not heard of the USS *Michigan*, a vintage paddle steamer, launched in 1843, with which the only hope of firing a cannonball that could touch Fredonia would be if she were capable of navigating Canadaway Creek, a small inlet that provided sufficient water for small boats and barges to float cargoes for local consumption. As for the marriageable maidens of China, particularly Ross Browne's daughters, one can only speculate that they were either exceedingly homely or ravishingly attractive. One can ponder whether Kate smiled on reading her naval hero's attempt at lighthearted humor or dismissed it with an exasperated frown.

Cushing warned his beloved that he did not wish to be teased. "That will do," he admonished, "very well for lovers whose fickleness requires occasional piques — and who might weary without the spice of a quarrel once in a while." He then warned that "some men, I know — many — cease to value what they had to strive to gain, and when they have accomplished their purpose." He continued his stern commentary by adding a note that "while there is anything ahead to be pursued they are eager and excited — earnest to win — but when all is attained then look for fresh excitement — forget vows and oaths and look around for some new adventure." Such was not the course of true love, Cushing declared, but one that was dictated by unbridled vanity and pride, attributes of a flawed character. As a result, such men were consumed by constant pangs of jealousy that encouraged their ardent pursuit of the next target. Men of that species, Cushing counseled, "are not worth the having."[6]

Cushing concluded his commentary on Kate's resolute defense of her conduct, as well as her firm but tender proclamations of unswerving affection, by reflecting in a prayerful mood, "It must be that God has been merciful to me in this, and has permitted my love to draw you to me — that I might be saved from my follies and temptations — and elevated into a purer, nobler and better life." "Such love as mine is a religion," he intoned, for "there seems to be nothing that I would not attempt that is brave and true and unselfish now that I have you and am sure of your heart."[7] Having reached this pious note, Cushing finished on a sacramental theme: "I wish I might realize all your hopes of me." "I will," he promised, "pray that I may be truly a Christian." He then affirmed his pledge with a vow that "I know that, with my great love for you, I can never be truly contented until I can kneel with you at the altar — thinking and believing with your thoughts and beliefs, and confident of a union with you hereafter as well as now."[8]

Having concentrated thus far on expressing his great joy in reading time and again Kate's correspondence, in which she repeated in many affectionate sentences her abiding devotion and love for her long-absent lover, Cushing turned to practical matters. He once again brought up the subject of the rare and expensive fur coat of Russian sable that he had bought in Beijing, he reminding her that it had been made for a brother of the late emperor — a palace intrigue had deposed this brother, and, consequently, much of his possessions were sold. The coat had not been worn. Cushing intended to send it to Kate on a naval ship returning to the United States. As part of the cargo of a warship, custom duties would undoubtedly be less than if it were sent by a merchant ship. He suggested that it could be altered to make a cloak, cape and muff. Such a transformation could be suitably accomplished in New York or

Boston. In the latter city, he suggested that the firm of Burt and Bush could probably undertake the project for approximately one hundred dollars. He asked Kate not to be upset by receiving such a handsome present before marriage, for such a rare sable was not usually acquired at a bargain price. As was the case with other presents that Cushing had acquired in China, especially the dinner set that he had commissioned at Hong Kong, the coat had been purchased at an opportune time. He further argued that when the sable had been altered into a style appropriate for a young woman, it would be worth at least $1,500 or possibly even $2,000.[9]

Cushing went on to observe that, "I don't know whether I shall be able to get down in India and procure your cashmere shawl or not." He preferred not to send for such articles, because there was a good chance that he might be cheated. If Kate did not feel comfortable wearing such expensive gifts, he could readily sell them. He made, moreover, a shrewd move to gain support from Kate's parents: "I did intend to keep that leopard skin robe. But since your father admires it so much you may have the pleasure of presenting it to him as a gift from yourself—only he must lend it to us when we want to go sleighing."[10]

He was careful to send an affectionate greeting to Kate's mother, in which he stated that he was quite willing to purchase any exotic object that she might crave. He undoubtedly would find an opportunity to send it on a returning naval ship and thereby escape any tariff. He likewise remembered that Kate had admired the diamonds worn by her friend Mrs. Carrie Jones. The sale of the Russian sable furs would easily provide enough cash to buy a collection of diamonds far more pretentious than those of her friend. As for Mrs. Hamilton's (a doyenne of Fredonia) sharp rebuke on his extravagance in writing on heavy paper, "it hit me like a hundred pound shot." He found that "very thin paper is hard to write upon—and I write so impetuously that my pen point would go through it at every stroke."[11]

Undaunted by the envious comments of Kate's married friends, who were displaying pangs of jealousy over the good fortune of a young maiden who had not yet ascended to the noble elevation of marital status, Cushing charged ahead, possibly recalling Farragut's famous reaction to annoying interference ("damn the torpedoes; full speed ahead"). Cushing announced that he had sought an album of photographs at Beijing and another at Yokohama; these pictures would provide visual reinforcement for his narrative. Finally, he reminded Kate that he intended to have an oil portrait made from the ambrotype photograph that she had given him, whenever he returned to Hong Kong.[12]

When Admiral Rowan arrived at Nagasaki to assign and prepare the ships of his fleet for their winter chores, he organized a panel of officers to inspect the *Maumee*. Their report brought an abrupt end to Cushing's expectation of an extended stay in Asian waters. The surveying officers stated that the *Maumee* was "rotten above the water line — and unfit to further cruising service." As Cushing explained to Kate, "It seems that many parts were built during the hurry of war of green timber — and the 'dry rot' has found these out and disabled us." He then reported, "So my cruise is virtually broken up — and, though I will probably take her to Yokohama; and may remain there for some months."[13] Quite naturally, he felt the tug of conflicting emotions. He lamented the shock of losing his beloved ship, on which he had sailed across many waters and had experienced many adventures; on the other hand, there was a good chance that he might embrace his dispirited sweetheart sooner than either of them had anticipated.

Cushing was well aware of Kate's bouts of melancholy. A high-spirited young lady might succumb to moments of depression whenever she recognized that her hasty engagement to Cushing had deprived her of the joyful frivolity of her youth. She had contracted an alliance with a celebrated American naval hero, and consequently she had the promise of a radiant future as a navy wife who would move in social circles more exhilarating than those provided by a small village nestled in a rural community. Yet at the moment she faced the sterile prospect of a tedious stretch of seemingly endless waiting for an always-elusive reunion with the man who was the key to this dazzling prospect. Cushing recognized the cause and legitimacy of her depression. "I don't like what you wrote about your health," he confessed, for "you are languid and thin — do not sleep well." He sought to comfort Kate with a cry of desperate concern. "My precious one," he wrote, "if anything were to happen to you I should die or go crazy." He pled, "Will you not be very careful for my sake?"[14]

Reflecting on the shocking and unexpected turn of events, Cushing speculated on his immediate fate:

> My vessel looks as sound as ever, but the appearance is deceitful. And the strong tough-looking beams, knees and timbers are eaten with decay. I do not know what the official action will be — but I do know that if she is not soon sold, otherwise disposed of — and if they expect to station her here or at some one's port, where she can remain at anchor until her cruise is up, I will get detached and go home. If she is condemned, or sold or put out of commission — any officer can be ordered to other ships — but there is no place in the squadron where there is a vacancy for a commanding officer, and I must return to the United States.[15]

Again, his sorrow over the desperate condition of the *Maumee* was tempered by the realization of the great peril in which his ship's plight had put him. He related to Kate his fearful musings:

> When I saw my ship's inside timbers and planking laid bare yesterday, I was amazed — yes — and very thankful to the good Providence that kept us through so many days and nights of storms and darkness — floating securely upon the

water — with but the shell of a ship under us, which might have crumbled at any moment, and sent us unprepared into eternity. But my first sensation in realizing our past danger was in thinking of the terrible possibility of losing you — and it was with a shudder that I told myself that "I might never again have met her." Caught in the open sea in just one of the fearful storms that prevail here, and we should have certainly gone to pieces — and yet I was confident of the strength and fine qualities of my beautiful command; and rather wished for a "typhoon" to show my Seamanship. How little we know of our nearness to hidden danger. It is often like the lightning flash coming from a clear sky.[16]

For his immediate future, Cushing did have several options beyond those that might be offered by the naval bureaucracy. If Grant became president, Captain Ammen, who was the chief officer of the flagship of the Asian Fleet, was likely to be appointed as head of the Bureau of Detail at the Navy Department. "That Bureau issues all orders and as Capt. Ammen is a great friend of mine I can get ordered home, I think," Cushing predicted.[17] Such an ambitious scheme to obtain preferment was a natural impulse for Cushing, who fervently championed the political fortunes of General Grant. Cushing reassured Kate, "Of course I, as an American democrat, laugh at all, and do as I see fit," as he related the British social conventions that he encountered in the foreign enclaves in China and Japan. However, he was careful to caution that "I don't intend you to understand that I call myself a party democrat — a 'Seymour Man.'" He stated emphatically, "We all hurrah for General Grant out here and laugh at the foolish party who mix with rebels and then commit suicide by nominating such a fellow [as Seymour]." He declared, "If Seymour is elected as my Commander in Chief, I'll resign and dig coal before I'll submit to such a disgrace."[18]

There was another alternative that was truly audacious. The Japanese were anxious to develop a modern naval fleet. To jump-start such an ambitious undertaking, the newly reconstituted imperial government at Tokyo was recruiting American and European officers to supervise the construction of yards and ships. They also sought expert consultants to assist in the launching of a naval academy and to supervise the compilation of a code of discipline for the responsible maintenance of their nascent fleet. The reward would be breathtaking. "If I wished it I could easily get one of the high positions now being given out in the Japanese naval service," Cushing claimed, announcing that "several naval Officers and Europeans have secured them." However, he would have to surrender his career and contract to remain in Japan for five years. Cushing predicted that he could easily procure the rank of admiral, and even if his services were not required for the full term of five years, he would still be compensated at the rate of fifteen thousand dollars a year. Cushing was, he admitted, sorely tempted, but his love for Kate and his deep attachment to his own country's navy prevented him from seriously considering this battery of richly funded opportunities. Indeed, a fellow officer, Walter Grinnell from

New York, had resigned his commission to accept a position as inspector general at fifteen thousand dollars a year. "He tried to argue the matter with me, but he doesn't know that I am in love," Cushing told Kate. Prudently, he added, "Besides I should not like to throw up so fine a position as mine in so big a Service as ours, and trust these heathens for recompense."[19]

Before the arrival of the commander of the Asian fleet had dramatically altered the expected trajectory of the duration and duties of his assignment to the Asiatic Squadron, Cushing had passed the time pleasantly with daily exploratory ventures on shore. In the morning, after a leisurely breakfast, he would work in his cabin, where he reviewed correspondence and wrote official reports. In the afternoon he ordered his "gig" to transport him to the Japanese side of the port, where he could explore the shops and examine the various articles for sale, including those offered as "curios" usually translated today as "souvenirs." He always carried his revolver, which he displayed prominently whenever he encountered a band of gentry. These gentlemen invariably belonged to a particular clan, and advertised their allegiance by carrying two swords, one long and the other short. Even young boys of six or eight years were seen frequently with these weapons. As a rule, these bands presented no challenge, even when some with stern visage glowered and made disapproving gestures. The principal reason for a foreigner to take precautions was that the members of such bands sometimes consumed ample potions of saki (rice wine), particularly during festive occasions. Then their customary discretion gave way to primitive passion. Ordinary men and women invariably reacted cordially to Americans, and Cushing found their children to be friendly, even to the point of accepting some teasing.[20]

At first Cushing had difficulty in assessing the Japanese. Not only did they have differing social structures, but their views of behavior and morality were not comparable to those he knew. Although the Chinese did exercise limitations on the public display of their bodies by wearing various gowns and tunics, the Japanese were oblivious to their nakedness in many public places. "For instance," Cushing had observed after his first arrival in Japan, "there are the public bath rooms — perfectly open to the street, in which one cannot help seeing a naked crowd consisting of men, women and children — of all ages and sizes — bathing in company, and utterly careless of all observers."[21]

He pointed out further that the Japanese bought and sold their women in the same nonchalant way in which they selected their horses. Strangely, he discovered that women did not object to this seemingly callous treatment. Indeed, they were flattered when they commanded a good price, and they received approbation from their friends and family, and claimed that their position in society had been elevated. A similar convention applied to children, who were sold readily, particularly girls. Nevertheless, Japanese parents exhibited great affection for their children, as testified by the practice of carrying them tightly bundled on their backs. Not only did adults follow this habit, but they also frequently had their older children engage in it.[22]

One Japanese practice that Cushing did not appreciate was the custom of encouraging young women to blacken their teeth. The result was that in their later years, they often lost their teeth. Meanwhile, they presented a visage that exposed a black mouth incongruously marring a face that otherwise was quite attractive.[23]

While at Yokohama, Cushing took excursions into the countryside, which was a risky enterprise, because when the Japanese had recognized that they lacked sufficient strength to repulse their unwanted visitors, they had restricted their presence to specific enclaves or treaty ports. In these ports foreign merchants could anchor their ships and construct warehouses and residences on nearby shores, but they were not permitted to venture beyond a perimeter of 25 miles. By the time Cushing arrived in 1867, Japanese authorities were gradually relaxing their stringent regulations. However, among the governing clique and regional clans, hostility toward foreign intruders remained unabated.[24]

Cushing joined a number of fellow explorers, all of whom were "armed to the teeth," to ride for some fifteen miles on the Tokaido toward "Dai-Bouts" (Daibutsu), which is the site of the celebrated statue of Buddha at Kamakura. Cushing explained that the Tokaido "is attractive from being through nearly its whole length one continuous country lane — although a broad-level and well-kept one — raised here and there by some picturesque thatched cottages, so rural in appearance amidst the shade, that they do not indicate the populous towns of which they form the border." Continuing his lyrical account, Cushing wrote, "The romantic dells are never disturbed by rattling carriages, or teams of fast horses." "No buses thunder along urged by excited jehus, to cut the road into ugly and defacing ruts," for "only foot passengers and horses shod alike in straw — and coolies bearing the native 'norimon' or chair — are to be met."[25]

Cushing acknowledged, "The road is a favorite one with the Daimios or Japanese nobles — and we met quite a number of these — some of whom passed us in a haughty or indifferent manner — while others went by with threatening face and hand on sword." However, Cushing and his companions were well prepared to respond with formidable force. "Our party," he explained, "was too strong to attack — and to that fact, and a wholesome fear that they have acquired of the terrible Yankee revolver — we owe our safety."[26]

Cushing and his entourage demonstrated a clever strategy to ensure their safety by breaking their journey into two segments and finding overnight accommodations within a large Buddhist temple. Clearly, they reasoned that any scornful and arrogant nobleman would be reluctant to violate the sanctity of a temple and its inhabitants. As Cushing wrote, "The first night we took up our quarters at a large temple in the town of Mayonashi — where the priests made us welcome — and where, for one, I slept soundly — until awakened by the Buddhist chant in the morning — and after breakfasting we proceeded slowly on to 'Dai-Bouts' — In no hurry — because every foot of landscape was too beautiful to lose."²⁷

At ten o'clock the hardy explorers arrived at Kamakura, where they could survey a colossal statue of a jolly Buddha. "It is probably the largest and oldest in Japan — and is very imposing," Cushing noted. He described the setting of this gigantic Buddha: "It is built on a hillside — and the broad front with its pillars, curves and odd ornament, is approached by an ascent of 200 stone steps — some 40 feet broad." He then recounted the legend of the reason for its construction. "The temple," he had learned, "was built twelve hundred years ago by the prime minister of the Empire — who dreamed while resting there on a journey that a sickle was buried at Mount O'Kura." Cushing informed Kate that "the Japanese name for sickle is Kama," and that the omnipotent councilor of the Japanese emperor subsequently "built a temple; and there to this day lies the sacred sickle." Hence the name is Kamakura — "the Mount of the sickle." Cushing explained further, "It is now dedicated to a God corresponding to the Bacchus of heathen mythology."²⁸

Cushing provided a description of this ancient portrait of a Buddha considerably different from the customary serene composition. He stated, "The idol is a colossal one built of wood — about sixty feet high, and entirely gilt." As he recalled, "It is a jolly looking old god, with head wreathed in grapes and grape leaves."²⁹ However, Cushing asserted, "But the great curiosity — and that which had prompted the journey was the great bronze statue of 'Dai-Bouts' — the most wonderful bronze in the world."³⁰ Cushing discussed this statue and its setting at some length:

> The figure which represents the God of that name — is that of a man — seated and in an attitude of meditation — with a solemn, pensive look in every line of the great face is truly impressive. It is situated in a pretty grove — and approached through an avenue lined with camellias, oaks &— that strive in vain to hide it. The statue is fifty feet high — 98 feet in circumference — the face is 8 feet long and 18 in breadth. The eyes are four feet long and the ears are seven feet. The length from knee to knee is 36 feet and each thumb is four feet in circumference. Isn't that a delicate little piece of bronze? Inside of it is a temple — and many other statues and images — five men can sit comfortably on one thumb. It is much more curious than the Egyptian Sphinx. All in all the expedition "paid" — even if we did make it at some risk of coming back a head the shorter.³¹

When Cushing returned to Yokohama, he continued to explore the many avenues of Japanese daily life. One of the more spectacular was a "matsuri," a public festival that fills the Japanese calendar with ample opportunity to indulge in colorful ceremonies commemorating a plethora of subjects ranging from joyful family events to observances of grave religious rites. Cushing had the pleasant experience of watching a matsuri that recognized male children who had been born during the year, in which large paper fish attached to bamboo poles were hoisted over any house where a young male child dwelt.[32]

From describing a picturesque and merry celebration centering on young children, Cushing descended to discuss the grim status of the lowest rank of the Japanese population — the coolies. Each category of this level of laboring class had its particular characteristics. "Amongst the most curious are the 'Bettors' or grooms," he observed, and then proceeded to supply a commentary:

> When I ride or drive one of these fellows is sent along to hold the horse and however far I may go or however fast, he keeps up on foot. I drove ten miles last night, on a fast trot — and my Bettor seemed much fresher than the horses when we got in. They wear no clothing except a slight hip cloth and an elaborate lot of tattooing. This is done in red and blue — a suit of such clothing is somewhat expensive, costing about a hundred "boos" or thirty-five dollars — but it must be admitted that it is durable — and will outwear many coats of other material.[33]

Although Cushing revived his probing of the countryside and its inhabitants upon returning to Japan, he occasionally interrupted his shore excursions to enjoy the tranquility of his cabin in the afternoon. Then he could reflect on the contents of Kate's letters without being constantly diverted by the chatter of his fellow officers, most of whom were only too pleased to escape the monotony of routine activity on an idle ship for receptions organized by some twenty youthful but married women of the foreign colony at Nagasaki. The usual entertainment at these social functions was indulging in a series of flirtatious conversations with a mixture of American, British, and French representatives.[34]

However, the levels of wealth and status in these enclaves were considerably more restricted than those accepted in relaxed and informal America society. Cushing advised Kate that the rules governing social standing in the foreign enclaves of Asia followed the criteria practiced by "Hong Kong snobbishness in the closest manner."[35] Despite Cushing's reservations on the stratification of British society in general, Americans gravitated toward the hospitality offered by British clubs and the receptions in their residences. On the whole, Americans were accepted as welcome additions to the British presence.[36]

Cushing sketched the hierarchy of British colonial society: "Their social rank is established as follows — First the Governor, then Army and Navy Officers — next Judges and barristers — after which came the large millionaire merchants — and clergymen — then merchant's clerks." Cushing proceeded to caution Kate, "You observe that the clerks of Wholesale shipping firms are admitted at the foot of society while the heads of large houses who dabble in retail are excluded."[37] Kate was being warned that her social rank (according to prevailing conventions in the foreign communities in Asia) might be jeopardized if her lineage was discovered to be rooted in the family of a small town merchant who sold material suitable for clothing as well as for household use.

In other words, she should be sure to hang on the arm of a husband who was in the upper echelons of a society. Actually, the layers of the society that Cushing described were roughly those that could be observed in most English towns and cities of that period.

Turning to nautical topics, Cushing sketched an account of the operations to be undertaken by the Asiatic Squadron during the coming winter months. He reported that the *Iroquois*, *Oneida*, and *Maumee* were remaining in Japan, but the *Piscataqua*, *Ashuelot*, *Monocracy*, *Unadilla*, and *Aroostook* were being dispatched to the Chinese coast. The *Maumee* was an impressive gunboat in size and armament, and her two companion gunboats, though somewhat lighter, had considerable firepower. These three ships could readily watch over American interests at Yokohama, Osaka, and Hyogo. The *Piscataqua* was a powerful frigate; she was accompanied by two Civil War gunboats, which belonged to a category that had acquired the nickname of "ninety-day wonders," and by two paddle-driven gunboats, both of which had become obsolete by the time they were commissioned, although they could still perform useful service in riverine excursions. Unfortunately, Admiral Rowan had the misfortune to discover that the *Piscataqua*, his flagship, had dry rot as a result of green lumber used in its construction. No wonder he had been prompted to order an inspection of Cushing's ship.

Overall, the disposition of the fleet reflected a careful reconciliation to the number and quality of the ships under Rowan's command and the tasks that they had to accomplish. Obviously the geographic extent of China, particularly along the winding coast (with its numerous rivers that connected it to the interior), claimed more attention than the more compact character of Japan. Moreover, the tea trade with China remained the significant factor in American trade with Asia, as did opium. After the conclusion of the Second Opium War, the Treaty of Tientsin in 1860 permitted opium to be exported with little interference from the central government, and, equally important, water routes to the Chinese interior, particularly the Yangtze, were opened to foreign navigation. In 1861 the cotton fields in the vicinity of Shanghai provided a lively export market to cotton-starved European factories, since the American Civil War had destroyed the lush plantation economy of the southern states through the Union coastal blockade or the actual destruction of plantations and their rail connections. Cotton and tea became the primary Chinese commodities and made Shanghai the sixth largest port in the world. Shanghai had become the great emporium for North American and European merchants in Asia. The dominant position of the American firm Russell & Co., both in Shanghai and on the Yangtze River, was far more important than the still-modest scale of commerce with Japan. Equally important was keeping a careful watch on the slow dissolution of imperial authority at Beijing.[38]

In the immediate aftermath of the Civil War, Americans confronted the taxing issues of Reconstruction and the challenge of mastering the vast landscape between the Mississippi River and the Pacific Ocean. Moreover, the economy of iron, steel and coal had replaced the former economy of timber, grain, cotton and fish. The old mercantile world of importers and exporters who obtained raw materials for direct shipment to the marketplace for popular consumption was replaced by a system of mass production of uniform products that were the result of transforming metal ores into tools and appliances, frequently propelled by steam power, some of which were employed to twist primitive fibers of wool and cotton into yards of cloth ready to be fashioned into apparel or material suitable for household use. In retrospect, it may be argued that in the decade following the end of the Civil War, the American commercial center changed from the port and its harbor to the factory and its rail junction.

As the nineteenth century drew to a close, a militant and aggressive Japan was still in its embryonic stage. Western nations remained secure in their comfortable enclaves, such as Hong Kong and Shanghai. Paradoxically, after the humiliating capture of Beijing, the coast of China was controlled by a *de facto* alliance between the British and the imperial regime at Beijing. In the interior the Manchu government developed a network of alliances with Chinese administrators who mutated gradually into warlords who absolutely controlled their respective territories.

With the major exception of the Boxer Rebellion in the latter years of the nineteenth century, America remained a neutral observer. Absorbed by the lucrative opportunities provided by the growth of manufacturing in their rapidly swelling urban centers, as well as by the challenge of exploiting the potential of the trans-Mississippi frontier, Americans preferred to root their Asian foreign policy in loyal adherence to a traditional spirit of isolation that discouraged any entanglements with ancient lands far removed from the modern civilization of the "new world." It was an age of boisterous confidence fortified by limitless innocence, which readily turned aside the robust arguments of Commodore Perry. After concluding negotiations in 1854 that opened Japan to trade with the United States, Perry had urged the implementation of an expansive policy in the Far East supported by a sizeable and aggressive navy. In this view, the island of Formosa, occupied by American merchants, would serve as the hub of American commerce with Asian powers. Perry's exhortations received a chilly reception and disappeared from view in the turbulence of the Civil War.[39]

The condition of the post–Civil War Navy reflected the insular mentality of politicians and their constituents. The *Maumee*'s plight was to be shared by many of the ships of the Asiatic Squadron. Constructed hastily, they had been labeled "90-day wonders" in the period of their construction. Little attention was paid to the timber employed; contractors had simply used the quickest sources of supply. The result was the liberal use of green lumber, which was likely to become afflicted with dry rot. These ships were not replaced with new vessels made of iron. The United Sates Navy soon became impoverished in both numbers and quality — a relic of the past. Not until 1883 did the political circles in Washington recognize that their antique navy was too feeble to protect American diplomatic policy and commercial interests in the Caribbean and South America, as well as those in Asia. By the time of Theodore Roosevelt and the celebrated White Fleet, the United States had become a leading naval power. America could defend its economic interests and political objectives beyond Atlantic and Pacific shores as its citizens recognized (albeit in hesitant steps) that an age of steam communication had made their cherished belief in perpetual insularity an illusion; henceforth, their security and prosperity would be integrated with that of the world community. Their age of innocence was over.[40]

Cushing left Nagasaki to sail through the Inland Sea to reach his assigned stations at Hyogo and Osaka. Apparently, this excursion provided an opportunity to participate in the extensive surveying of the Japanese coastline that was being conducted to ensure the safe navigation of coastal channels. At the end of October, he sat in his cabin on a dark and rainy day, reading once again Kate's letters that he had collected in Yokohama. As he rehearsed his litany of affection, Cushing informed Kate, "You tell me to burn those unloving letters to Hong Kong that greeted me last May." "Do [you] think that," he queried, "I could destroy one word that you have written?" On the contrary, he argued, "If so, you know not the worship of my entire affection." Cushing proceeded to declare, "The paper that your hand has touched is sacred to me." Flamboyantly, he likewise proclaimed that "I would burn off my right hand in flame, before I would deface one word that you have written," wondering whether Kate had ever pondered on the strange turn of events that had transformed the "egotistical Captain Cushing" into her sweetheart and ardent lover.[41]

His reverie was interrupted suddenly by a summons to the admiral's ship, where he was ordered to prepare for immediate departure, which took place after the steamer from San Francisco had delivered mail. Joyfully, Cushing told Kate that he had received several letters from her. Thereupon, the fleet executed the admiral's commands and departed to sea. Cushing was ordered to proceed to Hyogo. Unfortunately, at 1:00 in the morning the *Maumee* shuddered to a stop. She was stuck on an uncharted sandbank. Cushing observed that it was fortunate that his ship had struck a sandbank rather than crashing against one of the rocky barriers, which were more prevalent. Indeed, he claimed only too frequently they provided "items for the papers as 'Wreck of the *Maumee*— Total Loss.'" He added, "That is the way that most of the surveying is done out here. A ship gets her bottom knocked out every few weeks and science benefits by it. I am not anxious to be a professor in those kinds of demonstrations. Surveying is very pleasant amusement in such beautiful waters as these, but I decidedly prefer the ordinary instruments for sounding instead of my ship's keel."[42]

Cushing described the lyrical beauty of the scene that he viewed from the deck of his ship. He could gaze upon verdant hills covered with cultivated terraces with "picturesque villages nestled at their feet like timid children at the side of a mother and the emerald-green water is alive with high storied junks of the natives." His attention, however, focused on an imposing spectacle: "On our left two miles away the shore is bordered by the stern looking walls and towers of a 'Daimyos's' [sic] fortress — one of the great Princes — who has certainly shown excellent taste in both selecting its position and designing its construction." He continued his descriptive narrative, adding, "The high walls extend, I think at least a mile along the sea front — and twenty majestic towers or pagodas crown its angles. Below a grim masonry fort looks sullenly at us from the muzzles of fifty cannon, as if the jeopardy of our position were too great a temptation for it to withstand. I wish that they would 'open' for a few minutes — just for a little excitement: I think that just a wee bit o' fighting would do me good."[43] Clearly, Cushing found routine parading on patrol a tiresome occupation. On a pacific note, he suggested, "If I could afford to leave my ship at this critical time, I would call on my friend the Daimyo prince and take a little 'Saki' with him." Cushing ended his account of the panorama before him with a claim that "the scenery all through this Sea for two hundred and fifty miles is said to be much finer than that of the Rhine or the Hudson.... It is certainly more moving. You would be enchanted with it I am sure. How I wish you were here."[44] Cushing then announced that he had reached his 26th birthday. He found it difficult to realize that five years had elapsed since the celebrated episode in which he sank the *Albemarle*. At that time he had not met Kate. Little could he envisage that she would become far more significant in his memory than his climactic destruction of the Confederate ironclad and the subsequent accolades heaped upon him. For Cushing, the war was over; the dawn of new life greeted him.

Unfortunately, the dawn had not been placid. Cushing was the recipient of a stern rebuke from his beloved, who had been sufficiently upset to read his commentary on naked Japanese women to her mother. He pointed out to Kate that Japanese dressing habits were part of a national convention in the same customary sense as a style of architecture or political conduct. European and American ladies became accustomed to such sights, even to the extent of commenting on the physical attributes of various Japanese that they encountered on the streets. Officers sometimes reminded their ladies of the "Japanese pants" that were a prevalent form of dress in summer: a small cloth band wrapped around the loin.[47]

Cushing attempted to comfort a weary Kate, who had taken on the burdens of the household due to her mother being indisposed. "I can feel what you feel in the fear of losing one so dear," he commiserated. "No one can replace a Mother; and it is terrible to think that those whom we love so much are on life's descending road and that in a few years we shall miss them." He revealed that he suffered from remorseful sorrow at the thought that some of his behavior in the past had caused his mother heartache. He hoped that Kate's mother would recuperate and that, meanwhile, Kate would be restored to her customary cheerful outlook as she resumed pleasurable activities.[46]

Kate, however, had more woe pressing on her slender shoulders. Her piano teacher, Miss Starr, was unhappy with her pupil's keyboard skills. In mock exasperation, Cushing queried, "Aren't you a foolish, nervous girl to write so earnestly about your music?" "Is it necessary," he continued, "to our happiness? Is that what you deliberately ask me?" He provided her with a prompt response: "Music is a pastime — love is a religion." Cushing further told her that "I am fond of music; but I am a million times more devoted to one glance of sweet blue eyes." He promised, "We will enjoy music made by others; and take our fill of concerts and operas whenever we like — and you need never fear that I shall give one regret to the thought that you do not play."[47]

Apparently, Kate had decided that the solution to her dilemma with Miss Starr was to divert her querulous instructor's attention with a suitor. She sought assistance from her own ardent admirer. Cushing's reaction to her request is best presented in his own masterful language:

> And so I am to find a naval man of 40 — a Naval Officer to make love to Miss Starr. My dear pet I have yet to meet one of that age who has not long been married; or who is not so conceited as to feel confident of securing some young and pretty girl to share his fate. You ladies forget, in New York, that in Massachusetts and other Eastern States there are about four women to every man; among whom are wealthy, pretty, and anxious to get married — and that when a Navy Officer has enjoyed his younger days in Clubs, cruising and flirtations, he may still find chances there for advantageous and charming reformation. For your friend, Miss Starr, to whom I have just written, I profess the most profound respect, but if I can judge the Navy by myself, I should be obliged to tell you, confidentially, that she hasn't a chance, even with such a miserable old bachelor as you described. Naval Officers have a decided weakness for pretty girls; whom they convert into pretty wives; and of whom they are very proud and fond, and, consequently, I fear that Miss Starr will be forced still to enjoy the looking-glass pleasure of self admiration.[48]

Cushing was flattered that one of Kate's friends asked for his autograph. He argued that the only signature he thought worthy was one that was attached to a thousand-dollar check, which was payable promptly at a bank. Nevertheless, he promised to award Miss Brown with a *carte de visit* endorsed by his signature. On the other hand, Cushing scoffed at Kate's trust in a machine called a "planchette." This device consisted of a triangle upon which was suspended a pencil-shaped pointer; when this pointer was touched gently, it sent coded messages to the mind. Kate claimed that she had received a signal that caused her to recall china. Accordingly, she wrote to Cushing on the subject of the china he had purchased in Canton; it would seem that Kate had reservations about the design. In turn, Cushing labeled Kate's mysterious device a "queer machine," "but so long as it answers so truly as to the questions that you tell me, I can't say a word against it." He added, however, "Of course it is a scientific humbug, but when it answered 'China' to your inquiry it did hit the nail right on the head. Give it my thanks." Evidently, Kate's major concern on the issue of china was whether it was possible to order a set of dishes for her mother. Cushing replied that he would be only too pleased to acquire a set of china for Kate's mother if he had an opportunity to visit Canton again. He warned that the operation was a slow process, because the Chinese produced their china by hand. Consequently, Cushing advised, "It will take four months, at least to bake and paint a dinner set." Cushing completed his dissertation on the making of china by emphasizing that he would attempt to secure the tinting that Kate's mother preferred, but he repeated that "my present set can't be changed" and even if "it is not just what you wish," she would discover that it was a most impressive composition.[49]

Resuming his travelogue, Cushing described the city of Osaka, which had been recently opened to foreign trade. It was a community of some million inhabitants, many of whom lived on boats anchored on the river, which split into many streams and inlets as it flowed into the sea. It reminded Cushing of the romantic descriptions of the legendary Venetian scene. Like Venice, it had a communication system linked by countless bridges and a ceaseless procession of boats that glided along the web of interconnecting waterways. Cushing chose to remain on dry land and crisscross the picturesque landscape on horseback over one bridge after another. For two days he wandered like a legendary stranger in paradise. Osaka was celebrated for its handsome women. Alas, Cushing missed this charming spectacle. He remarked disconsolately that "its pretty girls must have all been out calling, as I failed to notice one." However, he did purchase several bronze pieces, for Osaka had a considerable reputation for skilled work with that metal. He also "visited and wondered at that stupendous work of science and art — the Tycoon's [Shogun's] castle."[50]

On his return to his ship, once again Cushing had to cross the treacherous reef, where a mistake calculating a safe gap would undoubtedly capsize or smash most boats. As Cushing navigated his gig toward the reef, which was obscured by towering breakers propelled by gale-force winds, several of his passengers pleaded with him to abandon his attempt, but Cushing was resolved to try: "Silence gentlemen! You are in my boat, and must take your chances — I am going through! My judgment proved correct and we got safely off — but they said that they would have given thousands to be out of the gig during that five minutes."[51]

Although Cushing was fortunate, he witnessed the smashing of several Chinese junks the next day: "At least fifty men perished before our eyes, half a mile away on this bright afternoon."[52] Cushing's skill and bravado commands praise, but a single mistake would have condemned him to a grave in a distant and strange land far from the sorrowful face of his beloved Kate. It would seem that he had forgotten that he had pledged his first allegiance to her happiness with him. There was no excuse for irresponsible heroics.

By December 1, Cushing returned to Yokohama, where he passed his time enjoying the ceaseless round of social engagements, during which he met the American minister, visited the residence of the head of the Pacific Steamship Company, and was invited to a reception given by the legendary Sir Harry Parkes, now the British minister to Japan. Besides traversing the sparkling circuit of the diplomatic and commercial society of the foreign colony at the site of the new Japanese government, Cushing took advantage of the opportunity to explore the pleasing landscape of lush valleys and the spectacular vistas offered by rolling hills and towering mountain peaks. Clad in brilliant autumn foliage, the hills and dales of Japan presented a stunning tapestry. Indeed, Cushing was sufficiently impressed to exclaim, "The foliage is much more brilliant than ours at home during this season." To facilitate his scenic excursions, he purchased a horse, and he actually rode to "Daibout" (Daibutsu), which was some fifty miles in distance from his point of departure.[53]

Cushing ceased his lyrical tribute to the dazzling beauty of the autumnal foliage in Japan to note the stately passage of the emperor from his ancestral retreat near Kyoto to Tokyo, where he intended to install himself in the citadel of the recently deposed shogun. It was slow progress over a distance of some 300 miles at an average rate of 16 miles a day. If Cushing's figures are reasonably accurate, the young emperor's march must have taken slightly more than nineteen days. Cushing indicated that he was at Yokohama during the last week of November, when the emperor, seated in a sedan chair, was carried by husky retainers along the famed Tokaido road, the main artery between the two major centers of authority in Japan, Kyoto and Tokyo. Cushing described carefully to Kate that the processional routes "had been prepared for weeks before; and were all as clear as a parlor floor or a New England kitchen; houses were placed in repair; bridges rebuilt and no one was permitted to travel on the Tokaido until after this Japanese God had passed by — for he is a god to the people who fully believe that his ancestor was heaven-born and that he is celestial."[54]

Cushing described the long, winding cavalcade as both splendid and "shabby." He was taken aback when he observed that the soldiers of the imperial army wore adapted foreign uniforms and carried Springfield, Enfield, and Spencer rifles. However, they still carried their massive two-handed swords. Daimyos (nobles), on the other hand, were mounted on horses, and feudal princes were accompanied by faithful retainers. The feudal nobility were garbed in their traditional ceremonial costumes, as were the officials of the court, who marched on foot on either side of the imperial litter. It was a truly splendid tableau of the magnificence of the traditional ritual and elaborate vestments pertaining to the imperial heritage.[55]

The emperor's litter, which was not the state version, but one that was less pretentious (and probably more comfortable), was located directly behind the ceremonial rig. When it reached the end of the Tokaido at the edge of the bay leading to Yokohama and then to Tokyo, it was greeted by Cushing, who had lined up his officers and crew in their formal uniforms to present an official salute. A mischievous impulse struck Cushing: If he had a launch waiting, he and his merry men could have seized the helpless emperor and shoved him in the launch and sped to their ship. Then swiftly sailing out of Japanese waters, they would be in possession of the ultimate authority of Japan. A stunned Japan, lacking a navy, would have been in a truly humiliating predicament, and the United States would find itself in an untenable situation. There would be, however, one certainty in the ensuing confusion — Commander Cushing would have been abruptly cashiered from the Navy. Cushing, fortunately, had sense enough not to take his juvenile daydreaming seriously.[56]

Cushing concentrated on learning about the collapse of the shogunate at Tokyo and the increasing stability of the revived absolute authority of the Emperor Meiji. He reported to Kate that the resistance of the daimyos in northern Japan to imperial legions had been shattered. Yet opposition to the imperial squadrons had not disappeared because, although the northern feudal potentates claimed that they were the true advocates of the emperor, "they fight because they do not believe that the armies are his; but that they belong to Southern Dunois [sic] who have got possession of him." On the other hand, Cushing informed Kate, "We had news, a few days since that the Southern forces had been successful, and that Aidzu [sic] and his allies had all surrendered."[57]

It is difficult to believe that Kate relished her fiancé's commentary on current Japanese political strife. It was far removed from the heated debate on the condition of the Fredonia Normal School or the strident 1868 presidential election campaign. Determined to add a more cosmopolitan outlook to his rural sweetheart, Cushing proceeded to describe political behavior in Japan. Grassroots politics in Japan were really combative struggles among contentious loyalists who resembled the rambunctious clansmen who populated the Scottish highlands. In Japan, "every Daimyo has, also, an immense castle or fortification, capable of containing an army — surrounded by three lines of moats and walls, some twelve miles square," he explained to his untutored mistress.[58]

Cushing then arrived at the sensational climax of his exposition:

> The Mikado's army, fifty thousand strong, marched north; and approached Aidzu's castle from three directions through three mountain passes and proceeded

to besiege it. No sooner had they encircled it and were ready to commence warlike operations, than the main gates were opened; and out walked in slow and solemn procession, twenty nobles — clad in robes of ceremony and unarmed, except with the short sword, or hari-kari instrument. They approached the hostile army, and asked permission to speak — which, being granted, they said that they alone were responsible for this war, and all the difficulties that had caused it, and that, according to Japanese custom they had come out to atone for their crime by committing hari-kari in the presence of the Mikado's army, and to surrender the Castle.

Upon this, nineteen cut themselves open in the most approved style — and the remaining one said, "I am left to conduct you into the castle. I will then commit hari-kari also." A thousand of the choicest men of the Mikado's force were then sent in to take possession; headed by some of the highest nobles — but no sooner had they entered the castle than the gates were closed, and they were cut in pieces. At the same time a signal was made, and the dams of some mountain streams were cut away, and the whole plain was converted into a lake of water. Upon the Mikado's army attempting to retreat, they found the three mountain passes full of armed men; and could not break through; so they were seized with panic, and broke into squads, attempting to escape across the mountains — but at least twenty-five thousand were cut off; and, as these people take no prisoners — were all killed.[59]

Another version of this event reported that the rebel leader, Aizu, had surrendered, and, therefore, the last formidable supporter of the Shogun had been removed. Cushing's dramatic account can only be interpreted by conjecture. It may be a Romanesque tale from a legendary narrative or possibly a sequel to the major conflict. Cushing had received a report of Aizu's capitulation and, evidently, the accounts of the several sensational events involved in his downfall have at least a ring of truth. Aizu was the last member of the shogun's dynasty to stubbornly resist Meiji's assumption of actual sovereignty. The full and unyielding wrath of the Mikado lashed out at the hapless Aizu, whose territory was confiscated and whose adherents were exterminated or forced to live in closely watched sites. Obviously, Meiji was resolved to obliterate all remnants of independent feudal power. Soon after the destruction of the shogun's family citadel and the dissolution of his followers, the authority of the daimyos was abolished to make way for a system of prefects appointed by the Mikado. These officials were directly responsible to the central government and the districts over which they had jurisdiction had no association with the feudal territories that they had replaced.[60]

Cushing's account of the gruesome battle strategy that caused the destruction of a considerable segment of the Mikado's armed forces was suddenly interrupted by a cannon shot from the senior ship in the American squadron that announced the arrival of the mail steamer. At midnight Cushing dispatched a boat to obtain any messages for him from the U.S. consul. Cushing received six letters — two were from Kate, one from his sister Mary, and three from his mother. Doubtless, Kate was relieved to learn that her swain intended to abandon his lecture on Japanese current events. The receipt of her letters prompted her lovesick admirer to fix his thoughts exclusively on her. Probably the U.S. consul was comforted by the departure of Cushing's emissary at two in the morning.[61]

Cushing was much amused to read Kate's narrative of village trials and tribulations. Evidently the rumpus in the Normal School still commanded lively debate. Her friend Herbert continued to have miscarriages with nuptial protocol, and even the obsequies associated with the sorrowful demise of Charles Higgins occasioned some bemusement. However, Cushing abruptly changed his course of customary chitchat and flowing tributes to his beloved. He did not wish to be admonished by Kate on the subject of money. His reprimand was prompt and starkly harsh. He had read Kate's strident and unequivocal denunciation of all those "weak and 'detested fools' who are weak enough to lend money to their friends, brothers or mothers." Moreover, Kate sought to receive a promise from her fiancé that he would abstain from lending any money even to his most trusted friends. Bitterly, Cushing protested, "What would poor Charles Higgins have done, so far from home, if I had promised you never to lend money?" "He would have died abroad; and never have seen home or friends," Cushing remonstrated. "Then there was my old friend Capt. Joe Fyffe of the Navy, whom I met here: suddenly detached from command, and who could draw no money because his pay accounts had gone in a wrong steamer and missed him." As a result, Cushing revealed, "When the noble old fellow, who has so often stood by me in battle, told me of this, would you have me say that 'I was sorry that I couldn't help him'?"[62]

Apparently Kate's stern request had been inspired by an uncle's recent calamitous experience. Cushing responded with the blunt assertion that her relative's unfortunate experience, for the most part, had not been duplicated in his transactions. "In the Navy," he explained, "we often have occasion to borrow of one another. An Officer may be traveling for months to meet his ship; and cannot draw a cent of pay until he finds her." "Suppose I meet him," Cushing reasoned, "and he says, 'My dear old fellow, lend me a hundred dollars' he should have it — and in any event indorse [sic] anyone's note." Cushing reassured Kate that he was firmly resolved not to jeopardize her financial security and blight her marital happiness through reckless deposition of his Navy income. Thus, he could claim comfortably, "When my friend wrote that he would like to keep the five thousand that I lent him, until my return home, I answered 'No!' I am going to be married when I go home; and I must begin to think for the future." Then Cushing rebuked Kate's strictures in no uncertain language: "I do not intend to say anything unpleasant, my dear little pet; but I am at a loss to comprehend the meaning of the two pages you devote to money lending. Unless you mean to infer that I am reckless in such matters.

I hope that I may always be willing to lend both money and blood if need be, to anyone whom I can truly feel and call 'friend.'"63

As Cushing continued his lecture, he (probably unwittingly) veered toward his first major spat with his beloved sweetheart. "I don't think it at all a compliment to have such a little village tailor as Philo Stevens," he complained, "pointed out to me as a guide in my worldly affairs." Returning to his proclamation to remain steadfast in observing his responsibility for Kate's security and happiness, Cushing commented that "I see in what you write a fear that I will not properly regard my responsibilities to you." He replied, "If my love is not pledge enough for you I can give no other." "Now do not pout and be cross," he admonished, "at what I write, for I perfectly understand myself, and have had a good deal more experience in life than you have." Finally, Cushing did offer this pledge: "I promise you never to borrow money, and that is twice as noble a pledge as the other."64

Cushing was sufficiently upset to end his bitter tirade. He provided a list of the main contentions that he perceived in Kate's letter:

> First then I am a man who lends money. Secondly — a man who does is weak foolish, and worthy of contempt as the tool of others. Thirdly you despise such a man. Fourthly you hold up as models such noble, elevated characters as Philo Stevens; to show how a man may be a rascal and appear like a God. Fifthly you enumerate amongst the excuses to be made on a borrower's application. 'I have no money,' saying that no one is supposed to know how we are situated as regard finances. That would be a falsehood, and I prefer to tell the truth."65

Cushing then produced several further examples of his charity toward friends who were facing pecuniary problems. A naval officer returning to the United States required financial assistance; Cushing supplied the necessary sum, but requested that repayment be sent to his mother, who received it promptly. On a more dramatic note, Cushing had lent five thousand dollars to a friend who had a young wife and child, and whose business had failed. On the very day that the loan became due, Cushing received payment. "I trust that none of the penny-worshiping Fredonianites," Cushing exploded, "have been offended because I have invested five or ten dollars in friendship." He queried, "Did you hear that you ought not to trust yourself to me — that I am a reckless spendthrift &?" Bringing the exposure of his sore feelings to a close, Cushing warned that though he might give an impression of being careless and happy go lucky, he was in reality a man who is careful to "look out for No 1."66

A letter from Mary Barker Cushing to her son in October confirmed his claim of loyalty to friends who were in temporary duress: "Your good friend Capt. Tuffle promptly forwarded me your generous present of one hundred dollars in gold and has since written me a most gratifying letter; very interesting — because so much was said in praise of my Son." Mary Barker then elaborated her report of the laudatory salute to her son by a comrade in arms, explaining that "Capt T. wrote that being ordered home and without any money, you lent him one hundred dollars." Mary Barker acknowledged her son's constant concern for her financial security and revealed that her son-in-law, Gayle, supervised her expenditures, particularly in charging her only 30 dollars a month for board and room. She also revealed that Gayle took care of Cushing's financial interests, especially in the investment of his award money. Following the hallowed tradition of many grateful mothers, Mary Barker Cushing urged her son to take care of his health. "Other Officers get good stations upon shore; Why not you," she counseled. She admonished further, "Do not, my Son, remain abroad long if you are not well, but come home, marry Kitty, and take comfort for awhile; You have had a hard course and have done work enough for twice your age — rest awhile."67

Having thus defended his character and his loyalty to the responsibilities that he owed to his fiancée, Cushing invited Kate to "transfer our thoughts to the mighty matter of Mrs. Tillinghurst and her professorship." He strongly supported the reservations that Mrs. Hamilton and Mrs. Wheelock exhibited on the latest scheme of Mrs. Tillinghurst, who had introduced a program to instruct the youth of Fredonia in the skills of acting. From that venture she had moved to offering a studio where the young ladies of the community could practice dancing in tights in the company of the resident gallants. Cushing without hesitation condemned Mrs. Tillinghurst as a "tainted" woman, whose society should be avoided by any woman wishing to preserve her good name; as he reminded Kate, "A man may do many things with impunity that would ruin any woman." He then launched a ferocious denunciation: "Scandal is so common in Fredonia that it truly shocks me to have you there — you. Who seem pure as Heaven to me — and whom I so idolize." "But there are some Souls" Cushing contemplated thoughtfully, "that might live in Hell and not be tainted; and yours is one of them — but, for my sake, don't associate with such persons as Mrs. T."68

Turning from commenting on the doubtful state of morality in Fredonia, Cushing confessed his sadness on learning of the death of his former secretary, Charles Higgins. He had promised to write to the father of Higgins, "but I did not write to him simply because he was not my personal friend and I never correspond with any others." Nevertheless, Cushing acknowledged his good opinion of Higgins:

> I liked Higgins and pitied him, but I did not think that a letter from me would interest a man amongst his family and dying. In fact, I did not know whether he liked me or not, for he was never demonstrative. I did nothing especial for him. I am always kind to my Officers if they behave themselves. Of course I thought that he would die; and I did doubt his reaching home, but I knew that he must try it; and that it would be a comfort to him and to his parents if he could spend the last of his quiet life at home.

Cushing also asserted that he did not realize that Higgins was engaged to Leilly W. In fact, Cushing had been convinced that the precarious condition of Higgins' health would persuade him to postpone such a momentous step until his recovery was achieved.[69]

Shifting away from such a mournful topic, Cushing focused on the subject of procuring silk dresses in the patterns and colors that Kate's mother desired. He repeated his former assertion that if he returned to China, he would be able to purchase a fine grade of silk dresses in black and white checks, and probably also in shades of yellow and green or even brown. In Japan, however, such colors were not available, but he could acquire a black and white pattern in a very heavy silk cloth. On the other hand, Cushing was quite happy to announce that he had already purchased a white silk crepe dress before he had received a specific request. Again, he warned that since he was returning by a commercial ship, he would undoubtedly be required to pay the customary duty of sixty percent in gold.[70] This figure causes some amazement for modern American tourists, who are subject to a moderate duty for most goods. Sixty percent would be exorbitant to a contemporary consumer, and to demand such a rate could be judged absurd. In the nineteenth century gold coin was rare; consequently, most tourists would husband their supply carefully. In that light Cushing's purchases in Asia have a costly allure, as well as a touch of the exotic.

However, Cushing was not allowing himself to be discouraged by high tariffs and the problems of appropriate packing. He promised to search for a silk lavender dress for Kate, and he revealed that "I tried to find a handsome writing desk, but found that all were of common lacquers, so I went to the agent of the most reliable Yeddo [Tokyo] firm and he said that he would make me the handsomest that he could for forty Mexican dollars." Proudly, Cushing announced, "I gave the order, and it will be done in a month — that's the way I obey my Admiral's orders." He added to his salute a pledge that "if the Jap does not make a handsome one I'll 'raise Ned' with him."[71]

As for his immediate plans for the future, Cushing suggested that although the decks of the *Maumee* were being caulked and tightened, the hull was beyond repair and, consequently, within six months she would probably be sold. "There are so few ships kept afloat now," he further stated, "that all the old Officers are fighting for commands, and I won't fight, so some of them will be ordered out." As a result, Cushing informed Kate cheerfully that "I can get any amount of leave when I get back, and long shore duty after." "Isn't it jolly? Are you glad?" he exclaimed.[72]

For the moment, however, Cushing had to respond to the pressing responsibilities of his position in the Asiatic Squadron. The *Oneida* was sailing for Hiogo, and Cushing would become the ranking senior officer. In this position he would be enforcing the neutrality agreement with the Japanese authorities for the United States government. Various foreign governments had participated in drafting and ratifying this agreement, which affirmed that those foreign governments that accepted the treaty would not interfere in the struggle between the youthful Mikado and the Shogun whose descendants had, for some centuries, exercised sovereign authority. In turn, the Mikado, who had recently defeated the shogun, would guarantee the security of foreign merchants and their representatives. Sir Harry Parkes, head of the British delegation, usually served as the spokesman for the foreign community.[73]

Cushing inherited the responsibility of keeping the *Stonewall Jackson* in American hands until she could be legitimately turned over to the recognized government of Japan. Eventually, the *Stonewall Jackson* joined the nascent Japanese fleet and served in the coastal waters of northern Japan, where she assisted in reinforcing imperial authority. Cushing believed that by staying on course he would shortly be promoted to the rank of commander, which would provide 700 additional dollars to his annual pay. "Not bad at 27," he chirped.[74]

In a buoyant mood, he could not resist delivering a flirtatious lecture to Kate:

> The only thing that I shall stipulate is that you shall not give me any Candle lectures on lending money. But earnestly speaking, pet, I am a different man in my financial affairs from what I was before becoming engaged to you. I don't spend much money now excepting for you — and I am sure that is lending, since I have only your word of honor. I never see anything pretty but I say — "how I'd like to see that on Kate"; or "how prettily Kate would arrange that," and forthwith I get it, of course — Am I to be scolded?[75]

After this, Cushing left Kate in peace until the end of the month, when he sent a Christmas letter in which he described the festivities that he had been invited to attend. To comply properly, he had been compelled to wear his formal attire consisting of a cocked hat and a resplendent coat with gold braid and epaulets. He had his Christmas dinner at the house of Mr. Phelps, the agent for the Pacific Mail Steamship Company, and to reciprocate the generous hospitality of the foreign community, he arranged for the ship's minstrel performers to give a concert at a theater on shore. They had a full house, and Cushing was able to present a contribution of five hundred dollars toward the funding for a hospital to serve the medical needs of Western government officials and merchants and their families. For New Year's Eve he received an invitation to attend a ball at the residence of Sir Harry Parkes.[76]

When he was not absorbed in holiday revelry and naval chores, Cushing explored the never-ending sprawl of Tokyo. The center of Tokyo was dominated by the former shogun's fortress, now occupied by the Mikado, which was "an immense fortification of stone, twelve miles square — some of the stones in the wall are thirty feet square; and there are nine walls; each surrounded by a wide and deep moat." From this nucleus Cushing traversed the numerous roads that led to the remote outskirts of the newly anointed imperial city. He mounted a horse and rode at a gallop for six or eight hours in various directions, but never discovered a definitive boundary to Tokyo. Instead, he passed through a succession of small towns that dissolved into their neighbors, separated only by groves and gardens. The entire vast expanse was at this time called Yeddo.[77]

Cushing used his Christmas letter to Kate to inform her that he was sending her a white crepe silk dress packed in a tin case, by way of a fellow officer who was leaving for the United States. When this naval officer arrived in New York, he would ship the package to Kate. Cushing revealed that the feminine contingent at Yokohama had assured him that the silk dress would be most suitable as a wedding gown.[78]

In his closing words to Kate, Cushing speculated that within three months he would be sent to the United States. The *Maumee* was fast deteriorating and could not continue very much longer on active sea duty. He added ominously that his health was unstable, and the climate was not favorable to his condition. Strangely, in this letter written during the holiday season (particularly since Cushing, in recent letters to Kate, had dwelt on Christian principles), he made no effort to send her any festive greetings. The only mention of the holiday season was his description of a series of dinners and formal balls to which he had been invited. Surely it is an unsettling observation with which to end an account of Cushing's adventures with the Asiatic Squadron of the United States in 1868.[79]

CHAPTER 8

Surveying the Landscape
and the Inhabitants of Japan

As the New Year slowly matured, Cushing acquired a more balanced perspective of the festivities that celebrated the seasonal passage from the fading old year to the youthful glow of its successor. Although he repeated his announcement that he had attended a constant series of receptions and dances, especially the memorable one that was given by Sir Harry Parkes, he was careful to assure Kate that he was, at this time, the senior U.S. naval officer, and therefore had to substitute for the ailing American minister to the Japanese government. Cushing, accordingly, escorted the minister's wife and daughter to Parkes' grand fete.[1]

"I enclose my card; from which you will see that I danced but four times — two of them being mere matters of semi-official etiquette," Cushing explained in defense of his conduct. He declared further that "I thought of you constantly, all through the holy days, <u>so</u> tenderly, and my heart ached to be with you." He confessed, "I felt sad all the evening, thinking how far I was from you — and as the music filled the room, and the bright and graceful forms of the dancers swept past, I thought 'Oh if my darling were but one of the throng how happy I should be.'" Cushing wrote that he could picture Kate "handsome and graceful" in command of "the center of attraction and admiration." He wondered whether as Kate sparkled in the glitter of seasonal frolics, she may have regretted that she was "fettered by an engagement to a lover so far away." Cushing reminded Kate:

> You write very sad letters to me, complaining of your sufferings from the loss of gentlemen's society, and the letters make me very sad also. It pains me that you are not contented and happy, my pet, and that I am in a measure, the cause, for I presume that it is my jealousy that has prevented your acceptance of the attentions of many gentlemen — but how can I help being jealous, when I have so much at stake — such a dear <u>precious</u> sweetheart — in whom my whole life and soul is bound up. It seems like sacrilege to me that one of those coarse, country

louts should presume to kiss you, even at a wedding. I suppose though, that you had been so long without an embrace that theirs were welcome. I presume that Harrison Parker amongst others enjoyed the honor and felicity. If you had only mentioned the number of those favors bestowed by you, I would try to make it all even by taking as many at weddings (or on other occasions) as I pass through San Francisco.[2]

In spite of his threat to rival Kate's acquiescence in occasional flirtations, Cushing put aside such an impulse, vowing, "If I were to drift near a flirtation now I should feel dishonest and despise myself as a weak and unprincipled man." Apparently Kate had demanded to know whether her fiancé had, from time to time, been tempted to disregard his status as an engaged man. Cushing's response was straightforward. "Everywhere that I go into society," he asserted, "I say that I am engaged for I am proud of it, and have not the least desire to pay any more attention to ladies here than the most formal courtesy demands." He concluded his resolve with this simple pledge: "My one earnest hope and desire is to quickly return to you."[3]

Cushing, however, could not disregard the news that his beloved Kate was succumbing to increasingly severe spells of loneliness, which were made all the more bitter by her observation that most of her youthful girlfriends had found their way to the matrimonial altar. Kate, however, had only the memory of a hasty engagement to a man who quickly disappeared from her familiar horizon and now appeared only in ink-and-paper communiqués narrating his passage through strange lands and among curious inhabitants. Small wonder that she reported to Cushing that she had suffered a nightmare in which he appeared as a cold and indifferent suitor who had grown weary of an unpolished country maiden. Cushing reiterated quickly that such dreams and the reflections that they prompted were not reality. "My love, truly given," he claimed, "does not fade like that; it has become a part of me." Then Cushing hit the nail firmly on its head: "And so, everybody is being married at home ... isn't it strange that you are the last 'Miss' of the four young friends I remember — two with different ties and changed name and one in the church-yard — only my darling left." In the next stroke of his pen he promised Kate that she would become far happier than her two married friends after he returned to claim her.[4]

Abruptly changing the subject that was uppermost on his mind, Cushing reacted as perhaps Kate wished to her none-too-innocent query on his feelings about the recent presidential election. "Of course you could answer the question yourself," he exclaimed. He then launched into a diatribe on his convictions. "Never the less I am going to tell you," he declared, "that I rejoice at the result more than at any battle of the rebellion — and that I never uttered a more earnest 'thank God!' than when I heard the news." He added firmly, "It was another and final victory over traitors." He then unequivocally denounced the Democratic candidates:

It is my firm belief that if Seymour had been elected we should have returned to a state of Civil War — and I know that I would have felt so dishonored by having such a Commander in Chief that I would have resigned my Commission. I believe Grant to be a firm, honest, moderate man — who will execute the laws without fear or favor. As to New York State, I claim it no longer for my home. I am from the West — from brave old Wisconsin. A state governed by a city mob of ignorant Irish convicts, blacklegs and traitors shall never be my home. I took an oath that if New York upheld in this election such villainous cutthroats as Wade Hampton and traitor Seymour, that I would never again acknowledge myself a New Yorker. That's what I think of the election! And as for your conversion, if you do not see that all the traitors were in one party and all the patriots in the other — I can say nothing to change your opinions. I am no politician but I love my Country from my very Soul — and I hate those who hate her. There was a time when "democrat" meant democracy — now the name alone is left — and the interpretation is Aristocracy and treason.[5]

Although Kate's inclination to extend some sympathy to Grant's opponents, perhaps to tease Cushing into a sturdy apology for the cause of the Union, might not have been a mere feminine provocation, even at the conclusion of the titanic struggle that had engulfed world attention, the final chapter of which ended on a mournful tribute to the stature of the fallen leader, Lincoln, there was a considerable residue of contrary opinion regarding his administration's policies and their execution. Kate, of course, was aware of her father's record in the Civil War, and even if it lacked the luster of that of her fiancé, it demonstrated a genuine conviction of the righteousness of the Union cause.

After repeated declarations of his abiding love for Kate and promising again to curb his envy of Kate's forays into the rustic pastimes of young men and women during winter days, Cushing declared emphatically that he was resolved to quit Asia, whether the *Maumee* was sold or retained for coastal patrolling. He hinted once more that he would deploy connections, particularly those in Washington, that could relieve him from enduring the full term of his assignment in Asia. Meanwhile, he would again visit Osaka, and then traverse the Inland Sea to Nagasaki. With some confidence, he predicted that he would not visit China again and therefore would not have an opportunity to purchase the silk material that Kate's mother so desired.[6]

Cushing concluded his rambling missive by surmising that his brother Milton by this time had been married to Nellie, who had once entertained aspirations for an alliance with Cushing himself, but after some shuffling had settled on Milton. "I suppose that Milton must have been married by this time — lucky fellow!" Cushing mused, adding a sigh that "I wish it were me instead — not with his sweetheart though — though Nellie is a very nice girl." Cushing admitted, "I laugh every time that I think of Milt as a married man — he used to be such a model old bachelor, and so avoided ladies [*sic*] society." He remarked further that he had been acquainted with Nellie for some time in the past and thoroughly admired and respected her. Cushing then returned to Kate to deliver a final benediction and warning. "I hope," he prayed, "that you are enjoying this winter in every way — with skating, sleighing and society — for I shall not be jealous any more — unless you dance a dozen times in an evening with the same gentleman, and then send me your dance card and — what do you call flirting if that is not?" He admonished, "If I got as many dances with one young lady as Mr. O. did with you — I would flatter myself that I had made an impression; and should expect everyone to call it a flirtation."[7]

Not wishing to end his long and rambling commentary on a sour note, Cushing again reaffirmed his love for Kate and reiterated his pledge of absolute loyalty. He prayed, "May Heaven bless you and keep you my darling Kate and keep in your heart many tender recollections of one who truly loves you. Please love me Kate!"[8]

A week later Cushing composed a letter to Kate in which he repeated his declaration of unceasing love for her, along with revealing that he continued to be distraught by fears that her search for male companionship to ease the loneliness forced upon her by the prolonged absence of her wandering lover might well signal an end to their engagement. At length, though, Cushing realized that his anguished pleas for a sympathetic recognition that they shared the common ground of isolation from the customary romantic prelude to marriage could cause Kate to conclude that he had become overwhelmed by doubt and self-pity. Consequently, he shifted back to the familiar narrative of his experiences among the strange and wondrous sights and sounds of the Far East.[9] "This has been a beautiful, bright day — just the one for a horseback ride," he wrote, "which I have been taking, all over the Country, in company with an old Classmate of mine, Mr. Stewart and Paymaster Tullock: and as it is the first time that I have been on such an excursion from Hiogo, of course I enjoyed it keenly." Cushing provided a lyrical description of his trip:

> We rode at least thirty miles through fields and woods, and dozens of rustic villages — until we came out on the shore of the Inland Sea — lying fair and blue in the Sunlight. There in the little place called La-ka-I — we entered a "Tea house" to refresh "the inner man" with a cup of tea, a little "saki" and a few oranges — and to laugh and chat in the few words of the language which we comprehend, with the pretty "Moosemeds" or young ladies — daughters of the house. The "tea houses" are places of refreshment, something like our "taverns"; and are very plentiful along all the roads, and in all towns and Cities. We sat down on our heels on the matted floor among the Japanese, smoked their comical little pipes, complemented [sic] the girls by affirming they were "Tyson" — or very pretty — and generally endeavored to make our society most agreeable. We were all in high spirits after our invigorating gallop and laughed all the time; and as the Japanese are a people who always laugh when a stranger does you can imagine that we were a merry seeming party. One of the young women was really

pretty — I think the prettiest woman I have ever seen in Japan — and Stewart, whose handsome black beard seemed to be an object of admiration — jokingly asked her father "Will you sell her to me? I want a wife and will give you plenty of money for her." The old fellow immediately assented to the proposal, but asked three hundred "boos" for her; or about one hundred dollars — which is a very high price. We laughed and changed the subject — but isn't this a queer country, where one can go into any Merchant's house and buy his daughter as easily as a curio? When purchased they leave their own homes and become the "Japanese wives" of the buyers — keeping house for them; sewing on the shirt-buttons — and generally fulfilling duties of good wives. At any time the purchaser may sell her, or send her back to her parents, where she is looked upon as a dutiful daughter and an honor to her friends. All the foreign merchants here live that way.[10]

Turning from his review of the position of Japanese women in the households of the shopkeeper class, Cushing launched a discussion of Japanese house construction. "The Japanese in winter are a very different people externally," he observed, "from what they are in Summertime — for they are all warmly and neatly clothed, and their houses are closed and more comfortable looking." The principal reason for this transformation was that "the paper window, which makes up about two-thirds of a Japan house, [is] carefully pasted in, and the big 'Shebaches' or fire boxes, around which they sit are full of bright, cheerful charcoal." Cushing further commented that undoubtedly the Japanese would have little use for glass in the construction of their houses, for they preferred to employ an oiled paper, which was in plentiful supply and inexpensive. "If a pane is torn," he remarked, "it is but a moment's work to paste in another, and in the Summertime when the heat is intense, and those Orientals want ventilations and fresh air, all they need do is to give the dozen babies in each house the intense juvenile enjoyment of dashing their interesting little fists and toes through every window, until all are gone and the habitation is ventilated at an expense of five cents."[11]

His description of the manner in which the Japanese solved their ventilation problems during the summer's heat prompted Cushing to dwell on the bountiful supply of small children and infants he saw in his travels through the Japanese landscape. "I am more and more lost in amazement," he reported, "at the immense, *fabulous* number of small children and babies in this country." Cushing elaborated further, "Men carry babies; every woman and girl carries babies — babies carry babies — every one's back is loaded with animated petite humanity. Children of three years old stagger along under a responsibility for the safety of a hopeful 'one year old' and look as wise as if they were their parents. I call them 'double babies.' Every one of them, old enough to keep a word sings out to us as we ride along 'Ohio!' or 'Good morning' which is the interpretation of the word — and the scream is taken up by everyone from the toothless old women down."[12]

Cushing then repeated an anecdote of what had occurred shortly after his arrival in Japan: Accompanied by a naval colleague, he had entered a curio shop, where he was greeted by a warm cry of "Ohio." Cushing replied, "Wisconsin," adding, "It is my friend here who has the distinguished honor to hail from that State." The memory of this amusing incident encouraged another anecdote involving this common Japanese greeting. An elderly commodore in the Navy who came from the state of Ohio and who had acquired a lackluster reputation in the Civil War, on arriving at his posting, made a courtesy call on the local Japanese governor. On being greeted cordially, the old naval officer exclaimed, "Well, gentlemen, it's astonishing! I certainly did not dream that I was already so well known, away out here! Who would dream that this man had read the history of our War?"[13]

Cushing had to fall back on recollecting humorous incidents in lieu of recounting routine naval duties. The *Maumee* was not fit for protracted services on the high seas, and survey and patrol chores were dull work. Hiogo was not a very exciting setting, for there were few Western women in the region to host pleasant receptions and lively parties. Cushing could only offer his ordinary daily schedule, which he had concocted to avoid the tedium of successive days of boredom. He rose at 7:30 in the morning and, after having consumed a hearty breakfast of soft-boiled eggs, coffee, and oranges, he waited for the sun to evaporate the chill and damp from the customary fog that had accumulated during the night. Then he was rowed to a landing pier that was only a hundred yards from where the ship was anchored. There he mounted his horse to take a ten-mile gallop along the beach. Although he had restricted his equine exercises to the shore, he felt confident that his familiarity with the surrounding terrain had become sufficient to explore beyond the coast without losing his direction.

On his return Cushing had an "eastern" breakfast (or tiffin) at noon, and devoted the early hours of the afternoon to fishing, shooting, or making any official social calls. "Towards evening," he wrote, "I take another gallop of six miles; and then dinner at seven; having every night either someone to dine with me or else, dining out myself." After dinner, Cushing smoked and chatted with friends. The frequent subject of their conversation was recent news of their families and friends. Such was the monotonous rhythm of his existence in the small port of Hiogo.[14]

To relieve the tedium of his daily activities, Cushing continued his explorations into the countryside in the neighborhood of Hiogo and Osaka. He discovered that this part of Japan did not receive much snow. The winter climate was raw and cold, but overall Japan did not experience dramatic changes in seasons. As a result, the Japanese could cultivate their acreage throughout the year. Cushing admired their intensive cultivation. "Every inch of country," he commented, "that is available is beautifully cultivated," with "Every hill and slope being terraced and supplied with water from artificial lakes."[15]

On the other hand, he scorned the business tactics of Japanese merchants. "Nevertheless, these Merchants are the smartest in the World," he admitted, "and a little rascal of ten years' age will swindle a foreigner 'out of his eye teeth' with a keenness and gravity that can only be comprehended after experience." Cushing underscored his judgment by arguing that "lying is considered an absolute virtue by all Japanese — and the man who can lie and deceive in the most plausible manner is thought the most promising citizen." Such was the circumstance in China, "and in both countries it is impossible for a foreigner to judge what a fair price is for anything they may desire to buy."[16] Cushing recounted an incident in which a Japanese silk merchant refused to sell a lavender silk dress for fifty Mexican dollars, instead demanding approximately ninety dollars. Later the same merchant walked three miles to the American consulate, where, after two hours of agitated bargaining, he sold the same dress for forty dollars. Ruefully, Cushing acknowledged that he had acquired a fairly sophisticated appreciation of variations in pricing. He predicted that most of the curios (generally bronze ornaments and lacquered boxes) would cost somewhat less in New York than the cost of purchasing them in China. To illustrate the shenanigans practiced by these merchants, Cushing related the tale of a Chinese merchant who was selling a lacquered box that he claimed was quite old and rare. When Cushing informed him that his customer preferred a modern copy, the indefatigable merchant quickly responded, "Dis piece — velly fine, number *one*, new piece — alla same price!"[17]

As he did frequently, Cushing shifted suddenly from a merry subject to a somber one. He described a Buddhist funeral, in which the climax was the burning of the deceased in a public square in the central part of Hiogo. The body was placed in a small brick structure that resembled an American farmer's smokehouse, which caused the whole square to be filled with smoke and fumes, carrying a stench that reminded bystanders of the grim proceeding. Cushing surmised that since the population was enormous, the marginal soil was strengthened by the ashes of the departed. He also noticed that a goodly number of the participants were prepared to turn the occasion into a convivial outing.[18]

Toward the end of January, Cushing was still engulfed in clouds of boredom and depression, brought on by the deteriorating condition of his ship, the leaden routine of inaction, and, above all, anxiety over the equivocal state of his engagement to Kate. Possibly, he debated whether he had made too rash a gamble. Yet if he had not seized his only opportunity, it now seemed that an uncommitted sweetheart could easily have slipped from his grasp. He admitted to Kate that he was desperate to return to her embraces. "Brother Officers," he wrote, "say to me: Why Cushing — What on Earth do <u>you</u> of all men, want to go home for? You have a splendid position abroad. Travel, do just as you please, live afloat or ashore as you see fit, are lionized, dined and wined. I don't see what more you can want."[19]

This seductive argument apparently failed to capture Cushing's imagination, which remained focused on Kate. Meanwhile, Cushing decided to alter his routine. He would no longer live on his ship; instead, he would reside at the home of the American consul, Colonel Scott Stewart, who was a year older than he. They belonged to the same generation and apparently shared similar interests. Stewart lived in a former residence of the local Japanese governor who had entertained Cushing. Stewart was described by Cushing as a handsome, wealthy man who demonstrated considerable familiarity with fashionable society, and Cushing was puzzled as to why such a promising young gentleman would decide to take on such an isolated post. Perhaps, Cushing speculated, Stewart sought to advance in the diplomatic profession. Meanwhile, Cushing resolved to enjoy the company of his newly acquired friend and his gracious hospitality. Certainly, there was ample food and drink, for game was quite plentiful; consequently, their table was regularly supplied with snipe, venison, wild boar, duck, pheasant, and woodcock. California oranges and apples were likewise in great abundance. Under such circumstances, Kate's grip on Cushing must have been truly firm.[20]

Cushing, indeed, remained anxious that Kate's bouts of self-pity might well propel her from him. He wrote, "I am very anxious to hear from you this month — for your last letters were so very gloomy that I have been worried ever since I received them." Once again he confessed, "I am truly unhappy when I think that you are so — and I am the main cause — and my heart aches with my impatience to go to you on the instant, and show you how fondly and faithfully I have loved and do love you." He begged, "Be true to me dear Kate — and do not permit your loneliness to induce you to drive me from mind and heart by association with others. You say," he added disconsolately, "that you find gentlemen's society indispensable; and that you cannot do without it."[21]

Reasoning diplomatically, Cushing responded, "I am sure that I do not wish you to give it up for my sake — and all I ask or expect is that you will not flirt or encourage particular attention as you certainly did with at least one gentleman since I have been gone," explaining that "I refer to the one who danced all the evening with you at a certain ball — when you sent me your dance card." Cushing declared, "I should not love you if I did not feel hurt at such things as that — and you know my love that my whole heart clings to your memory with the most intensive passion and devotion."[22]

Despite his anxiety over Kate's desperation at being cut off from the normal pleasures of an attractive young woman, Cushing did not neglect discussing once again the difficulties encountered in shipping his purchases back home. A baffling issue was just where home was to be. Large and bulky articles, such as servers or cabinets, could not be carried as luggage — they had to be shipped, preferably to Boston, where his brother-in-law Gayle could collect them. His sister Mary could then store them until Cushing and his bride had obtained suitable accommodation.[23]

In the first week of February, Cushing received a mail bag that contained two letters from Kate and ten from Navy colleagues announcing their nuptial celebrations. He also received seven newspapers; unfortunately, he did not record their titles. At least one was probably the *Fredonia Censor*, but quite possibly papers such as the *Times* and *Herald* from New York, as well as some from Boston, were included in the collection. Cushing found Kate's correspondence delightful, but it failed to soothe his tormented spirit. He speculated that the following year Kate and he would be able to announce to distant friends their own nuptials in the same manner that he had received such notices in his most recent batch of mail: "We may be able to reciprocate their politeness — that is, if you do not too far yield to that vanity and love of general admiration which is frankly acknowledged — and get into a flirtation with that young man whom you describe in such glowing terms — whom 'All the girls are crazy over, and who is ready and anxious to be my beau.'"[24] Cushing once again dispatched a forthright response:

> And then you tell me, earnestly that you can not do without the constant attention of the gentlemen; and half reproach me that you should. Now listen to me — You can, so far as I am concerned, go anywhere and everywhere with any gentleman in or out of town — even with the fascinating fellow who sets crazy all the girls — and when his attractions become so great as to become necessary to you — when you can no longer resist them — just write it to me — and if I am hurt — you at least will never know it. Am I cross? Am I naughty? Then why do you try to pique my pride continually? Mine is not a love that needs jealousy to keep it true. You say that we are as much man and wife, in the presence of Heaven, as if we had taken vows before the altar and, so far I agree with you, but if this is true am I not right to be provoked when you speak, often, so lightly of your self? I wish you to receive the particular attention of gentlemen well and good. My wife should not.[25]

Cushing complained that Kate's frivolous commentary on her romantic impulses that were readily ignited by the attentions of youthful admirers augmented his loneliness and increased the pain of separation from his true love. With a mischievous stroke and touch of maliciousness, he offered a compromise: "You may <u>receive</u> all the attention that you please from gentlemen — if I may <u>pay</u> all I like to ladies — and neither will write anything about it."[26] His proposition was lopsided, Cushing admitted, for he did not intend to launch any campaigns of a romantic nature. In short, he had fired a smokescreen, not a real salvo. He ran the risk, therefore, that Kate would conclude that she had the upper hand and could continue her frivolous behavior, which gave her the opportunity to explore new horizons while maintaining steadfast loyalty to the old.

8. Surveying the Landscape and the Inhabitants of Japan

Meanwhile, Cushing had left his ship to take up residence at the comfortable mansion of Colonel Stewart, where he reported that his two dogs, Fanta and China, had gleefully changed from sailors to "landsmen." A major occupation of these two dogs was chasing quail and woodcocks on the ample grounds surrounding the mansion. Apparently, Cushing had plenty of time to move at a leisurely pace, for he had been left alone at Osaka with the responsibility of protecting American merchants and overseeing their trading operations. Hence, he was able to live on shore without fear of censure, and consequently he remained inside the insulated mansion of the consul during two days of torrential downpours that dominated a dark and forbidding landscape. Happily, the climate did offer an occasional break in the dour Japanese winter, allowing Cushing to invite a number of residents of the foreign enclave to sail with him across a narrow neck of water that separated Hiogo from Osaka. Leaving the *Maumee* at the entrance to the harbor at Osaka, he ferried his company in his gig to a small French hotel.[27]

During their excursions in Osaka, Cushing and his companions were escorted by an interpreter from Hiogo whose name was Marowaski. He took them to a succession of temples, palaces, castles and parks. The tour culminated in a stop at an imposing nine-storied pagoda, which provided at its top a spectacular panorama of Osaka. Again, Cushing described the city as the Japanese Venice on account of the meandering streams and rivers that divided the countless sacred edifices, fortified structures and inviting palaces into a multitude of enclaves surrounded by lanes of water.[28]

At the end of an exhausting day the tourists sought refreshment at a tea house, where they encountered a number of nobility. With their swords resting next to them, the men straddled their mats to eat with chopsticks their bowls of rice and to sip their tea. As at Hong Kong, Cushing seized an opportunity to become informally acquainted with those in authority in a society with which his own country sought to establish official relations. He ordered a bottle of champagne and invited the Japanese nobles to dine with the American party. The invitation was accepted, "and that made sport for the evening; for we so filled them with Champagne that their jollity overcame dignity; and soon they were roaring out their national songs and joining in ours with a heartiness that is rare amongst those smaller nobles." "Late in the evening," Cushing additionally reported, "the elder one invited us all to go to his house and have another supper; and all went but myself, and did not get home till four in the morning."[29]

Possibly, Cushing declined to follow his companions because he suspected that, as a representative of the U.S. Navy, it would not be prudent for him to continue in riotous communion with Japanese civilians whose background and character remained unknown. At any rate, he returned to the hotel, where he spent nearly four hours with the landlord shooting foxes. The Japanese refused to kill foxes, for they believed that they were companions of the devil, "but when slain by a foreigner they rejoiced greatly both at the death of an evil thing and the idea that a foreigner has got himself into unpleasant relations with the Devil."[30]

On their return to Hiogo, Cushing and his friends were invited to their guide's residence, which was several miles beyond Hiogo. There they observed the Japanese custom of removing their shoes in order to keep the white mats that covered the floors immaculately clean. After having smoked their pipes, they had the signal honor of being greeted by the pretty wife of their guide, an unusual event when a foreigner was entertained in a Japanese household. The entertainment then commenced, with a band playing for several dancers (although Cushing characterized Japanese music as a noisy racket produced by various metal objects), followed by a juggler who was especially skilled in top spinning. Then a snack consisting of fish, eggs, tea, and saki with oranges and candies was served. The conclusion of the evening's entertainment was a ceremonial fan dance performed by three girls dressed in elaborate and richly colored costumes, who displayed graceful agility in using their fans to express their movements.[31]

Near the conclusion of his letter, he included an account of a visit to a temple dedicated to children who had died. Sorrowful parents left behind toys of their departed children, who they believed fervently would return in spirit to play with these offerings. Cushing was genuinely touched by this Japanese custom, and certainly it was a chronicle that Kate would likely prefer over a recital of an encounter with a group of Japanese nobles that turned into an uproarious party fueled by an ample flow of alcohol. It would seem that Cushing had overlooked earlier vows of abstinence, which she might readily recall.[32]

Apparently, she did, for Cushing in May wrote that "I absolutely refrain from both smoking and the use of any wine or liquor." "Yes, my pet," he claimed, "I some time since came to the conclusion that I would not taste any intoxicating beverage, even as a matter of courtesy with my guests." He swore, "I keep all sorts of wines just the same for my friends, but always tell them frankly that I've given up everything but tea, coffee and water," although he admitted, "They laugh and ask what I am going to do on the 4th of July—but I know that I am right, and I don't mind joking. I shall be looked upon as a wonder—out here in the East, where all are so dissipated. You do not set me a very good example, though; for I remember you once wrote me that you drank 'whiskey punch' at a sort of late o'night spree at a married gentleman's house in Buffalo."[33]

At the beginning of March, Cushing was at Yokohama. He had left the *Maumee* at Hiogo and taken a land route with a number of companions to explore the surrounding mountains; possibly he had surveyed the legendary Mount Fuji during his trek. He informed Kate that he had met Captain

Ammen, formerly the commander of the flagship of the Asiatic Squadron, who had examined the *Maumee* and recommended that it should be decommissioned. Since, as Cushing had speculated, Ammen, a close friend of Grant, had been promised leadership of the bureau that assigned officer postings for the Navy, he could provide reliable information on naval programming. Indeed, Ammen suggested that within several weeks Cushing should know the fate of his ship and his immediate future. However, if such orders failed to materialize, Ammen promised to expedite their settlement.[34]

The *Maumee* had been in commission only seventeen months, during which Cushing had served as her captain. Now he had to face the disheartening threat that his ship was no longer fit for service in the U.S. Navy. Although such an event was not uncommon on account of slipshod and hasty construction during the Civil War, nevertheless, it was a sad conclusion to a challenging mission for a youthful officer seeking to build his career. Compensation, of course, was an early return to his beloved Kate. Hopefully, Cushing's agonizing over the disposition of his fiancée would not cause his superiors and colleagues to question whether the celebrated hero was too young to be advanced to responsibilities that required the maturity of a truly seasoned commanding officer.

Fortunately, Cushing's doubts were swept aside by successive letters from Kate. With reckless impetuousness he declared his eternal gratitude to her charitable spirit and unequivocal expressions of her unrelenting love for him. He was pleased that Kate had become the confidante of Miss Starr, who had found a local swain who provided a long-anticipated opportunity to escape the drought of romance, even though the piano teacher was some years beyond the usual time for such a refreshing event. Cushing lamented that he was unable to attend Milton's wedding to Nellie, but pictured Kate as the real ornament of the occasion, and he also had an opportunity to reinforce his indictment of Mary White as spreading idle and sometimes outright malicious gossip about his past behavior.[35]

Then Cushing launched into a further discussion about the high price of consumer goods in the Far East. He informed Kate that "I am going to Osaka again in a few days and will look for the satin that you desire. I hear of some heavy silk of satin (white)," he explained, "which costs about five silver dollars for a yard — or seven and a half in green backs." He suggested further that "the best price of the silk crepe which I sent you would be in the United States (if I had paid duty) seven dollars and a half a yard. So you can see," he argued, "the queer idea at home, that everything in the East can be bought for a mere nothing, is all 'moonshine.'"[36]

He also straightened out a previous shipment of tea to Kate's mother — a box of a superior quality was now on its way. Apparently, it contained some forty pounds of this extraordinary variety. He likewise requested Kate to discover whether Albert Barker was likely to be in Fredonia, particularly when Cushing and Kate would celebrate their nuptials. Cushing asserted that Barker was an admirable man. Kate should make him available to several promising young maidens, and Cushing would like him to be a groomsman. Sadly, Cushing reminded Kate that Barker's sister, who had married a missionary, had died recently at Ning-Po. In recalling that he had entertained this couple at Hong Kong, where he had bought some books for them as a present, Cushing reflected, "How glad I am that I met her and was kind to her."[37]

Meanwhile, Cushing had to wait impatiently for orders that would determine the length of his tour of duty in the Far East and the fate of the *Maumee*. He spent a considerable amount of time lying on his bunk in his cabin, daydreaming about the various naval posts that Kate and he should consider as suitable venues for their first years of marriage. "It seems to me," he mused, "that New York is the finest place — for there, one is never at a loss for amusements," although it occurred to him, on further contemplation, that "the society at the Naval Academy is very pleasant as there are at least forty officers there with young wives; and balls and parties, sailing excursions and picnics are frequent. And then it is very near Washington and Baltimore — either of which can be visited in two hours time."[38]

Apparently, it did not occur to Cushing that the superintendent and staff at Annapolis might hesitate to accept him as an instructor, since he had been dismissed abruptly from the academy on the charge of refusing to prepare adequately for his examination in the Spanish language. Although Cushing could be exonerated on account of youthful temperament and his later heroic conduct in the Civil War, the Naval Academy has never bestowed on him an honorary diploma, despite his eventual burial on the grounds of that institution.

Kate's letters, alas, did not spare him from a renewal of gloomy musing that was encouraged by gloomy weather and his isolation in a minor port and city. He was, moreover, afflicted with a debilitating fever that recurred from time to time. Her most recent letter, he complained, was but a hasty note, which she had ended by literally tearing the bottom of a sheet off in order to join a social excursion that summoned her participation. He acknowledged that Kate's letters were as melancholic and despairing as those he wrote in which he described a boredom that matched an ever-present loneliness, but he realized that he was responsible for Kate's frustration over her lack of progress in her study of music. He confessed, "You know that I <u>love</u> music and I know that you have talent for anything — so I asked you to try and please me — but I now see that I am selfish to try to gratify my pride, by forcing your inclination — and I am shocked at the earnest, unhappy manner in which you write your fears about our future, basing them upon that subject."[39]

However, Cushing did occasionally experience some excitement that broke up the deadly routine of his customary schedule of duty. One day a group of

Chinese sailors loading powder onto their warship insisted on smoking their clay pipes, and as a result their ship blew up and promptly sank. The luckless men were tossed skyward until their momentum slowed and they tumbled into the water, although some had the misfortune to experience a hard landing on the shore. Further excitement was provided at the Kobe races, when the roof of the grandstand collapsed suddenly. Although, luckily, no one was killed, many were seriously injured by the crashing planks and beams. Cushing had the good fortune to land on a fat English captain, who thereby suffered considerable damage. Except for a few bumps from flying timber, Cushing escaped unscathed, but he was able to catch a young child who had become detached from his mooring and, being stuck between two boards, was in danger of being snapped in two. As Cushing fell, he retrieved the child by reaching up and pulling him into a safe landing in his own arms. Shortly thereafter, Cushing found the weeping and hysterical mother, whose husband informed him "that she was 'much obliged,' and I took his word for it — so I came away from the 'Kobe' races serene and satisfied — never telling the husband that it was the pretty lady that I wanted to save, on the principle that a charming, grown-up woman is worth a hundred babies — however as Madame la Mere came down from aloft with few injuries, and the child would have otherwise required a coffin, I suppose that is all right." Cushing added that the rescued family left that evening for China.[40]

The month of May opened on a gloomy note. Cushing was now quite desperate. It had been nearly three months since he had received any significant news from Kate. He had been the recipient of two brief notes in which Kate excused her brevity by pleading pressing social engagements. Moreover, she had not inquired about the schedules of the steamers from San Francisco, and consequently her letters had reached California after the steamers had departed on their voyages to various Pacific ports, so that her letters came to Cushing three months after they had been posted. Although they had been dated later, even newspapers from Fredonia arrived before Kate's letters. It appears that Cushing's misgivings had legitimacy.[41]

Nevertheless, a spell of bright and cheerful weather permitted Cushing to enjoy the picturesque scenery that unfolded along the Tokaido and its winding connecting lanes. On his latest visit to Yokohama, he had purchased a new horse, "and he is such a splendid joy that I do not let a day pass without trying his mettle." He made daily excursions of ten to twenty miles, frequently in groups of four or five, and he and his companions took care to be well armed, for the feudal nobility and their warrior retinue did not tolerate foreign inspection of their territory.[42]

He described in some detail the execution of a Japanese woman who had cooked her infant child and served it to her husband well seasoned with poison. Such a gruesome episode was not likely to persuade Kate to share her fiancé's adventures with her friends and their families, as it would probably be considered as unfit for young ladies and their mothers. However, perhaps unwittingly, Cushing retrieved his precarious predicament by returning to the subject of silk cloth. Not trusting that his judgment on color and texture corresponded to the preferences of Kate and her mother, Cushing resolved to purchase some material in a color that reflected his preference:

> It is to be done in thirty days more — is to be fifteen English yards in length — and is to be the best that can be made in Japan. So my contract reads. I am to pay sixty five "rios" in silver for it — or, about ninety dollars silver. I don't intend to pay duty on it — but, if I did, its price, turned into currency in the United Sates, would be about two hundred dollars. It ought to be a nice dress ought it not — for the best black silks to be had in Yokohama cost but thirty dollars. I have not quite made up my mind what to do with it when finished; but I suppose that it will do as well for my wife as for anybody.[43]

Cushing then inquired as to whether Kate had received her silk crepe dress, which he had sent by a fellow officer, Lt. Commander McFarland, who was returning home at Christmas. As for the writing desk, he explained that Colonel Curry, a mail agent, had volunteered to take it to New York but, unfortunately, this gift had traveled no farther than San Francisco, where Curry shipped it to Kate's address by collect charges. When he had been informed of this transaction, Cushing asserted that he had been greatly embarrassed by the realization that Kate's father had to pay the invoice. Contritely, Cushing promised that he would compensate Kate's father with some article from the Far East. Moreover, Cushing had persevered in his other shipping tasks, for he told Kate that he had sent some black silk material to her mother. Again, a friend had promised to carry it to New York, at which point it would be sent to Fredonia. "Its price was thirty Mexican dollars — and I think it was one of the best pieces that I have seen in the East," he announced proudly. He concluded his letter with an announcement that he had bought a silver baby set in Hong Kong for his young nephew that consisted of a mug, knife, fork, and napkin ring patterned in a dragon motif.[44]

However, Cushing did not send this lengthy epistle, even though it contained much useful information for Kate and her family. He explained later that he had locked it up in his desk, because he had exposed far too much gloomy uncertainty and anxiety. Writing a week after he had composed his bitter and sorrowful missive, he told Kate that on his return to Fredonia he would quickly arrange the requisite formalities, and immediately after the wedding ceremony he would take her to New York or Boston, where they would make their home for three years. Cushing speculated jubilantly on "how the miserable old gossips of Chautauqua will stare when they see all their predictions falsified, and 'that dissipated and inconstant Capt. Cushing' married to the sweetheart that they pretended to imagine he would tire of and forsake."[45]

8. Surveying the Landscape and the Inhabitants of Japan

Cushing's daughters, Marie Louise and Catherine Abell, in the beautiful costumes of a bygone day. The dresses were worn by their mother, the widow of Commander Cushing, naval hero of the Civil War, who brought the fabrics from the Orient.

Cushing also wondered about Kate's piano instructor's matrimonial ventures. Was Miss Starr's suitor, evidently a cleric, following the "Evening Starr" toward the safe matrimonial port? Why had he not received his customary quarterly report from Miss Starr on Kate's musical progress? (Apparently, Cushing had more than perfunctory involvement in the development of his fiancée's musical skills.) As mentioned previously, he feared that he was largely responsible for Kate's frustration in her musical enterprise. In a guilty mood he underscored his contrition:

> I wonder if you have yet escaped from that goblin of music that has haunted you so since I have been gone. If you have not it is your own fault; for I tell you, truly that it does not trouble my mind in the least. The proof is that the most beautiful woman in the world, and the most accomplished musician could not draw my heart from you for one instant. Music is but a limited and fleeting

pleasure — while love is infinite. Music is a cultivated taste — and we can do without it as we dispense with tobacco or wine — but love is Nature itself, and as necessary to my happiness and life as is the blood coursing in my veins or the brain which governs the body. It has been a latent power in me until I met you, but, since then it has become a moving force, strong and imperative, that governs every heartbeat, and thrills every nerve. I look upon musical talent as a personal adornment than a thing to create or sustain affection. I should be proud of it for your sake, since anything beautiful becomes you; but I would not love you more for its possession — just as I would be glad to see you clad in rich silks and jewels — since they are due to grace and beauty — but I would not love you one iota more than when in calico. It is your dear little self to whom I surrendered — and I am grateful enough to realize, always, that I received much more favorable terms than ever before were bestowed by conqueror upon a helpless foe. Please, Miss, I did not make love to "music," and music did not promise to become my wife — and I'd like to know what the impertinent thing means by trying to persuade you that she is a necessity to our happiness. So! Music or no music — in silk or in calicos — give me the dear, sweet, charming Kate Forbes that I fell in love with in that dearly remembered Summer."[46]

Cushing's somber mood came to an abrupt end shortly after this letter was written. After an almost five-month stay at Hiogo and Osaka, he received orders to proceed to Nagasaki, where the Asiatic Squadron was ordered to rendezvous. Admiral Rogers was shortly due to arrive from China. Cushing picked up rumors that quite possibly an assault on the recalcitrant Korean kingdom was contemplated. His combative spirit revived promptly, and he cheerfully informed Kate that "if I am to join the expedition, I will try to make myself conspicuous — although, (as I wrote to someone, lately,) I am not half so ready to be shot as I was before I met you."[47]

Within a few hours of receiving his orders, Cushing sailed toward Nagasaki. Following the Inland Sea for thirteen hundred miles, he reached his destination on May 20. Most of his trip was on a smooth sea, the surface of which appeared to resemble a mirror of reflecting glass. Cushing installed himself on the quarterdeck in a comfortable armchair, where he could survey a constantly changing landscape. He wrote lyrically of the romantic vista, which reminded him of a storybook ramble in fairyland. "Threading our way," he recounted, "amongst hundreds of emerald islands — girdled with terraces and mountain-set villages — a panorama of harbors, hills, valleys, temples and huge castles that created ceaseless interests."[48]

Unfortunately, the final twelve hours of his journey were through fog and mist that concealed this treacherous course through open waters to the protected harbor of Nagasaki, where an exhausted Cushing slept soundly for sixteen hours. On waking, he found that Admiral Rowan had not arrived, but several reports read by senior officers suggested that the Navy Department had decided, if possible, to send the *Maumee* home. Cushing speculated that she would be ordered to San Francisco, in which case he would be able to again visit the

Sandwich Islands. Yet, as his tour of duty in Japan was drawing to a close, Cushing had no definite knowledge of his future. He did not know whether his sojourn in Asia would be terminated or whether he would remain until the end of the full term of his original assignment.[49]

On May 31, Admiral Rowan, who had finally arrived at Nagasaki, dispatched his cruising order to Cushing. It clearly settled the duration of Cushing's term of service with the Asiatic Squadron. He would remain as the commander of the *Maumee* until the end of his contracted term of duty, at which time the fate of his ship would be resolved. Meanwhile, Cushing's orders stated, "The '*Maumee*,' under your command being ready for sea, you will proceed to Fou-Chow, China for the purpose of affording protection to Americans and American interests." His instructions further advised, "You will communicate with the American Consul and learn the state of affairs, and also preserve a good understanding with all foreign consuls." Cushing should also contact American consular officials at Amoy and Ning Po, who were to be informed that Cushing was at Foochow, and therefore could readily come to their aid. If Cushing encountered fair weather, he should likewise visit Keelung and Jamisin on the island of Formosa. Above all, in his cruising Cushing should exercise considerable caution in his consumption of coal. As a general practice, he should use wind power for sailing and keep one or two boilers with banked fires that could provide hot water. These boilers could be activated to furnish steam for navigation but, his orders stated, "Run your ship while under steam with one boiler only, and let her speed not exceed eight knots. The great object is to economize coals that weigh so heavily in the expenses of the Squadron."[50]

Chapter 9

A Lingering Farewell to the Far East

As Cushing commenced his final cruise, he was confronted with baffling dilemmas. His naval career was not in jeopardy, but he was enmeshed in the routine chores of patrolling that did not readily present the heady drama of naval engagement. Piracy was a draining problem, yet its practitioners were careful not to expose themselves to a definitive challenge. Watching over the activities of missionaries did not reveal a landscape in which heroic action was demanded, although Cushing could seek out the comfortable solace offered by the luxurious mansions of the mercantile community. The precarious condition of his ship, of course, further restricted the scope of his activities and complicated the timing of his departure from the Far East.

Possibly, Cushing had contemplated a series of exhilarating adventures in a mysterious and exotic Orient, all of which would be capped by a triumphant return to the rapturous embrace of an adoring sweetheart. Instead, he had been stricken with a prolonged period of torment marked by bouts of disillusionment and the fear of humiliation while he waited in vain for letters reaffirming Kate's tender love. As he drifted slowly down the Chinese coast, he still remained uncertain of the loyalty of his despairing and bored fiancée, who apparently feared that she had embarked far too hastily on an engagement to a man who had dropped off her horizon soon after making his pledge of steadfast commitment. She had to accept that he still was true to his promise by messages of paper and ink that could not take the place of a physical presence and spoken declaration. In desperation, Cushing attempted to turn ink and paper into passionate proclamations of loyalty to his beloved. Hymns of Christian devotion reinforced assertions of the purity of his love, which he sought to install on a sacramental level. In angry frustration over Kate's persistent reliance on casual flirtations with youthful rustics, Cushing denounced the society of Fredonia and declared himself a citizen of Wisconsin, the state of his birth. His outburst was childish, for he had not had any association with Wisconsin since leaving it as a baby. If he wished to legitimately invoke a genuine allegiance to a childhood home beyond western New York, he should have recalled Chicago, where a youthful accident had bestowed upon him the nickname "Coons," which his brother Milton still called him. Cushing should also have paused to remember that both Alonzo and he had been launched into their respective careers through the kindness of their local congressman. Above all, Cushing's mother remained firmly attached to Fredonia.

He also should have reviewed his contacts with the fair sex in San Francisco and the persistent reports of an abundant supply of comely damsels in New England, who would respond readily to any matrimonial invitation from successful naval officers. Cushing undoubtedly recognized that as a youthful and handsome Civil War hero, wealthy and influential families would promptly welcome him into their circle. His loyal affection for Kate, an innocent and still uncertain young adult whose knowledge of the world scarcely stretched to the nearby regional metropolis of Buffalo, is truly an enigma. Cushing had become a denizen of a sophisticated and cultured world. He may have been still a neophyte, but he was rapidly gaining stature. On arriving at Shanghai, Cushing easily appreciated the imposing splendor of the great metropolis of the Far East. He wrote enthusiastically to Kate, "We spent a most delightful week there; and left with much regret; for it is *the* American place of the East; and full of hearty, hospitable people."[1] He continued his narrative with a description of the dramatic approach to Shanghai's harbor from the sea. The mouth of the Yangtze River is generously wide, and it is not until a ship reaches the Whangpoo River (a tributary of the Yangtze that provides a sheltered waterway to Shanghai) that it has truly left the turbulent waves of the Pacific and the uncompromising currents of the Yangtze's mouth. Like many fellow mariners, Cushing was awestruck by the graceful reception that the shoreline of Shanghai, called the Bund, offered its visitors.[2]

Cushing wrote, "The appearance of Shanghai from the water, is very imposing — since the river-bank bordered by a wide avenue, forming the fore ground [*sic*] to a mass of houses truly palatial. These merchant princes of the East live in a style of luxury that surpasses anything that I have before seen abroad. I was a guest during my stay, at one of the large 'hongs'— and was almost ruined for a sea life in a single week."[3] Although Cushing enjoyed the abundantly luxurious hospitality of his Chinese merchant hosts, he favored the generosity of his countrymen. One family in particular attracted his plaudits. He had received letters of introduction to a Mr. Eames, who lived approximately two miles beyond the urban configurations of Shanghai. Every day Cushing visited the Eames family at their comfortable residence well removed from the noise and smells of the bustling entrepreneurial environment. "Mrs. Eames," he reported, "is one of the most charming ladies that I have ever met — and one of the finest musicians." Cushing announced further, "She sang all

my old favorites to me to my hearts content [*sic*] — and coming, as the music did, after the many long and lonesome months when I have been without it — it gave me the keenest pleasure and truest enjoyment that I have found in the East." To express his gratitude to his hostess for her charming reception and, above all, for her recitals featuring many of his favorite melodies, Cushing gave her children a pet deer that he brought from Japan. In the course of his travels, he had collected an unusual menagerie — several exotic birds, a monkey, and various dogs, but, thankfully, no roaring lions or tigers. He might have been tempted to experiment with the feline breed, though, if they and other formidable predators flourished in his corner of Asia.[4]

Cushing viewed the contemporary scene in Shanghai as an unusual situation where Americans and their commerce were the predominant influence. This was evidently a valid conclusion at the time of Cushing's visit. However, historically Shanghai had been developed by the British. In 1843 William Jardine and James Matheson, who soon became partners, and were later joined by other British merchants, launched a mercantile community on 140 water-soaked acres adjacent to the nearby Chinese trading city on the Whangpoo River. By driving countless wooden piles to reinforce the foundations of their buildings, the British and their American competitors were able to transfer the center of their trading operations to the great region dominated by the Yangtze River.[5]

Shanghai was constructed on a sandy swamp, but its shore on the Whangpoo became a glamorous citadel of Western commerce that proclaimed the technology and business skills of Western enterprise to a reluctant and suspicious Chinese regime. It was, moreover, separated from its Chinese neighbors and enjoyed a cultural and social segregation from the prevailing customs of imperial China.[6] From the start, American merchants had joined the migration of merchants and shipping interests from Canton and Hong Kong to Shanghai and the Yangtze. The most prestigious of these firms was Russell & Co., which soon constructed an imposing headquarters on the Bund. The architects of this impressive enterprise were a brotherhood of Providence, Rhode Island, financiers who also made significant investments in the American transcontinental railroad project that was completed in 1869.[7]

Russell & Co., however, had been challenged by the same intransigent problem that had almost wrecked the operations of Jardine and Matheson: the Chinese had scant interest in the commodities offered by Western merchants. Comfortable with the wares of their culture, the Chinese and their Ch'ing emperors at Beijing regarded Western products as curiosities and, occasionally, gadgets for the distraction of idle minds. Certainly, such materials had no place in the lexicon of Confucian teaching, which provided the essential rules of governance in China.[8]

Opposite: American company headquarters, 1860s.

As a result, British and American merchants were seriously crippled by an imbalance of trade that was clearly pinpointed by a steady flow of specie from domestic coffers to purchase tea, pottery, and silk. Scarcity of cash and certificates of credit threatened the solvency of government tax accounts. Monetary starvation prompted Western governments to get involved with military intervention and acquisition of privileged territorial stakes. An immediate source of relief was the predilection that prevailed in all strata of Chinese society for the pleasure of opium. Cultivated in hospitable regions surrounding the Yangtze, the domestic crop within China had long exercised an unchallenged monopoly. Now the supply of opium became more abundant and less costly. The result was two armed conflicts between the imperial army and Western naval and military forces (discussed in an earlier chapter). European and American diplomats established treaty ports and liberal acceptance of their opium imports. The Chinese populace was assured of a liberal supply of narcotic escapism from the humiliation of subservience to foreign dominion.[9]

Although tea remained the all-important substance the British sought in the Far East, the American Civil War had blocked the most reliable source of raw cotton for their factories in South Lancashire. As a result, many factories were forced to curtail production or even to close, and unemployed workers and their families faced desperate hardship. The end of the American Civil War did not revive a dislocated plantation economy. At this time, however, fortune smiled on a principal engine of the Industrial Revolution in Great Britain — a sure and steady supply of cotton appeared in the lush terrain surrounding the Yangtze. China claimed a truly vital link with British commerce that promised far more endurance than the luxury traffic in porcelain and silk.[10]

Nevertheless, as Cushing observed, American influence was pronounced in Shanghai. Russell & Co. had ventured into the steamship business by operating a line of ships navigating the Yangtze. There was a paradox: many of the ships that had been constructed for the Navy during the Civil War were now coming apart because of slovenly construction and failure to use properly cured timber; however, American engineering on shallow draft ships suitable for service in riverine commerce was superior to that of their British competitors. HMS *Warrior* was far superior in size and weaponry to the wooden hull capital ships of the Americans, but she was much too large for service in the uncharted and cluttered waters of the Chinese interior. The American steamers had been built to reflect the American navigation challenges on the rivers of the North American continent, whereas the *Warrior* had been designed to meet the challenge of European rivals, principally the French Navy.[11] The sleek American paddle steamers that plied the eastern rivers of America, such as the Hudson, were more suitable for the rivers of China than the celebrated steamers of the Ohio and Mississippi, which were propelled by paddle wheels attached to the rear of their hulls. Also, the larger steamers of the Hudson variety were able to make the long passage from San Francisco to the Chinese coast, although many were shipped across the Pacific and then assembled in Chinese ports. At the height of its prosperity, Russell & Co. dominated the Yangtze River traffic with a fleet of sixteen ships.[12]

Unfortunately, American dominion in the commerce of Shanghai was short-lived. The financial status of Russell & Co. was tenuous. Much of the investment capital in the United States was soaked up by land speculation and the lucrative rewards of successful acquisition of railroad stock. Investment in the markets of Asia was not reassuring, as they were distant and their potential was difficult to gauge, although there was far too much risk and tawdry shenanigans in the home markets, which did flourish in well-known domestic territory.

Much of Russell & Co. business was conducted on a commission basis. After a six-year hegemony, the American firm was overtaken by Jardine and Matheson, which confirmed the preeminence of the British presence in the commerce and governance of Shanghai. Actually, the Chinese compradors—the merchants who served as intermediaries between foreign firms and Chinese traders and producers—gained control of the commercial relations of Western financial and commercial interests seeking to practice business in China. Perhaps, therefore, claims that Western nations exercised a masterful control of the Chinese economy are more of an illusion than a fact.

Moreover, Cushing was well aware of the catastrophic destruction of the American merchant marine during the Civil War. When he arrived at Foochow, he quickly observed the absence of American ships. "I noticed with regret," he commented petulantly, "but one American flag in the fleet," lamenting, "All the rest are English." He then launched a tirade against the disheartening spectacle and its perpetrators. "It was not so a few years since," he remonstrated, "when the stars and stripes covered most of the Eastern carrying trade—but English perfidy sent out the *Alabama* and her consorts and ruined American commerce." Continuing his bitter denunciation, Cushing asserted, "When I see such examples as this—twelve thousand miles from home, of the injury that England has done us—I can't help longing—with all my heart and soul—for a grapple with our 'cousins' that should wring the life blood out," and he went on to vow that "no treaties can be made that can cover up such wrongs as we have received." "In our hearts," he intoned, "we hate and scorn England and Englishmen, and always will—until the backdrop is shredded by sword points." Cushing's angry outburst reflected the evangelical spirit of his provincial agrarian heritage, which was far removed from the sophisticated commercial and financial enterprises of the cosmopolitan mercantile society of Shanghai that had so lavishly welcomed him.[13]

As he moved down the Chinese coast, Cushing ran into another prominent Western phenomenon in the Far East—the missionary. He reported to Kate, "There are few foreign inhabitants in Ning Po—excepting missionaries—but they swarm like unto the locusts of Egypt." He then expostulated, "I can see — the more I travel — where my five-cent piece used to go — in my innocent Sunday-school days of happy infancy. I think if I had known as much as I do now — that I would have invested in molasses candy or marbles." Cushing pleaded teasingly, "Keep your diminutive green backs, Kate — Yea! And entice not the juvenile Episcopalians under your charge to subscribe for tooth powder or fine tooth combs for the heathen — for to tell the truth — the said pagans don't get the benefit of it."[14]

Despite his reservations on the legitimacy of clerical evangelism in the Far East, Cushing remained steadfast in his allegiance to behaving chivalrously toward those that duty required him to serve. "What do you think of my playing croquet," he asked Kate, "with a party of ancient Missionaries headed by old Mr. Lord?" "It was," he reminded her, "my first game since I played with you." He then exclaimed, "Well — I did — and notwithstanding my long neglect of the game I beat them all." Cushing did not neglect to touch on a nostalgic memory: "Think what a lively and frolicsome game! Alas on the present occasion there were No pretty gaiters and neat ankles to inspire me with enthusiasm! Bald heads and No 14 boots formed the sad contrast to my memories of Auld Lang Syne."[15] Mr. Lord was, however, not only an elderly missionary, but also the American consul at Ning Po. J. R. Goddard, whom Cushing had encountered at Hong Kong, had introduced him to Lord. Cushing had visited Goddard to console him on the recent loss of his wife, to whom Cushing had presented a package of popular novels (which he was sure did not exist in the collection of books belonging to a devout cleric). Cushing discovered that Lord had several children who lived on the same street in Fredonia where the Forbes family had their residence. Cushing informed Kate that the home of these children was near a family named Lewis, and then he recalled vaguely that he had heard the name Gusty or John used to identify these natives of Fredonia. As for Cushing himself, he lamented that he had experienced considerable difficulty in recovering from the sober mannerisms of the missionaries. "I haven't got over," he confessed dourly, "feeling long-faced and solemn."[16]

Cushing's somber mood was fortunately dispelled by the formalities of an official visit to the residence of the provincial governor. Although Ning Po lacked the commercial vibrancy of Shanghai, it still enjoyed a steady mercantile nexus. Situated in a snug harbor that was at the mouths of two rivers, it provided a convenient route to the fertile plain of the province of Tche-kiang. This province was noted for abundant harvests of rice and cotton, which were sustained by an extensive labyrinth of canals. It also had elevated terrain in its interior, which supported a comfortable acreage devoted to the production of tea, and sponsored a healthy industry in cattle and the production of silk. Cushing informed Kate that he had observed that many of the local shopkeepers he had encountered were well stocked with finely carved and lacquered wooden ware.[17] Ultimately, the British gained command of the city during the several wars that established the network of treaty ports. Initially, the British had been repulsed by Portuguese and Russian traders, who had established a firm foothold.[18]

Cushing's account of his formal visit to the governor of the Province deserves to be recorded here, for it illustrates the tenuous relations between the conquering West and the stubborn defenders of the traditions of the East:

> We rode in Chairs for some two miles, followed by an excited and enthusiastic crowd of Chinamen whom my full-dress uniform attracted; and entered the "dragon gate" amidst a burst of barbaric music, and a confused salute from Chinese cannon — passing, as usual, through three or four court yards, until we were deposited, chairs and all, in an ante-room of the house — by our coolies, who had been shouting themselves hoarse to notify everyone of what "a swell" they had on their shoulders. Being shown into the audience room, through a line of blue, gold and white button Mandarins, the Governor appeared an old man — richly dressed in heavy silk — with a hat displaying the high and mighty "red button" and the ornamental end of at least two peacocks [feathers].

Cushing continued his narrative with a description of the governor's costume: "Around his neck were two strings of beads — of various materials — such as carved nuts — jade-stone — amethyst, emerald etc. — the richest ones I think, that I have seen on any official in China. The immense thumb ring — of jade-stone an inch and a quarter broad was said to be worth four thousand dollars. It is a green stone — and valued by the Chinese very much as we value diamonds — although it has no value as a jewel out of China." He then proceeded to describe the liturgy of the interview:

> Upon my being seated upon the raised couch, the place of honor on the left — the old fellow placed himself in the lowest chair; and tea was produced. This is the first ceremony in a Chinese call, where you shake your own hand instead of your host's; and keep on the hat to indicate respect. We soon commenced our "confab" through two interpreters about as follows — (Captain C.) I am happy to be able to pay my respects to the famous and far-known Governor of this Province. (Governor) "The small and unworthy official whom you see — rejoices to see you at Ning Po." Then a sip of tea — and pipes are introduced. (Governor) "What is your distinguished and happy name?" — Ans. "The humble and insignificant title of your guest is Capt. Cushing" — Governor "Ho!" (more smoke and more tea) — (Capt. C) — "What is your honorable and venerated age?" Ans. "My mean and boyish age is sixty years." The last are two of the most polite questions in a conversation with a Chinese.[19]

Cushing explained, "After this the chat became general — cakes, sweetmeats and 'samshu' (native wine) were brought in — and in half an hour we took our leave, amidst the same ceremonies that attended our entrance — the Governor at the same time, notifying me that he would be happy to pay his respects to me on board at ten o'clock the next day." When the governor appeared the following morning, Cushing was pleased to announce that his illustrious guest "was highly delighted with everything; and looked open mouth [*sic*] at the working of the cannon, the machinery and the ship's deck which was canopied in the flags of all nations."[20] The governor, indeed, was so impressed with his hospitable reception that he spontaneously invited Cushing to a banquet honoring his visit. When Cushing declined the honor on account of his schedule, the governor pledged that the invitation would be renewed whenever Cushing came again. Cushing noted that the *Maumee* was the first foreign ship that the governor had inspected.[21]

Cushing was in a reasonably cheerful state because he anticipated that his tour of duty in the Far East was drawing to a close, but also, and more immediately, on account of being able to canvass the meandering coast of China, where, despite the prospect of a humid and fiercely hot summer, fascinating sights were in plentiful supply. He informed Kate, "Tomorrow I shall be in Foochow — and settled down for a month at least. I hear that there is quite a pleasant American society there and that will compensate for the heat of a Chinese summer." He then mused, "After I have been to Amoy and to Formosa my view of the Chinese coast will be nearly complete."[22]

Cushing quickly added that "I am glad, while I am forced to remain here, to be again on the coast of China, for there is much more of interest to see and to write about — since my place in the Empire has some customs peculiar to its own limits." "Living, too," he further commented, "is much cheaper in China than in Japan — beef, poultry, eggs & being very abundant."[23] Yet, he admitted, "I dreaded coming to China at this season, because of the heat — but, thus far it has proved as cool as Japan. Unfortunately, Cushing acknowledged, "My throat still troubles me — but is nothing serious — and my general health is good." Moreover, he reported cheerfully, "My ship has had no sickness, thus far, in this country of epidemics — and I trust our good fortune may continue." The following morning Cushing announced that the *Maumee* had anchored at the mouth of the Min River, which flowed majestically through a lush delta toward the harbor of Foochow. Cushing remained at this spot until a pilot arrived the next morning to guide his ship along the ten-mile route into the actual harbor. Meanwhile, Cushing could take refuge from a dark and rainy day with speculations of sights to come. "We are anchored a few hundred yards," he told Kate, "from a fine pagoda — seven stories high — which I would like to visit and examine, but rain and mud prevent."[24] At this time, Foochow was a leading treaty port because of its flourishing market and shipping prominence in the tea trade. It was at this port that the spectacle of a lone American ship surrounded by a flotilla of vessels flying the Union Jack had prompted Cushing's previously noted outburst against the behavior of Britain toward the American republic during the Civil War.

Despite Cushing's fascination with the panorama of the Far East and the strange behavior of its inhabitants, the quality of Kate's affection for him remained a constant torment. "Indeed, indeed, I love you!!" he cried, insisting that "nothing can change me in this — Time can not mar it, your silence does not change it — nothing but death can come between it and you, my darling, darling little wife." Nevertheless, Cushing's passionate affirmation of his undying love could not conceal the agony of his fear: "And yet, with all my devoted love I am not happy — even while I feel that you are well and trust me, for how can I be happy or even patient when I no longer hear from you! Your last letter is dated nearly five months ago — and I sometimes fairly tremble to think what five long Months may have brought forth. I ask myself, now and then — 'When Kate was expecting me and I failed to come, may not the disappointment have caused her to blame me — and may not coldness grow with long neglect of writing?' Alas dear Kate — love, such as mine is jealous of the air — and I am miserable without your continued assurance of fidelity and affection."[25]

Looking to the future, Cushing saw some rays of sunshine to chase away the gloomy clouds of the moment. He realized that he could begin to count weeks, not months, before his term of duty in the Far East came to an end. In addition, he had been informed that the new secretary of the Navy had stated emphatically that when an officer had completed three years of sea duty, he was assured of three years of shore duty. Cheerfully, Cushing speculated that since he had accumulated nine consecutive years of sea duty, he could legitimately apply for a longer shore assignment. He then steered his discourse into a colloquial direction by asking Kate to provide an updated report on the gossip that she had sent in her last letter. Had Mary White at long last consented to become a bride? Had the piano recital in which Kate had participated been an accomplished success? What was the state of Miss Starr's matrimonial campaign? Did Kate have any news of the Reverend Lord's relatives who lived on her street? Thus, Cushing managed to complete his long rambling on a bright note, which might spark a ready reply.[26]

On arriving at Foochow, Cushing anchored close to the island of Mantai, which straddled the River Min. This site provided suitable security and insularity from the undesirable aspects of a Chinese community. These considerations had led the foreign colony to establish its headquarters away from the long-established Chinese marketplace.

Staying loyal to his lighthearted mood, Cushing narrated for Kate's amusement an anecdote from a conversation with an Irish missionary. As Cushing was relating some of the more dramatic events of his *Albemarle* adventure, his pious auditor exclaimed, "But you weren't killed were ye?" Cushing informed Kate, "I hastened, in the midst of a somewhat audible smile, to assure him that I was not, and it is owing to that fact that I am now seated in my cabin, by candle light, warding off numberless mosquitoes with one hand, while I write to you with the other."[27]

The *Maumee*, however, was not being sprayed and netted against the elements and harmful insects encountered during a tropical summer in southern China. Instead, Cushing heard the merry conversation of his officers in the wardroom as they entertained their dinner guests, and the ship's band was playing from the stern deck melodic waltzes and heart-rending operatic melodies for romantic ambiance. The *Maumee* was the only foreign ship anchored at the settlement reserved for merchants and representatives stationed at foreign legations. The main part of Foochow was situated on the shore directly opposite the island. Since the American warship would be at this anchorage on the Fourth of July, she would be decorated colorfully, and at noon she would fire a twenty-one gun salute, which would be repeated at the end of the day. This festive occasion would encourage a parade of receptions and dinner parties, all of which served to provide relief from the normal tedium of commercial and official business.[28]

Meanwhile, pandemonium flourished on the river, where junks and sampans produced a noisy racket as they jostled for a favorable position close to the *Maumee*. Cushing hired a sampan for a month's service to ferry officers and crew into port, as well as to bring supplies to the ship. This craft was twenty feet long and only five feet wide. The family, the members of which spent their entire lives in this circumscribed space, consisted of two men, a wife and a grandmother, and four children less than five years old. These children were given a safety device, which consisted of a small log tied to their back and a rope twenty feet long, which connected each child to the boat. If a child fell overboard, it would neither perish nor float away. Instead, the unfortunate youngster would simply receive a good soaking.[29]

This clever strategy for protecting children living in the midst of the much-traveled river, alas, was confined to the family circle. Beyond the rim of that modest craft a raging, and frequently brutal, competition flourished among junks carrying cargo downriver to the ocean-plying ships of sail and steam. "If a junk capsize or a boat go down," Cushing explained, no thought was given to rescuing the crew or collecting their abandoned goods, "although a thousand boats are at hand." On the contrary, "The San pans make a wild dash to steal the floating articles; and, as soon as the plunder is secured, they hurry off to conceal it; leaving the unfortunate survivors to get out or sink, just as it happens."[30]

Cushing explained the background of this rapacious behavior, having discovered that "it is river Law, here that anything picked up in the stream is the property of the finder." "Even if the boat containing the true owner," Cushing clarified, "is but a minute behind him in reaching the property, it matters not — it has changed owners."[31] Cushing then underscored his commentary by describing a dramatic incident that had swirled around his ship:

> This phase of Chinese life was illustrated yesterday. A tea junk was coming down the river loaded with boxes of fresh tea when the strong current carried her across the bow of another junk and then and there capsized her. Away went the boxes of tea, by thousand floating down with the tide, while an assorted family of seven was plunged into the swift river, screaming for aid. A hundred san-pans [*sic*] were instantly in the midst of the tea, their crews frantic with excitement, and yelling and fighting for plunder as no one but a Chinaman can, but all seemed utterly oblivious of the drowning wretches in the water. Of course I had expected to see these unfortunates instantly rescued but as soon as I saw how things were I hastened to lower boats to save them. My aid was only in time to save four out of the seven, however — and the tea was stolen to the last box. Hurrah for the Chinese![32]

Cushing fortified his scathing description of Chinese navigation customs with an observation of a sailing routine prevalent on rivers. Conventionally, Chinese boats were propelled by wind, and as soon as wind currents revived, the noise of waking men and ships quickly reached a crescendo. Cushing narrated a tableau of the confusion and racket manufactured by clashing boats and men: "In a second every thing starts into life — sails are hoisted — anchors weighed — and on each junk are four or five excited Chinamen, dancing about, with outspread limbs and sprawling fingers, beating gongs with all their might until the ear is almost deafened by the din."[33]

The pandemonium of this spectacle left the unprepared onlooker speechless, Cushing cautioned, "and the rush is so great that many fall foul of each other, and the noise of rent sails and crushed timber is mixed with the wrathful yells of the crews [who] seem ready to eat each other with-out cooking, but would never strike a blow." The lack of outright combat, he explained, was due to the fact that "a Chinaman's tongue is his weapon, and the most noise gains the victory."[34]

Cushing did venture into the city of Foochow, where he found that rain-soaked terrain had become flooded. The streets were small streams. As a result, customary modes of transport had to be set aside and small boats were employed to paddle travelers to their destinations. Cushing remarked further that Foochow was "principally famed for its wonderful and unprecedented combination of offensive odors — which almost smothered me in one afternoon." To escape a further threat to his physical constitution, Cushing declined a dinner invitation from the provincial governor, who had extended an invitation to a "trifling entertainment." Cushing had not forgotten that the last time he had accepted such an engagement, he "didn't get over it for a week."[35]

Cushing continued to be amused by the conventions of Chinese etiquette. For example, when received initially by his host as a guest, "A Chinese calls his Wife 'The mean one of the inner apartments' but expects the one with whom he is conversing to mention the unseen fair one as 'your favored one' — 'your honorable lady' or some such thing."[36] It was clear, however, that for the moment Cushing was resolved to enjoy the colorful and joyful entertainment presented by the *Maumee* in commemoration of July 4th, which would reach a climax with a production by the ship's minstrel performers. Moreover, Cushing looked forward to being the center of attention at numerous receptions and parties given by American and foreign residents to celebrate the great American patriotic event.

However, one event at Foochow provides an excuse for rethinking the customary interpretation of Sino-foreign interaction. Cushing reported, "I find that the head of the largest tea 'Hong' is an old acquaintance," going on to explain that "we were in company at a Country house, thirty miles from San Francisco in a party of a dozen young ladies and gentlemen who were spending a week there in what we called a croquet party." "His house here," Cushing elaborated, "is magnificent. My idea of an oriental house — and he is very hospitable."[37] This brief anecdote reminds readers that Western relations with China were not exclusively centered on blood-and-thunder exploitation of a decaying culture. Indeed, a defensible argument can be mounted that the Chinese traders were the essential link between Western shipping interests and native suppliers. Without the Chinese merchants and financiers, Western entrepreneurs would have confronted a dubious challenge.

Yet there was a dark side to the interaction between Western men of commerce and Chinese natives. The latter scorned the strange religious and cultural background of their uninvited guests, while the former looked upon the Chinese as stubborn loyalists to ancient and discredited philosophies and forms of worship that had no place in a modern industrial society. Cushing revealed that he had picked up a rumor that a cabal of the "Celestials" was attempting to foment an uprising of the Chinese community against the foreign colony, and the inhabitants were to be the victims of a mass slaughter. Most of the officials of the foreign enclave discounted the threat, for Foochow had never experienced any militant protest again the Western powers who had established the network of treaty ports. As a consequence, Foochow had enjoyed a peaceful coexistence with her Western guests, while her sister treaty ports had experienced devastating warfare between rebelling native insurgents and angry foreign military forces.

Many provincial centers' governing authority was shared by a Chinese executive and a Tartar caretaker, appointed by imperial councilors at Beijing to ensure loyalty to the Manchurian emperors and their entourage. At Foochow there was actually tripartite sharing of authority: a viceroy, a governor general, and a Tartar supervisor. They met to consider a request from the "Celestial" cabal to sanction a seemingly spontaneous uprising by an outraged populace. The Tartar emissary endorsed the request, as did the governor general. The viceroy, however, pointed out that he was seventy years old and then inquired of the Tartar his age. The reply was forty-five. "Then said the ancient one,"

Cushing recorded, "I was an officer of his Majesty long before you were born — and I tell you that (while these Western barbarians will bear much), if you attempt the least violence they will shell and burn your city over your heads."[38]

Having received this admonishment, the other two councilors consented to table the proposition. Cushing did not hesitate to approve their rejection of violence in favor of temperance. He recognized that "this is the only open port in China where such an idea would enter the heads of the people — for during all the war and trouble between China and our Western Nations, this city alone escaped a taste of powder and shell — and they have not the least idea of what powerful people we are."[39]

Cushing then expanded his waspish commentary on the innocence of the inhabitants of Foochow: "The foreign population is small and but few men o'war ever come here — and they retain all the insolent presumption of superiority that was common to them all, but a few years since. In consequence they are turbulent and quarrelsome — and will never improve until their City is bombarded once or twice. I wish that they had come. My ship is the only Man o'War here and I might have gained great distinction, if I would have opened their eyes by such a beating as falls to the lot of a few unhappy cities. Just think what a glorious 4th of July bonfire such a live Village would make!"[40]

Fearing that his belligerent tone would vex Kate, Cushing moved to a pacific topic. He related the invaluable service that many missionaries provided to their secular neighbors, being excellent tour guides for the staff of the *Maumee*. Many of the missionaries had acquired a respectable command of the Chinese language, which made them invaluable not only to foreign visitors but also to foreign officials and their entourages, as they provided an essential link between foreign delegations and Chinese authorities.[41]

Cushing found that some missionaries had very delightful families, which "go in for croquet and such vanities." "Two of these self-sacrificing individuals," he remarked, "are remarkable for faith — and evidently think themselves under special care of Providence." He then queried, "What do you think that they did — I should say dared?" The answer: "Having occasion to send home to the Mission board for various useful articles such as books, furniture &— they bethought themselves to send for wives, also — and coolly requested that such better halves might be immediately forwarded. The best of it is that two old Maids — gushing damsels!— were found to enter into pious speculation — and the four have become two. How it will turn out remains to be seen — but I think it about as cool a piece of business, as has ever come under my notice. There's still hope for Miss Starr, for Leilia, and all the rest — only let them make me their agent, and I'll pick out a Missionary for each of them."[42]

Cushing must have found the chronicle of a discarded conspiracy against the foreign colony at Foochow and the rollicking tale of the marriage market venture of two lonely missionaries an invigorating escape from constantly waiting for news of the two all-important issues that dominated his daily contemplations. First, the fate of the *Maumee*— was she to be condemned and sold at Hong Kong, or would she be sent to San Francisco for extensive repairs? If the first choice occurred, Cushing would be sent home within a month after arriving at Hong Kong, which he expected to reach a month after leaving Foochow. On the other hand, if he were ordered to sail to San Francisco, a journey that would take him a month to accomplish, he was unlikely to see Kate for another three months. There was, however, a third possibility: the *Maumee* might be assigned to river patrol, in which case, he could anticipate several more months of active service until his contract with the Asiatic fleet expired, an option that filled Cushing with considerable anxiety, particularly since a recent communication from the Navy Department had advised that all assignments to sea duty would henceforth be for a term of four years instead of the current two-year period.

Cushing's second principal concern was the strength of his engagement to Kate. He sought to make it a sovereign declaration of their loyalty and honor, asserting, "For three of us, who have condemned ships, are young men — and all engaged — haven't a heart amongst all three of us and were all groaning with impatience, and constantly writing to each other. What's the last news? When are we going home? Yes! Here are three Naval Officers — who at the end of two years are still 'dead in love,' and sighing like furnaces for home and sweethearts."

Cushing then declared emphatically, "Talk of sailors' fickleness! Why — there's not one landlubber in a hundred that would stand the test. They can't appreciate, admire and respect ladies as we do — and not one of a thousand is bred up with the same ideas of honor. Besides they don't travel enough to learn human nature, and to educate the judgment. When a Navy man does find the woman whom he wants to marry, there is no one truer in the World, and his mind compares her with others whom he has seen and known intimately in all parts of the World, and he acknowledges a superiority of grace, of beauty, of character of something — to which he freely yields. I notice that nearly all the married officers of the Service have wives to be proud of— and they all seem as happy as the day is long."[43]

Cushing's fears and anxiety, prompted by the dearth of letters from Kate, were fortunately set at rest ten days after writing his latest missive to her, when he received two reassuring messages from Kate. One had been written in February and another toward the end of April. Both letters underscored her continuing affection for him in tender and consoling words. "Such delicious letters," Cushing exulted, "they would have melted a heart of stone — while in mine — which is so entirely yours — you can judge what emotion they excited."[44]

He was amused by her somewhat innocent argument supporting her pledge of enduring understanding of his lonely separation from her. In her letter written on February 6, Kate had asserted that she "had not received any attention from gentlemen this year." Cushing calculated this guarantee was actually for thirty-six days, according to the date of her letter, and teased "You actually did without beaux for five weeks!" He continued in this light vein, "You say that you thank me for never writing anything to make you jealous." "Why my precious girl," he exclaimed in a patronizing tone, "that is the last thing in the World that I want to do, and even if I did wish to gratify my vanity in that manner, I could not do it without lying; and a man might as well bite off his nose to spite his face."[45]

Despite Cushing's solemn preaching on the sterling character of U.S. naval officers, especially in regard to their unswerving loyalty to their wives and sweethearts, Kate might well have giggled when she wrote several later paragraphs in which she hinted that her fiancé did not really trust her, apparently in response to one of his letters. Cushing protested that she failed to read that letter correctly. "I have absolute faith in your truth, prudence, and womanly pride, but I think that my letter must have been an answer to one telling me of the promiscuous kissing at the Parkers' wedding." He invoked a literary reference in his defense. "If you wish to comprehend, my feelings," he argued, "I refer you to Shakespeare's 'Mark Anthony and Cleopatra'— Scene eleventh — where Anthony sees Thyrsus kiss Cleopatra's hand." Cushing confessed that "I am jealous of even such formal favors — and — (would) cut the ears off such a fellow as Harrison Parker for taking such a liberty upon any occasion or on any excuse."[46]

Knowing that his assignment with the Asiatic Squadron might be drawing to an end, Cushing began to reminisce on his experience, and quite naturally, as time telescoped his separation from Kate, he reflected on their prolonged courtship that had held firm, despite slow and sporadic sea and land communications. "Once, you know," he reminded Kate, " you were a little humbug, when your letters used to declare that you loved me; and you did not, really, care whether I sank or swam." Cushing explained, "I sometimes read those letters over — and wonder — those written just before my Rio letters reached you — and wonder how you could use some expressions there when you knew that your heart was as cold as an iceberg," and then went on to say, "How thankful I am that all that has gone by!" He speculated, "Is it true that love begets love?" "If so," he concluded, "I don't know how much I shall draw out of you during all our life — for I intend, always, to love you desperately."[47] Cushing had won his battle for Kate's true and steadfast love. For him, it was an accomplishment that matched his destruction of the *Albemarle*.

Meanwhile, he sought to escape from his reveries through the distractions offered by the landscape and populace of China. As the river became calmer, cormorant fishing resumed. The cormorant is a generous-sized aquatic bird with a hooked beak and webbed feet. Since it has a long, thin neck, the Chinese fashioned a ring that tightened a narrow passage. The cormorant could easily catch fish with its hooked beak, but if its ring was securely in place, it could not swallow its prey. Chinese fishermen trained their cormorants to carry their catch to them. As a reward, the ring was removed, and they were permitted to swallow a fish. "Several rafts made of bamboo," Cushing observed from his gig, "were on the fishing ground each containing one Chinaman, who had charge of a dozen or more cormorants." Cushing reported, "These were constantly sent into the water, and were diving with great success; each time bringing up struggling fish, which they carried at once to their master."[48]

There was an even more dramatic diversion at hand. An eclipse of the moon occurred, and the general assumption among the Chinese was that an evil dragon was attempting to obliterate the friendly pale ball that illuminated the dark sky of the night, "and there was an excitement," Cushing exclaimed, "that I never have seen equaled." "It is a custom, all over China in such a case," he interpreted, "to assist the persecuted Moon by beating gongs, shouting, firing cannon, rockets, and fire crackers, and making all din possible to frighten the dragon away." He explained further, "When you consider that there are a million or so of people jeering, averaging a gong apiece, and thousands of junks armed with cannon — you may faint to imagine the effect of the music." Cushing's final comment was that "a Chinaman seems to get crazy in beating a gong — he does it furiously — jumping and dancing about in the wildest excitement." This tale has a happy end, for after two hours of this cacophony, the sinister dragon "was, finally, forced to disgorge his prey and beat a retreat."[49]

The river saved Cushing from further clamorous performances of gongs. Receding waters prompted him to sail downstream to the Pagoda Anchorage of the Nin River. There, in sweltering heat of some 100 degrees Fahrenheit, Cushing received and read seven letters from his beloved Kate, who reassured him in letter after letter of her resolve to be steadily true to her vows of love and engagement. Cushing was sufficiently encouraged to break the rule of naval confidentiality by informing Kate that he had been ordered to sail the *Maumee* directly to Hong Kong by way of Amoy after leaving Formosa. Cushing would likely arrive in Hong Kong early in September, at which time Admiral Rowan intended to inspect the *Maumee* again to determine if she could be repaired to make the journey to San Francisco or whether she should be decommissioned and sold in Hong Kong. "If the ship is sold," Cushing advised Kate, "I shall start home in the October steamer." However, he warned, "If she is sent to San Francisco, she will have at least 40 days repair before starting, and, under sail it will be a two month passage, and could get her there by about sometime in January."[50]

"On the one hand," Cushing speculated, "I should like to be with you a month or two sooner, which is the first thing to be thought of, and, on the other I could carry home, free of duty, my large collection of curios and enjoy, also, the satisfaction of giving back into the hands of my government a ship entrusted to my charge."⁵¹

"Under the circumstances," Cushing claimed, "I do not see how I can fail to be with you in either Dec. Jan. or February next, but I wish you to continue to write — and not to be too certain about me — for something might happen." He then repeated his noted dislike for the climate of south China in the summer. "We have been roasting in the river, as patiently as possible, and are heartily glad that our stay here is coming to a close." He announced that "in three days I sail for Formosa, where I shall remain but four days, to enquire into the interests of Americans there — then sail for Amoy and Hong Kong. I feel as if it were my closing affair out here, and that I was homeward bound."⁵²

Emphatically, Cushing informed Kate, "No steamboats for me when I once get to San Francisco! The way that Cushing and all the trunks pertaining to him, will dash off to the railroad depot will astonish the City. I have not lived to the respectable age of twenty six without learning the difference between seven and twenty one days."

With a touch of mocking belligerence, he exclaimed, "You hard hearted young woman! What do you mean by advising me to go by Sea? Are you anxious to have me bringing home Panama fever or that I should be eaten up by cockroaches while I get nothing to eat myself? I have traveled on those Atlantic steamers before, and I assure you that I prefer to stick to Yankee soil, when I once more get on it."⁵³

Cushing also insisted that he had sent the white silk crepe from Japan not as material suitable for a wedding dress, but as cloth that could be turned into an evening gown. At any rate, Kate should not take it to Brocton, a small settlement that housed several spiritualists. Apparently she was anxious to employ the magic caressing of the white silk fabric for any sensitive evidence of treachery practiced by her lover in the mysterious Far East. Cushing, of course, denounced such suspicions, pointing out that he had long been the victim of salacious gossip. In this particular instance, he was convinced that Mrs. Higgins, the mother of his late secretary, had started a series of rumors about the continued dissipated conduct of Cushing, whose heroic naval career was tainted by scandalous behavior.

Small wonder that Cushing felt obliged to defend the honor of the officers of the Navy. He preached, "With us, woman is the superior; [sic] to whom we owe our devotion, protection, and tenderest care, even at the expense of life itself." "For they are the most persevering and unyielding lovers in the World," he claimed, "and once truly in love 'never give up the ship,'" rhapsodizing further, "They never 'lay an anchor to the windward' by marrying for money and not one in a thousand is influenced in that act to make a connection favorable to ambitious views." Cushing concluded his sermon by proclaiming that "Jack-tar and ladies' favors all go together."⁵⁴

On August 17 the *Maumee* anchored at a port named Tamsui, which is situated on the very northern tip of Formosa. It is close to Taipei, political capital of the modern government of the island. At this port the foreign enclave had settled. It was a small outpost comprised of some dozen foreign merchants who were engaged in purchasing tea and camphor. Cushing was quickly informed that the coastal waters of Formosa were infested with pirates. Having been foiled soon after reaching Hong Kong in a dramatic probe for pirates in the South China Sea whose lucrative excursions continued unchecked, Cushing readily seized an opportunity to crimp the style of the irrepressible buccaneers. He swiftly sailed to the nearby port of Keelung, which was on the eastern coast of Formosa. There he learned that his presence had already been reported to the pirates, who had fled down the southern coast of Formosa. In pursuit, he came to Soua Bay, which faced toward the coast of China. Alas, the pirates had slipped away to other hiding spots.[55]

Nevertheless, Cushing resolved to explore a nearby village on the margin of the heavily forested interior of the island. The Chinese community occupied coastal land next to the Pacific Ocean on the west and the South China Sea on the east. In their original invasion of Formosa, the Chinese had sought to subdue the indigenous population, whose ethnic roots identified them as belonging to a Polynesian background. They were a primitive people who were quickly defined as savages. Regardless of their cultural status, the savages repulsed the Chinese and held firm sway over the heavily timbered and mountainous interior of the island. They were on most occasions delighted to massacre hapless seamen thrown up on sandy beaches along with debris from the wreckage of their sunken ships.

In 1867 the U.S. Navy had dispatched an expeditionary force into the interior of Formosa, hoping to punish the particular tribe that had brutally slaughtered a number of shipwrecked American sailors. Sadly, this foray was a fiasco. Not only did the savages resist sturdily, but the stifling heat of the rainforest also substantially increased the casualties of the sailors and their officers.

Happily, Cushing's experience was far more pleasant. He encountered the chief of the local village, to whom he presented a musket. The delighted chief sought to reciprocate by presenting one of his daughters as a worthy bride. On learning that a significant part of the ceremony consisted of a ritual in which the groom's facial hair was pulled out, Cushing declined to proceed.[56]

Cushing reinforced his commentary on the unruly tribal chiefs in the mountains of Formosa with an anecdote regarding the adventure of an American consul at Amoy, "who once came over here to form a treaty with the Southern tribes, to induce them to protect foreign seamen who might be wrecked upon the coast. In order to make a show of force he took with him five hundred Chinese soldiers. He secured an interview with the Chief, some miles from the native towns; and stated his object. The old savage looked at the soldiers and said, 'You are a man and a Warrior. I respect the Americans as brave men, but who are these? The Chinamen are dogs, and no Chief or man can degrade himself by treating with them. Let them come on, and we will destroy them all. If they desire to treat for peace I will send my women to treat with them.'"[57]

As Cushing's sojourn in the Far East came gradually to an end, he became increasingly restless with the formalities of naval routine and uncertain pace of communications. At the same time, he became anxious about the nature of his reunion with Kate. He wanted desperately not to greet her at some formal occasion, even at her residence: "I couldn't bear, after this long and lonely absence to meet you with a hand shake and as Miss Forbes. But I'd rather meet you all alone in the parlor — and sit by you on our old seat, and not have one outside word or look to come between us."[58]

On August 28, 1869, the *Maumee* dropped her anchor in the harbor of Hong Kong. Cushing's cruise in Asian waters thus finished at the very port where it had commenced. The next day a restless Cushing sailed up to Canton, where he spent six pleasant days visiting the landmarks and shops from his inaugural introduction to the ancient culture and the society still devoted to its cultivation. He was fascinated by the Chinese and their reverence for their antiquity. When he paused briefly at Amoy, he had an occasion to remark, "How insignificant time seems in this old Empire!" He continued, "On every hand are the inscribed monuments of past centuries — going back and back until the birth of Christ is but an intermediate period."[59]

Fortunately, Cushing was able to reinforce his appreciation of the Chinese heritage through selecting additions to the collection of dinnerware that he had commissioned at Canton. Respecting several suggestions from Kate, he acquired six more soup bowls; two ornamental stands for fruits, flowers, or cake; a dozen tea cups; a butter dish; a sugar bowl; and a milk jug. Alas, he could not discover any sauce plates, but judged that the cheese plates he had ordered would serve the purpose. Cushing announced sadly that his Chinese potter would require three months to complete a similar set for Kate's mother; obviously, his imminent departure from China prevented such a commission. Cushing confessed, "The seven big cases of china ware frighten me every time I look at them, and think of the probable sixty per cent gold duties that I must pay upon them."[60]

Even at this early date, shortly after he had arrived in Hong Kong, he could tell Kate the happy news of the decision that the *Maumee* was to be sold: "There is no longer doubt about the sale of my ship — between this and November — and I can see no reason for the Chief to come down here unless sent to effect the transaction." Cushing employed the newly created title "Chief of the Fleet," which was held by the senior captain in a squadron. "It <u>must</u> be sold," he exclaimed, "for the *Maumee* is too rotten to repair, or to send to California."

He added several joyful shouts of "Hurrah!" Overwhelming longing for the welcoming caresses of Kate had erased the memory of his pride in his trim and sparkling gunboat as he had navigated her over strange waters toward exotic ports. However, the *Maumee*'s fate was no different from that of most other ships, both naval and commercial. Only very few survived as floating memories of splendid passenger liners or gallant defenders of their country.[61]

Meanwhile, Cushing submerged his anxiety over the time of his departure by enjoying the agreeable society of Hong Kong. "I am in very pleasant society," he wrote, "and dine ashore as often as I choose at the best houses." He presented a list of his hosts: "The Austrian Consul General called lately with a letter of introduction from my dear old relative Admiral Smith. I find him one of the most pleasant acquaintances that I have met in the East — and his wife is truly charming. I dine there to morrow [*sic*] evening at 8 o'clock — and the next day at the British Governor's. The next day I dine with the English Commodore." Nevertheless, he warned Kate, "You must not think that I forget my grudge against England because I accept such attention," going on to say, "It is my duty to exchange courtesies with high officials, but I still tell them frankly — and I am well known in the Orient as an uncompromising foe to British policy and British pirates." He completed his diatribe with a charge that the *Alabama* claims made John Bull wince, "and I delight in applying the caustic as often as possible."[62]

Although Cushing had exhibited considerable agility in diplomatic and military interaction with a wide range of public officials in the Far East, he allowed his wartime experience to override a natural flair for diplomacy. The Civil War was over. Alas, the bloody and bitter conflict continued to create divisive sores in domestic and international society.

As for his prolonged courtship of Kate, Cushing convinced himself that "Kate does love me now," and he hoped ardently that he would witness "the real love which you so long denied me (and of which my diaries are full). I don't think that we were truly united in dear fortunate old 'sixty seven.' Fortunate I say — not because we were not truly united; but because you gave the right to me then to try to win you. Have I done it? God grant it true!"[63]

Cushing not only had to withstand his own mood of impatient frustration, but he also had to reassure Kate that her second thoughts over her alliance with a man who now was essentially a stranger, and who, on close inspection, might expose a personality that did not match her dreams, lacked a sure foundation. He promised that he would learn to skate and, of course, would take her on sleigh rides, where they could cuddle under the warmth of a Buffalo lap robe.[64]

On September 13, 1869, Cushing informed Kate that Captain Law had arrived on his ship, the *Iroquois*, with an order to form an inspection board to determine the current condition of the *Maumee*. The squadron commander,

Captain Roe, who was to chair the board, was expected to arrive shortly from Shanghai. In a high state of anxiety, Cushing hoped that Admiral Rowan's suggestion that the *Maumee* might be repaired for river duty would be blocked, but he had plotted an escape route. Another captain, Hooker, a member of the inspection board, had his ship condemned recently, but he, unlike Cushing, sought to remain in the Far East. In that event, Hooker might replace Cushing as the skipper of the repaired *Maumee*.[65]

Four days later a jubilant Cushing told Kate, "My ship was surveyed yesterday and entirely condemned," adding the news that "Captain Roe said she is the most dangerous rotten ship he has ever seen in commission." If the *Maumee* remained in Hong Kong as a stationary ship, Hooker would probably be assigned to her. With his good humor restored, Cushing sent Kate a photograph of himself, in which he displays a truculent image. He explained that this severe portrait was the product of a tedious sojourn in the photographer's studio, during which a distressed mother attempted to restore a restless and sobbing child to a contented state and happy face. Finally, he announced that he had been invited to a gala welcoming ceremony for His Royal Highness, the Duke of Edinburgh. Hopefully, he had the common sense not to challenge a son of Queen Victoria on the *Alabama* incident.[66]

While Cushing waited, he hoped in vain that a steamer from Yokohama would bring a letter from Admiral Rowan stating that Cushing was detached from the *Maumee*, and ordering his return to the United States. Unfortunately, Rowan had been distracted from this simple task by a series of horrendous typhoons in the Pacific that had severely damaged his squadron. Four of his best ships had been disabled. "The *Idaho*," Cushing announced, "has experienced the worst fortune of all; for she was struck by a severe typhoon early last month and forced to make extensive repairs — and now the news is that she was caught by another, the other day, on her way here — which left her completely disabled — and the flagship has gone out to search for her."[67] Eventually, the flagship found the *Idaho*, which was towed into Yokohama. She was in such battered condition that any plan to have her again repaired for a trip to San Francisco was abandoned. She was decommissioned and sold in Japan.[68]

It would appear that during the immediate period after the Civil War, the Asiatic Squadron had neither sound ships nor a comprehensive naval policy in the Far East. Certainly its ships, survivors of coastal and riverine operations, were not of the appropriate design for navigating the considerable distances involved in ocean operations. Moreover, many of these ships inherited from the Civil War had been constructed of unseasoned timber. In operational policy, cruising here and there in an aimless and incoherent fashion rather than as part of a long-term strategic plan to advance the genuine interests of the American republic in the crumbling empire of China and a suddenly rejuvenated empire of Japan (which was resolved to master Western industrial and military technology in order to compete with Western nations on their own terms) was not in the political and military lexicon of the national political establishment. Americans remained transfixed by the searing tragedy of the Civil War, which had nearly destroyed the Union. However, the exhilaration of *Manifest Destiny* in the vast region stretching from the Mississippi River to the Pacific Ocean provided natural and easily understood relief from a tragic and bloody past.

There were practical obstacles to launching a pragmatic and unified naval program in the Far East. The American squadron had to rely on sails to provide the requisite power to move its ships. If winds were dormant, then ships were becalmed, but if the winds became turbulent, stormy waves could smash ships into useless wreckage. Steam engines could provide a promising solution, but they lacked sufficient strength and durability for constant use, and also required access to a considerable quantity of coal. American ships had to rely on coaling stations managed by British and other foreign interests. Also, the American squadron did not even have a semblance of territorial sovereignty. On the one hand, this was a genuine asset, for Chinese and Japanese authorities could be reassured that the United States could be trusted as a true neutral. On the other hand, unlike imperial Britain, the United States had no string of island and mainland harbors to provide sure communication and shelter its ships. As a result, chasing pirates was an aquatic sport akin to the foxhunt of the English countryside. Even the Royal Navy, from its formidable perch at Hong Kong, had been stymied in repeated attempts to bring law and order to the waters of the Far East.

As Cushing waited impatiently for an official response from Admiral Rowan, he had plenty of time to contemplate life with Kate. Although he continued to declare his undying affection for her, he began to concentrate on her ups and downs, realizing that she too entertained doubts about the future. "I am much troubled," Cushing wrote, "at what you write me of the sad decline of the many young ladies whom I remember so fresh and blooming but two years since." He reassured Kate, "You do, indeed, seem a wonderful exception amongst them." "Oh, how earnestly I pray," he cried, "May God keep my precious one — and spare her such a fate." He recalled, "When you wrote in the last of these letters you too were suffering from a severe cold, I trust that you soon recovered but I shall be in distress of mind until I am certain of it." Cushing vowed that "I wish from my very Soul, that in taking you for my Wife, I might take upon myself every sickness and sorrow of your life."[69]

"My darling! Take great care of yourself for my sake," Cushing exhorted Kate, "and I will soon be with you to take care of you. It frightens me to think that you may be ill, for I have no hope in life if I am not to share it with you." He assured Kate that he was in good health, "but I am thin in consequence of the intense heat to which I have been exposed all the Summer." Nevertheless, he was sure, "I shall readily attain to more than your standard of 150 pounds as soon as I get into a cool, bracing climate where I can exercise." He finished his commentary on a cocky note: "I fear that I can't please the good gossips of F— by appearing among them in a dying condition—but I hope that they may survive the disappointment."[70]

There was further evidence in this correspondence of the fragility of life in the nineteenth century. The medical knowledge of our era, at least in Western society, is far removed from the primitive conditions of Cushing's time. Apparently a family tragedy was narrowly averted, for Cushing informed Kate that "I learned of my nephew's illness by a letter from Mary as well as from you—and I am thankful that the youngster was saved." He swore furthermore, "I am going to see him a Middy before many years are over."[71]

In another direction, however, the sky was threatening, for Cushing hastened to assure Kate that "I sympathize with you earnestly and sincerely about your dear Mother's ill health." He sought to reassure mother and daughter by saying, "She shall not lose you dear, but we will unite in adding to her comfort and happiness." "She does not know me as well as you do; but I intend that she shall, and that she shall like me better for it."[72]

As Cushing's departure from the Far East meant he might be granted, for the first time in his career, a short respite from the routine of naval life, he became preoccupied with his forthcoming domestic obligations. He found himself counseling his fiancée on her wedding arrangements. Kate contemplated pushing the ceremony forward to spring, the legendary season of nuptial festivals. However, Cushing sought to dissuade her from pursuing such a gambit. "You say that you do not wish to be married in winter," he lamented, "while I have no dearer desire than to possess my self of my little Wife at the earliest possible moment." He argued moreover that "you know that winter is the gayest season of the year, the time for parties, operas, theaters, sleigh rides &— and why not enjoy all this together?" "<u>Please</u> do not keep me waiting when I get home," he beseeched his beloved, for "I have waited much too long already." "Are you afraid," he wondered, "that I cannot make you happy in winter as well as in summer?"[73]

Cushing's reaction to Kate's second thoughts betrays exasperation: "You say that I must remain your devoted love until the warm, bright weather comes again." Bitterly he snapped, "Then why might I not better remain out here than to be tantalized for months at home?" He then argued forthrightly, "The truth is, my darling, I am always to be your devoted lover, and you might as well surrender first as last."[74]

Cushing likewise had bouts of second thoughts. His, however, were prompted by the logistics of travel. Originally, he had emphatically rejected Kate's suggestion that the journey from the Pacific to the Atlantic could be more comfortably and safely accomplished by taking passage by water, including an overland trip across the narrow isthmus of Panama. But Cushing later reasoned, "I am not certain that I shall go by rail from San Francisco — for I may get caught in the snow amongst the mountains — and a ship is safer than a railroad, and don't want to get smashed up just now." His thoughts were not farfetched, for the popular lithographs of Currier and Ives that were published at the time documenting trains stalled by snowdrifts blocking the tracks were inspired by a well-known peril.[75]

Cushing was also preoccupied with the challenge of packing, familiar to many travelers returning to their native country. This particular chore becomes more tasking when the homeward trip is the climax of a long excursion or prolonged visit to foreign climes. Cushing informed Kate that he had sent a tremendous crate packed with "ornamental furniture — such as vases, cabinets &" on a merchant ship that was sailing to Boston. He made it clear to her that he intended to meet the ship when it arrived in Boston, and that he had to make similar arrangements for two more boxes of similar size.[76]

He was also involved in the complexity of satisfying feminine taste in dress material at a reasonable cost. The principal instigator at the moment of this issue was the ubiquitous Miss Starr, Kate's piano teacher, who was attempting to negotiate at a distance for material. An exasperated Cushing laid down the facts to Kate. "You cannot get a decent dress in Japan," he argued, "for less than thirty Mexican dollars — and if duty was paid, and the sale total converted into currency, said dress would cost in Fredonia 75 dollars." He explained further, "The Japan silks are, however, heavier and more expensive than those of China." "I can buy silks at all prices here from the gauze silk of 25 cents a yard to the light summer silk of seven dollars the dress, and the mandarin silk like I sent you at 18 Mexican dollars for fifteen yards." He also informed Kate that he had found several dresses in those colors that she had requested.[77]

Eleven days later he was able to tell Kate that although Admiral Rowan had been unable to send him information directly (having been compelled to focus his whole attention on the rescue mission for the *Idaho*), he had advised the fleet captain that Cushing was to be permitted to return to the United States. While he waited for definitive instructions, Cushing explored various coves and islands belonging to the colony of Hong Kong. He even explored that exotic remnant of the once impressive citadel of the Portuguese trading enterprise in the Far East — Macao.

He found Macao fascinating, even though the women were uniformly the most unattractive that he had yet inspected. The Roman Catholic Church held an impressive sway over the population. The clergy of that faith were "thick as blackberries," and they wore large "broad shovel" hats. Every day celebrated some particular festival with spectacular processions. While he was unable to overlook the fact that the inhabitants of this historic colony had a long-standing reputation of cooperating with Chinese pirates, Cushing did not neglect to pay homage to the tomb of the famous Jesuit missionary, St. Francis Xavier.[78]

A far more pleasant pastime, Cushing discovered, was to extend the scope of his daily walks in the mountains and on the islands surrounding Hong Kong. He explained, "The weather this month [November], is charming — being cool and bright with beautiful moonlit nights, and I intend to pick up much of my former health and vigor that the past summer has borrowed from me." He revealed, "Sometimes I clamber up the mountains — and then the view is my attraction." "Hundreds of islands meet the eye in all directions — from green sun-gilt ones close at hand to the far-away peaks, made blue and mirage-like by distance — while between and around, far as the eye can reach — the bright blue water lakes — a mirror to the mountains." To complete his lyrical tableau, Cushing added this spectacle: "Thousands of junks float idly on its bosom, their gay red pennants just moved by the coquettish air, their huge mast-sails flapping lazily as some huge fine fish; and the big eyes, painted on their bows, staring sleepily at each other." "It is, indeed, one of those scenes that might be a boys dream of the Orient ripened into a glorious reality — a sort of Aladdin's for the imagination, bright with real jewels."[79]

The major event in Hong Kong at this time was the arrival of Prince Alfred, the Duke of Edinburgh, the second son of Queen Victoria, who was the captain of the HMS *Galatea*. This ship was a screw propeller wooden vessel, with powerful boilers that could move her quickly, and carrying cannon capable of destroying the average frigate or gunboat. When the *Galatea* steamed into the harbor, Prince Alfred was welcomed to Hong Kong by an admiral. In response, he fired a seventeen-gun salute, but he received only a seven-gun

HMS *Galatea*, the Duke of Edinburgh's frigate in Hong Kong harbor in 1869. The purpose of this first royal visit was to open the new city hall. By kind permission of FormAsia.

salute, the same as that granted to Cushing and all other commanding officers. However, after an interlude of two days, the Royal Standard was hoisted on the *Galatea*. "Then what a change!" Cushing exclaimed that "National salutes" were discharged, crews stood at attention on the rigging of their ships, "all the masts in the harbor [were] brilliant with flags" and, of course, "Admirals, Generals, and Governors [stood] in attendance."[80]

At a cost of $50,000, a typical Chinese greeting was staged, composed of gyrating dragons and rumbling sea monsters, along with rockets, firecrackers, and cheering throngs. "The morning after all this idol worship," Cushing reported, "what does this fortunate and jolly young Briton do? He formed a boat crew of his Officers, himself being 'stroke oar,' and pulled the old Admiral Keppel, late commanding the English squadron, down to the mail steamer in which he was to take passage home." Cushing marveled, "Think of Victoria's second son actually performing the duty of a common seaman to honor an old Admiral who is only a Knight."[81]

Despite his reluctance to participate in the innumerable social occasions that commemorated the royal visit to Hong Kong, Cushing resolved to make peace with the defenders of the Empire. He asserted cheerfully, "Admiral Keppel is a jolly old dog—and very popular in the East." Cushing admitted that "I attended a great dinner given to him just before he left, by all the foreign community, where we sat down five hundred strong." "I am happy to state," Cushing declared, "that I got off the pun of the evening. It was only intended for my immediate neighbors at the table, but was circulated through the entire room, and tickled the good old Admiral mightily. Just before we broke up the Chairman read it, standing. Why is Admiral Keppel like one of England's greatest enemies? Answer: 'Because he's *Von Tromp*.'" Evidently, Cushing had suggested that Keppel was a turnip in fractured Dutch pronunciation of English.[82]

Cushing had thus made amends for his inexcusable breach of etiquette in neglecting to personally greet Keppel after dropping anchor on his initial arrival at Hong Kong. Cushing was also pleased to relate that Prince Alfred "is a fine, manly, jolly looking young fellow of about 25—carried himself very well." However, Cushing noted that "the Prince cares much more for cricket and ten pins than for all this extensive festivity." Indeed, Cushing observed that "he only danced twice, and then cut off to a private room to drink brandy and water and smoke until supper—then he appeared for a moment and was off again, much to the chagrin of the 'toadies' who long to feast their eyes on a live cub of the British Lion." Yet the curious public had another chance to gaze upon His Royal Highness when he conducted the orchestra in which he played a violin for an amateur theatrical presentation by the officers of the *Galatea* at the City Hall.[83]

Changing the subject of his letter, Cushing announced that he had located

9. A Lingering Farewell to the Far East

Cushing in ceremonial dress with sword.

some gold silk cloth at Canton and had ordered twenty yards. The cloth was approximately one yard wide. "I hope," he argued, "that will be that—but I shall not let you have it until after we are married," for it might, he urged, "aid me in coaxing you into some concessions regarding hurried proceeding when I get home." He revealed, furthermore, that he had twelve selections of silk goods. Among mandarin silks, he had yellow, black, and lavender. The only checked material he was able to discover were summer silks. He purchased both a white check and a blue and white. Unfortunately, he was unable to find a yellow and brown pattern.[84]

Although the greater part of this last letter to Kate from the Far East was dated November 13, the last page had a hasty addition that is dated November 18, at which time Cushing was still waiting for Admiral Rowan's order that would end his duty in the Far East. It obviously came shortly thereafter, informing Cushing that he had been detached from the command of the *Maumee* and should proceed to San Francisco. The letter was sent from Nagasaki and dated November 12, 1869. On January 19, the Navy Department at Washington acknowledged that Cushing had informed the department that he had arrived in San Francisco on January 13. Cushing had been granted a three-month leave of absence commencing from his arrival in Fredonia. The letter was sent to Fredonia.[85]

Cushing on his wedding day.

Kate Cushing just after her wedding day.
Courtesy Barker Library, Fredonia.

Kate in her Japanese crepe wedding dress with point lace and veil adorned with orange blossoms, February 22, 1870. By kind permission of Barker Library, Fredonia.

The *Wyoming* on its final trip at the end of Cushing's service.

The first sea-going torpedo boat in the U.S. Navy—named the *Cushing*.

When Cushing was leaving the *Maumee*, the crew had requested permission to shout farewell salutes, but Cushing had declined the tribute, claiming that such a courtesy was not permitted by Navy regulations. The crew, however, was resolved not to allow him to depart without a heartfelt display of their affection for him. After Cushing had walked down the line of men and officers on the deck, where he had quietly said goodbye to each man, he then went on the gangway. As he started to descend, "the sweet low strains of 'Home sweet home' struck his ear as, as he turned quickly; the entire crew stood there on the deck, bare headed and as near the gangway as they dared to come, the musicians (his favorite minstrel troupe) had concealed themselves behind the funnel, guns & on the opposite of the deck; there was not a sound except the low strains of music from the invisible minstrels. This farewell performance was too much for Cushing, he descended quickly to his boat and shoved off, crying like a child."[86]

The *Maumee* finished her service with the Asiatic Squadron on a sad note. After receiving $20,000 in repairs, she was sold for $70,000 to haul cargo on the coast and rivers of China.[87] However, the ending of this narrative is much more cheerful.

At six o'clock on February 22, 1870, Katherine Forbes, wearing a heavy white silk crepe gown, rustled

Top: William Barker Cushing from an engraving from "Naval Commands." *Bottom:* Widow Katherine Louise Forbes Cushing.

in a stately pace down an aisle that was flanked by a packed congregation to the altar of Trinity Episcopal Church. There the Reverend Mr. Arey heard the wedding vows of Miss Forbes and Lt. Commander William Barker Cushing. After an impressive reception given by the bride's father at the family residence, Cushing and his bride left on a train traveling to the East from the station at nearby Dunkirk. Cushing had proved to be an able naval commander and capable representative of the United States, and he had won his prize.[88]

Cushing family memorial at Forest Hill Cemetery, Fredonia. Courtesy Boltz Photo.

Notes

Introduction

1. Marie L. Cushing to Colonel Heimstreet, *History of Mary Barker Cushing*, Cushing Papers, May 13, 1928.
2. Marie L. Cushing to Colonel Heimstreet, *History of Mary Barker Cushing*, Cushing Papers, May 13, 1928.
3. Marie L. Cushing to Colonel Heimstreet, *History of Mary Barker Cushing*, Cushing Papers, May 13, 1928.
4. Marie L. Cushing to Colonel Heimstreet, *History of Mary Barker Cushing*, Cushing Papers, May 13, 1928.
5. Andrew W. Young, *History of Chautauqua County, New York: From its First Settlement to the Present Time* (Buffalo, NY: Printing House of Matthew & Warren, 1875), 482–84.
6. Theodore Roosevelt to Kate Cushing, May 11, 1897. Roosevelt was acting secretary of the Navy at this time. The actual secretary, John D. Long, had left Washington for a lengthy summer vacation. As a result, Roosevelt exercised unchecked sovereignty over naval issues. See Edmund Morris, *The Rise of Theodore Roosevelt* (New York: Modern Library, 1979), 590–667; Gideon Welles to Capt. Dorr, Hartford, July 17, 1876.
7. Albert Barker to Catherine or Louise (?) Cushing, USS *Oregon*, Manila, April 9, 1899.
8. Mark Russell Shulman's *Navalism and the Emergence of American Sea Power, 1882–1893* (Annapolis, MD: Naval Institute Press, 1995) includes a remarkable description of Mahan's distaste for active sea duty (76–84).
9. The interaction between Roosevelt and Mahan is described by Edmund Morris in *The Rise of Theodore Roosevelt*, 599–602.
10. Kate Cushing to H. H. Huntington, Fredonia, Aug. 19, 1882.
11. Kate Cushing to David Parker, Fredonia, May 31, 1883.
12. Kate to David Parker, Fredonia, May 31, 1883. Apparently, H. H. Huntington was distracted by his literary projects, and Kate turned to Parker, who was now the superintendent for the eastern division of the New England Telephone and Telegraph Company. Parker intended to assign the actual composition of the book to a New York writer named Townsend.

Chapter 1

1. There are several authoritative accounts of the U.S. Navy and its ships in the latter part of the nineteenth century. The monitors are given considerable attention because they represented far-reaching innovation in design and engineering, while steamers and ships belonged to the imposing heritage of sailing masts, spars and sails. The most balanced commentary on the post–Civil War Navy is found in Robert Gardiner, ed., *Conway's All the World's Fighting Ships, 1860–1905* (London: Conway Maritime Press, 1979), N. J. M. Campbell, "USA The Old Navy, 1860–1882," 114–15.
2. Cushing to Mary Barker Cushing, Aspinwall House, Panama, New Grenada, July 30, 1865, William B. Cushing Papers, Chautauqua County Historical Society and McClurg Museum, Westfield, New York. Subsequent references to the Cushing Papers will be identified by the nature of the document and its date.
3. Cushing to Mary Barker Cushing, USS *Lancaster*, Sandwich Islands, Dec. 4, 1865; Cushing to Mary Barker Cushing, Honolulu,

207

Sandwich Islands, Dec. 10, 1865 (henceforth, Mary Barker Cushing will be identified by the abbreviation MBC).
4. Cushing to MBC, Honolulu, Sandwich Islands, Dec. 10, 1865.
5. Cushing to MBC, San Francisco, April 17, 1866.
6. Cushing to MBC, San Francisco, April 17, 1866.
7. Cushing to MBC, San Francisco, April 17, 1866.
8. Cushing to MBC, San Francisco, April 17, 1866.
9. Cushing to MBC, San Francisco, April 17, 1866.
10. Cushing to Mary Edwards, Boston, June 25, 1861; Eliza Mary Hatch Edwards, *Commander William Barker Cushing of the United States Navy* (London and New York: F. Tennyson Neely, 1898), 91.
11. Cushing to MBC, Boston, April 8, 1863.
12. Edwards, *Commander William Barker Cushing*, 127–28.
13. Edwards, *Commander William Barker Cushing*, 128.
14. Cushing to MBC, USS *Maumee*, April 18, 1863.

Chapter 2

1. Gardiner, *Conway's All the World's Fighting Ships*, 128.
2. Cushing to Kate, Mansion House, Brooklyn, New York, July 21, 1867.
3. Cushing to Kate, Ebbitt House, Washington, DC, July 21, 1867.
4. Gideon Welles, Secretary of the Navy, to Cushing, Navy Department, Washington, DC, July 25, 1867.
5. Cushing to Kate, Astor House, New York, July 31, 1867.
6. Cushing to Kate, Astor House, New York, August 21, 1867.
7. Cushing to Kate, USS *Penobscot* at sea, Sept. 5, 1867.
8. Cushing to Kate, USS *Penobscot* at sea, Sept. 5, 1867.
9. Cushing to Kate, USS *Penobscot* at sea, Sept. 5, 1867.
10. Cushing to Kate, USS *Penobscot* at sea, Sept. 5, 1867.
11. Cushing to Kate, USS *Penobscot* at sea, Sept. 5, 1867.
12. Cushing to Kate, USS *Penobscot* at sea, Sept. 8, 1867.
13. Cushing to Kate, USS *Penobscot* at sea, Sept. 8, 1867.
14. Cushing to Kate, USS *Penobscot* at sea, Sept. 8, 1867.
15. Cushing to Kate, USS *Penobscot* at sea, Sept. 8, 1867.
16. Cushing to Kate, USS *Penobscot* at sea, Sept. 8, 1867.
17. Cushing to Kate, USS *Penobscot* at sea, Sept. 8, 1867.
18. Cushing to Kate, USS *Penobscot* at sea, Sept. 8, 1867.
19. Cushing to Kate, USS *Penobscot* at sea, Sept. 11, 1867.
20. Cushing to Kate, USS *Penobscot*, Sept. 22, 1867, and Oct. 6, 1867.
21. Cushing to Kate, USS *Penobscot*, Sept. 22, 1867.
22. Cushing to Kate, USS *Penobscot*, Sept. 22, 1867.
23. Cushing to Kate, USS *Penobscot*, Sept. 22, 1867.
24. Gardiner, *Conway's All the World's Fighting Ships*.
25. Gardiner, *Conway's All the World's Fighting Ships*.
26. Cushing to Kate, USS *Maumee*, Washington Navy Yard, Oct. 9, 1867.
27. Cushing to Kate, USS *Maumee*, Washington Navy Yard, Oct. 9, 1867, and Oct. 12, 1867.
28. Cushing to Kate, USS *Maumee*, Washington Navy Yard, Oct. 11, 1867, and Oct. 15, 1867.
29. Cushing to Kate, USS *Maumee*, Washington Navy Yard, Oct. 16, 1867; S. P. Lee to Cushing, Washington, DC, June 18, 1867; and Admiral Josh Smith, Navy Department, Washington, DC, June 18, 1867.
30. Gideon Welles, Secretary of the Navy, to Cushing, Washington, DC, Oct. 16, 1867.
31. Cushing to Kate, USS *Maumee*, Washington Navy Yard, Oct. 16, 1867.
32. Cushing to Kate, USS *Maumee*, Washington Navy Yard, Oct. 16, 1867.
33. Cushing to Kate, USS *Maumee*, Washington Navy Yard, Oct. 16, 1867.
34. Cushing to Kate, USS *Maumee*, Washington Navy Yard, Oct. 16, 1867.
35. Cushing to Kate, USS *Maumee*, Washington Navy Yard, Oct. 16, 1867.
36. Cushing to Kate, USS *Maumee*, Washington Navy Yard, Oct. 19, 1867.
37. Cushing to Kate, USS *Maumee*, Washington Navy Yard, Oct. 23, 1867.
38. Cushing to Kate, USS *Maumee*, Washington Navy Yard, Oct. 27, 1867, and Oct. 29, 1867.
39. Cushing to Kate, USS *Maumee*, Norfolk, Nov. 3, 1867.

40. Cushing to Kate, USS *Maumee*, Norfolk, Nov. 3, 1867.
41. Cushing to Kate, USS *Maumee*, Norfolk, Nov. 4, 1867; Cushing, *Diary*, Nov. 4, 1867.
42. Cushing to Kate, USS *Maumee*, Norfolk, Nov. 7, 1867.
43. Cushing to Kate, USS *Maumee*, Norfolk, Nov. 7, 1867.
44. Cushing to Kate, USS *Maumee*, Fort Monroe, Nov. 8, 1867.

Chapter 3

1. Cushing, *Diary*, Nov. 10, 1867.
2. Cushing, *Diary*, Nov. 12, 1867.
3. Cushing, *Diary*, Nov. 12, 1867.
4. Cushing, *Diary*, Nov. 15, 1867, and Nov. 19, 1867.
5. Cushing, *Diary*, Nov. 28, 1867, and Dec. 8, 1867.
6. Cushing, *Diary*, Dec. 11, 1867.
7. Cushing, *Diary*, Dec. 21, 1867.
8. Cushing, *Diary*, Dec. 27, 1867.
9. Cushing, *Diary*, Dec. 28, 1867.
10. Cushing, *Diary*, Dec. 29, 1867.
11. Cushing, *Diary*, Dec. 30, 1867.
12. Cushing, *Diary*, Dec. 30, 1867.
13. Cushing to Kate, Rio de Janeiro, Dec. 1867 (title page of letter is missing, and precise day is unknown).
14. Cushing to Kate, Rio de Janeiro, Dec. 1867.
15. Cushing to Kate, Rio de Janeiro, Dec. 1867.
16. Cushing, *Diary*, Dec. 30, 1867.
17. Cushing, *Diary*, Dec. 31, 1867, and Jan. 1, 1868.
18. Cushing, *Diary*, Jan. 3, 1868.
19. Cushing, *Diary*, Jan. 3, 1868.
20. Cushing, *Diary*, Jan. 3, 1868.
21. USS *Maumee*, Log Book, Jan. 5, 1868.
22. USS *Maumee*, Log Book, Jan. 6, 1868.
23. Cushing, *Diary*, Jan. 9, 1868.
24. Cushing, *Diary*, Jan. 9, 1868.
25. Cushing to Kate, USS *Maumee*, Jan. 2, 1868.
26. Cushing to Kate, USS *Maumee*, Jan. 2, 1868.
27. Cushing, *Diary*, Jan. 10, 1868.
28. Cushing, *Diary*, Jan. 11, 1868.
29. Cushing, *Diary*, Jan. 12, 1868.
30. Cushing, *Diary*, Jan. 21, 1868.
31. Cushing, *Diary*, Jan. 21, 1868.
32. Cushing, *Diary*, Jan. 30, 1868.
33. Cushing, *Diary*, Jan. 31, 1868.
34. Cushing, *Diary*, Feb. 1, 1868.
35. Cushing, *Diary*, Feb. 2, 1868.
36. Cushing, *Diary*, Feb. 9, 1868.
37. Cushing, *Diary*, Feb. 3, 4, and 6, 1868.
38. Cushing, *Diary*, Feb. 7, 1868.
39. Cushing, *Diary*, Feb. 9, 1868.
40. Cushing, *Diary*, Feb. 11, 1868.
41. Cushing, *Diary*, Feb. 15, 1868.
42. Cushing, *Diary*, Feb. 15, 1868.
43. Cushing, *Diary*, Feb. 15, 1868.
44. Cushing, *Diary*, Feb. 16, 1868.
45. Cushing, *Diary*, March 7, 1868.
46. Cushing, *Diary*, March 9, 1868.
47. Cushing, *Diary*, March 9, 1868.
48. Cushing, *Diary*, March 13, 1868.
49. Cushing, *Diary*, March 14, 1868.
50. Cushing, *Diary*, March 16, 1868.
51. Cushing, *Diary*, March 20, 1868.
52. Cushing, *Diary*, March 20, 1868.
53. Cushing, *Diary*, March 29, 1868.
54. Cushing, *Diary*, April 5, 1868.
55. Cushing, *Diary*, April 6, 1868.
56. Cushing, *Diary*, April 20, 1868. A printed clipping from a newspaper at Batavia is included with this diary entry.
57. Cushing, *Diary*, April 21, 1868.
58. Cushing, *Diary*, April 22, 1868.
59. Cushing, *Diary*, April 21, 1868.
60. Cushing, *Diary*, April 26, 1868.
61. Cushing, *Diary*, April 27, 1868.
62. Cushing, *Diary*, April 29, 1868.
63. Cushing to Kate, USS *Maumee*, China Sea, April 30, 1868.
64. Cushing to Kate, USS *Maumee*, China Sea, April 30, 1868.
65. Cushing to Kate, USS *Maumee*, China Sea, April 30, 1868.
66. Cushing to Kate, Hong Kong, China, May 1, 1868.
67. Cushing to Kate, Hong Kong, China, May 1, 1868.
68. Cushing to Kate, Hong Kong, China, May 1, 1868.
69. Cushing to Kate, Hong Kong, China, May 1, 1868.
70. Cushing to Kate, Hong Kong, China, May 1, 1868.

Chapter 4

1. Cushing to Kate, May 2, 1868.
2. Cushing to Kate, May 2, 1868.
3. Cushing to Kate, May 2, 1868.
4. Trea Wiltshire, *Old Hong Kong*, Vol. 1 (Hong Kong: Formasia Books, 1997), 9–47.
5. William Frederick Mayers, N. B. Dennys and Charles King, *The Treaty Ports of China and Japan: A Complete Guide to the Open Ports*

of Those Countries Together with Peking, Yedo, Hongkong and Macao, Forming a Guide Book and Vade Mecum for Travellers, Merchants, and Residents in General with 29 Maps and Plans (London: Trübner; Hong Kong: A. Shortrede, 1867), 9–23.

6. Cushing to Kate, May 2, 1868.
7. Cushing to Kate, May 2, 1868.
8. Cushing to Kate, May 2, 1868.
9. Cushing to Kate, May 2, 1868.
10. Cushing to Kate, May 2, 1868.
11. Cushing to Kate, May 2, 1868.
12. Cushing to Kate, May 2, 1868.
13. Cushing to Kate, May 5, 1868.
14. Cushing to Kate, May 5, 1868.
15. Cushing to Kate, May 5, 1868.
16. Cushing to Kate, May 5, 1868. Josh sticks (the modern spelling is "joss") are incense-burning sticks used in the worship of Chinese deities; they are used in Japan.
17. Cushing, *Diary*, May 5, 1868.
18. Cushing to Kate, May 5, 1868.
19. Cushing to Kate, May 5, 1868.
20. Cushing to Kate, May 5, 1868.
21. Cushing to Kate, May 5, 1868.
22. Cushing to Kate, May 5, 1868.
23. Cushing to Kate, May 5, 1868.
24. Cushing to Kate, May 5, 1868.
25. Cushing to Kate, May 5, 1868.
26. Cushing to Kate, May 5, 1868.
27. Cushing to Kate, May 14, 1868.
28. Cushing to Kate, May 14, 1868.
29. MBC to Cushing, Salem, March 7, 1868; Cushing to Kate, May 14, 1868.
30. MBC to Cushing, Salem, March 7, 1868.
31. Cushing to Kate, May 14, 1868.
32. J. R. Goddard to Cushing, Hong Kong, May 7, 1868.
33. Cushing to Kate, May 14, 1868.
34. Cushing to Kate, May 14, 1868.
35. Cushing to Kate, May 14, 1868.
36. Cushing to Kate, May 19, 1868; U.S. Department of the Navy, *Report of the Secretary of the Navy with an Appendix Containing Bureau Reports, Etc.* (Washington, DC: Government Printing Office, December 1868), xvii, xi–xiv, 5.
37. Frank Welsh, *A History of Hong Kong*, rev. ed. (London: HarperCollins, 1997), 12–13.
38. Welsh, *Hong Kong*, 32–38.
39. Welsh, *Hong Kong*, 6–10; Jonathan Spence, *Chinese Roundabout: Essays in History and Culture* (New York: W. W. Norton, 1992).
40. John King Fairbank, *Trade and Diplomacy on the China Coast: The Opening of Treaty Ports, 1842–1834* (Cambridge, MA: Harvard University Press, 1969), 74.

41. Fairbank, *Trade and Diplomacy*, 155–60; and Welsh, *Hong Kong*, 101–39.
42. Jacques M. Downs, *The Golden Ghetto: The American Commercial Community at Canton and the Shaping of American China Policy, 1784–1844* (Bethlehem, PA: Lehigh University Press, 1997), 65.
43. Downs, *Golden Ghetto*, 67–71.
44. Downs, *Golden Ghetto*, 65.
45. Downs, *Golden Ghetto*, 106, 114–15.
46. Downs, *Golden Ghetto*, 109.
47. Downs, *Golden Ghetto*, 106, 114–15, 119–20, 126–28.
48. Downs, *Golden Ghetto*, 127.
49. Downs, *Golden Ghetto*, 136–40.
50. Downs, *Golden Ghetto*, 305–18.
51. Downs, *Golden Ghetto*, 150–62.
52. Keith Laidler, *The Last Empress: The She-Dragon of China* (Chichester, UK: John Wiley & Sons, 2003), 73–98.
53. John King Fairbank, *The United States and China* (Cambridge, MA: Harvard University Press, 1971), 141–46.
54. Fairbank, *The United States and China*, 134–37, 146–49; Welsh, *Hong Kong*, 218–21.
55. Mayers, Dennys, and King, *Treaty Ports of China and Japan*, 416–18; Olive Risley Seward, ed., *William H. Seward's Travels Around the World, 1873* (New York: D. Appleton, 1873), 227–40.
56. Cushing to Kate, May 14, 1868.
57. Cushing to Kate, May 14, 1868.
58. Cushing to Kate, May 5, 1868.
59. The following anecdotes were related by Commander Z. L. Tanner for Captain Dorr and copied by Kate Cushing, and can be found in the William B. Cushing Papers, Chautauqua County Historical Society and McClurg Museum, Westfield, New York (henceforth, this source will be referred to as "Anecdotes").
60. Tanner, "Anecdotes."
61. Tanner, "Anecdotes."
62. Tanner, "Anecdotes."
63. Cushing to Kate, May 19, 1868.
64. Cushing to Kate, May 5, 1868.
65. *Fredonia Censor*, July 29, 1868.
66. *Fredonia Censor*, Sept. 16, 1868.
67. Sir Algernon West, *Memoir of Sir Henry Keppel, G.C.B., Admiral of the Fleet* (London: Smith, Elder, 1905), 127, 129–51.
68. Cushing to Kate, May 19, 1868.
69. MBC to Cushing, March 5, 1868.
70. Cushing to Kate, May 19, 1868.
71. Cushing to Kate, May 19, 1868.
72. Cushing to Kate, May 19, 1868.
73. Cushing to Kate, May 19, 1868.
74. Cushing to Kate, May 20, 1868.
75. Cushing to Kate, May 22, 1868.

76. Cushing to Kate, May 22, 1868.
77. Cushing to Kate, May 22, 1868.
78. Cushing to Kate, May 28, 1868.
79. Cushing to Kate, May 28, 1868.
80. Cushing to Kate, May 31, 1868.
81. Cushing to Kate, May 31, 1868.
82. Cushing to Kate, May 31, 1868.
83. Cushing to Kate, May 31, 1868.
84. Cushing to Kate, May 31, 1868.
85. Stanley Lane-Poole, *The Life of Sir Harry Parkes: Sometime Her Majesty's Minister to China and Japan*, 2 vols. (London: Macmillan, 1894), Vol. 1, 264–89.
86. Lane-Poole, *Life of Sir Harry Parkes*, Vol. 1, 264–89.
87. Seward, *William H. Seward's Travels*, 253–55; Valery M. Garrett, *Heaven Is High, the Emperor Far Away: Merchants and Mandarins in Old Canton* (New York: Oxford University Press, 2002), 125–37.
88. Seward, *William H. Seward's Travels*, 255.
89. Cushing to Kate, May 31, 1868. A good review of the formative years of Oliphant & Co. is provided by Downs in *Golden Ghetto* (118–209). In 1870 Seward listed the number of American mercantile establishments in China as 9. The largest was Russell & Co., which had offices at Hong Kong, Canton, Shanghai, Foochow, Kin-King, HanKow and Tien Tin. It was followed by Augustine Heard & Company at Shanghai, Hong Kong, Canton, and Foochow; Oliphant & Co. and Bull, Pardon & Company had stations in the same cities. Then came Smith Archer & Company at Shanghai, Hong Kong and Canton. Two companies, Silas E. Burrows and E. J. Sage, were in Hong Kong; two others, H. Fogg and A. C. Farnham, were situated at Shanghai. (See Seward, *William H. Seward's Travels*, 276.)
90. Cushing to Kate, May 31, 1868.
91. Cushing to Kate, May 31, 1868.
92. Cushing to Kate, May 31, 1868.
93. Cushing to Kate, May 31, 1868.
94. Cushing to Kate, May 31, 1868.
95. Cushing to Kate, May 31, 1868.
96. Cushing to Kate, May 31, 1868.
97. Cushing to Kate, May 31, 1868.
98. Cushing to Kate, May 31, 1868.
99. Cushing to Kate, May 31, 1868.
100. Cushing to Kate, May 31, 1868.
101. Cushing to Kate, May 31, 1868.
102. Cushing to Kate, May 31, 1868.
103. Cushing to Kate, May 31, 1868.
104. Cushing to Kate, June 9, 1868.
105. Cushing to Kate, June 9, 1868.
106. Cushing to Kate, June 9, 1868.
107. Cushing to Kate, May 31, 1868.
108. Cushing to Kate, May 31, 1868.
109. William Guthrie, *A New Geographical, Historical, and Commercial Grammar and Present State of the Several Kingdoms of the World*, 13th ed. (London: Charles Dilley, G. Gad, and J. Robinson, 1790), 668.
110. Guthrie, *A New Geographical, Historical, and Commercial Grammar*, 668.
111. Cushing to Kate, June 8, 1868.
112. Cushing to Kate, June 8, 1868.
113. Cushing to Kate, June 8, 1868.
114. Admiral Rowan to Cushing, USS *Piscataqua*, June 6, 1868, William B. Cushing Papers, Chautauqua County Historical Society and McClurg Museum, Westfield, New York.
115. Admiral Rowan to Cushing, USS *Piscataqua*, June 6, 1868.
116. Ellis King to Cushing, Consulate of the United States of America, June 10, 1868, William B. Cushing Papers, Chautauqua County Historical Society and McClurg Museum, Westfield, New York.
117. Cushing to Kate, June 13, 1868.
118. Cushing to Kate, June 13, 1868.
119. Cushing to Kate, June 8, 1868.
120. Newspaper clipping, Hong Kong, June 18, 1868, William B. Cushing Papers, Chautauqua County Historical Society and McClurg Museum, Westfield, New York.
121. Newspaper clipping, Hong Kong, June 18, 1868.
122. Cushing, *Diary*, Dec. 21, 1867.
123. Newspaper clipping, Hong Kong, June 18, 1868; Cushing, *Diary*, Dec. 21, 1867. A copy of the program presented in the *Maumee* can be found in the William B. Cushing Papers: "Amateur Mandrills on Board the U.S. Maumee this Evening," June 10, 1868.
124. Cushing to Kate, June 11, 1868.
125. Cushing to Kate, June 13, 1868.
126. Cushing to Kate, June 10, 1868.

Chapter 5

1. Cushing to Kate, June 15, 1868.
2. Cushing to Kate, June 13, 1868.
3. U.S. Department of the Navy, *Report of the Secretary of the Navy with an Appendix Containing Bureau Reports, Etc.* (Washington, DC: Government Printing Office, December 1868), xlv.
4. Cushing to Kate, June 13, 1868.
5. Cushing to Kate, June 13, 1868.
6. Cushing to Kate, June 13, 1868.
7. Cushing to Kate, June 13, 1868.
8. Robert Malcomson, *Lords of the Lake:*

Notes — Chapter 6

The Naval War on Lake Ontario, 1812–1814 (Toronto: Robin Brass Studio, 1998), 325–26.

9. Gerald S. Graham, *The Politics of Naval Supremacy: Studies in British Maritime Ascendancy* (Cambridge: Cambridge University Press, 1965), 9–10, 14, 22–23.

10. Graham, *The Politics of Naval Supremacy*, 16–24, 52–53, 61–62, 102–12, 113–25.

11. U.S. Department of the Navy, *Report of the Secretary of the Navy with an Appendix Containing Bureau Reports, Etc.* (Washington, DC: Government Printing Office, December 1867), 5–6.

12. *Report of the Secretary of the Navy* (1867), 6.

13. Mayers, Dennys and King, *Treaty Ports of China and Japan*, 84; Andrew Lambert, *The Last Sailing Battlefleet: Maintaining Naval Mastery, 1815–1850* (London: Conway Maritime Press, 1991), 66; Richard Hill, *War at Sea in the Ironclad Age* (London: Cassell, 2000), 27–29.

14. U.S. Department of the Navy, *Annual Report of the Secretary of the Navy Showing the Operations of the Department for the Year 1869 with an Appendix* (Washington, DC: Government Printing Office, 1869), 11.

15. *Report of the Secretary of the Navy* (1869), 12.

16. *Report of the Secretary of the Navy* (1869), 5, 10–13.

17. Cushing to Kate, June 15, 1868.
18. Cushing to Kate, June 15, 1868.
19. Cushing to Kate, June 15, 1868.
20. Cushing to Kate, June 15, 1868.
21. Cushing to Kate, June 15, 1868.
22. Cushing to Kate, June 17, 1868.
23. Cushing to Kate, June 17, 1868.
24. Cushing to Kate, June 17, 1868.
25. Cushing to Kate, June 17, 1868.
26. Cushing to Kate, June 17, 1868.
27. Cushing to Kate, June 17, 1868.
28. Cushing to Kate, June 17, 1868.
29. Cushing to Kate, June 21, 1868.
30. Cushing to Kate, June 21, 1868.
31. Cushing to Kate, June 21, 1868.
32. Cushing to Kate, July 3, 1868.
33. Cushing to Kate, July 3, 1868.
34. Cushing to Kate, July 3, 1868.
35. Cushing to Kate, July (5–6?), 1868.
36. Cushing to Kate, July (5–6?), 1868.
37. Cushing to Kate, July (5–6?), 1868.
38. Cushing to Kate, July (5–6?), 1868.
39. Cushing to Kate, July (5–6?), 1868.
40. Cushing to Kate, July (5–6?), 1868.
41. Cushing to Kate, July (5–6?), 1868.
42. Donald Keene, *Emperor of Japan: Meiji and His World, 1852–1912* (New York: Columbia University Press, 2002), 15–21; Marius B. Jansen, *The Making of Modern Japan* (Cambridge, MA: Harvard University Press, 2002), 63–98.

43. Keene, *Emperor of Japan*, 25–36; Jansen, *Making of Modern Japan*, 255–93.

44. Keene, *Emperor of Japan*, 194–209.

45. Alfred Thayer Mahan, *From Sail to Steam: Recollections of Naval Life* (New York: Harper & Brothers, 1907), 243–54.

46. Cushing to Kate, July (5–6?), 1868.

47. *Report of the Secretary of the Navy* (1868), xi–xiii.

48. Mahan, *From Sail to Steam*, 254–65.

49. Keene, *Emperor of Japan*, 128–46, 188–97; Jansen, *Making of Modern Japan*, 394–32.

50. Cushing to Kate, August 8, 1868.
51. Keene, *Emperor of Japan*, 189; Jansen, *Making of Modern Japan*, 333–70.
52. Cushing to Kate, August 8, 1868.
53. Cushing to Kate, August 8, 1868.
54. Cushing to Kate, August 8, 1868.
55. Cushing to Kate, August 8, 1868.
56. Cushing to Kate, August 8, 1868.
57. MBC to Cushing, June 16, 1868.
58. MBC to Cushing, Fredonia, June 20, 1868.
59. MBC to Cushing, June 20, 1868.
60. MBC to Cushing, June 20, 1868.
61. MBC to Cushing, June 20, 1868.
62. MBC to Cushing, Aug. 3, 1868.
63. MBC to Cushing, Fredonia, Aug. 3, 1868; *Report of the Secretary of the Navy* (1868), xviii.
64. Edwards, *Commander William Barker Cushing*, 24–35.
65. Milton to Cushing, July 17, 1868.
66. Milton to Cushing, July 17, 1868.
67. Milton to Cushing, July 17, 1868.
68. Cushing to MBC, Aug. 8, 1868.
69. Cushing to MBC, Aug. 12, 1868.
70. Admiral Rowan to Cushing, USS *Piscataqua*, Aug. 7, 1868.
71. Cushing to Kate, Aug. 26, 1868.
72. Cushing to Kate, Aug. 26, 1868.

Chapter 6

1. Mayers, Dennys, and King, *Treaty Ports of China and Japan*, 465.

2. Cushing to Kate, Sept. 17, 1868.

3. Cushing to Kate, Sept. 17, 1868; Mayers, Dennys, and King, *Treaty Ports of China and Japan*, 467–68 (Taku).

4. Cushing to Kate, Sept. 17, 1868. Mayers, Dennys, and King, in *Treaty Ports of China*

Notes — Chapter 6   213

and Japan, 468–71 (Taku), provide an account of those carts that reinforces Cushing's agonizing analysis.
5. Cushing to Kate, Sept. 17, 1868.
6. Cushing to Kate, Sept. 17, 1868.
7. Cushing to Kate, Sept. 17, 1868. Mayers, Dennys, and King give "Ho-si-wu" as the name of a place that provided nourishment and accommodations. They further state that carts usually departed at 4:00 in the morning to reach Beijing before nightfall (*Treaty Ports of China and Japan*, 487 [Tientsing]).
8. Cushing to Kate, Sept. 17, 1868.
9. Cushing to Kate, Sept. 17, 1868.
10. Cushing to Kate, Sept. 17, 1868. In *Treaty Ports of China and Japan*, the authors provide a similar description of a room at a Chinese inn that catered to travelers (487 [Tientsing]).
11. Cushing to Kate, Sept. 17, 1868.
12. Cushing to Kate, Sept. 17, 1868.
13. Cushing to Kate, Sept. 17, 1868.
14. Cushing to Kate, Sept. 17, 1868.
15. Cushing to Kate, Sept. 17, 1868.
16. Cushing to Kate, Sept. 17, 1868.
17. Cushing to Kate, Sept. 17, 1868. Mayers, Dennys, and King, in *Treaty Ports of China and Japan*, 508–11 (Peking), provide an interesting account of the Forbidden City at this time, but their information should be studied with caution, because access to the imperial court was seldom granted. Courtiers and servants were reluctant to volunteer their knowledge of the physical characteristics of the buildings, and, of course, any open discussion of current events within the sacred compound was taboo. In Xu Chengbei's *Old Beijing: People, Houses and Lifestyles* (Beijing: Foreign Languages Press, 2001) there are several photographs of the "Coal Hill" that Cushing and his companions scaled.
18. Cushing to Kate, Sept. 17, 1868.
19. L. C. Arlington and William Lewisohn, *In Search of Old Peking* (New York: Paragon Book Reprint Corp., 1967), 25–45.
20. Arlington and Lewisohn, *In Search of Old Peking*, 25–45.
21. Arlington and Lewisohn, *In Search of Old Peking*, 129–68.
22. Cushing to Kate, Sept. 17, 1868; E. Z. Tanner, "Reminiscences of Wm. B. Cushing," March 8, 1899, Washington, DC. The following anecdotes were related by Commander Z. L. Tanner for Captain Dorr and copied by Kate Cushing, and can be found in the William B. Cushing Papers, Chautauqua County Historical Society and McClurg Museum, Westfield, New York.

23. Arlington and Lewisohn, *In Search of Old Peking*, 234–286.
24. Seward, *William H. Seward's Travels*, 211–20.
25. John Bell, *Travels from St. Petersburg in Russia to Diverse Parts of Asia* (London: John Murray, 1806), 268–355. A very informative description of the Forbidden City is provided in a recently published book by Chuimei Ho and Bennet Bronson, *Splendors of China's Forbidden City: The Glorious Reign of Emperor Qianlong* (London: Merrill, 2004), which was published in conjunction with an exhibition organized by the Field Museum in Chicago. The character of the imperial family and the private relations of the imperial court are discussed in chapters 5 and 6. Qianlong ruled from 1736 to 1796. It should be noted that in a plan of the Forbidden City on page 166, the areas to the right and left of the emperor's private audience hall were reserved for the wives of the emperor. The inner court on the left side, as one looks toward the northern gate, was occupied by the concubines and other dependents of the emperor. All three areas were off limits to anyone who was not affiliated with the imperial entourage. Another account of Qianlong can be found in Gianni Guadalupi's *China Through the Eyes of the West: From Marco Polo to the Last Emperor* (Vercelli, Italy: White Star, 2003–2004), 164–83. This elaborately illustrated book is distributed by Rizzoli International Publications in the United States and Canada; the English translation is prepared by A.B.A. Milan.
26. Cushing to Kate, Sept. 17, 1868.
27. Cushing to Kate, Sept. 17, 1868.
28. Cushing to Kate, Sept. 17, 1868.
29. Cushing to Kate, Sept. 17, 1868.
30. Cushing to Kate, Sept. 17, 1868.
31. Cushing to Kate, Sept. 17, 1868.
32. Cushing to Kate, Sept. 17, 1868.
33. Cushing to Kate, Sept. 17, 1868.
34. Cushing to Kate, Sept. 17, 1868.
35. Cushing to Kate, Sept. 17, 1868.
36. Cushing to Kate, Sept. 17, 1868.
37. Cushing to Kate, Sept. 17, 1868.
38. Cushing to Kate, Sept. 17, 1868.
39. Cushing to Kate, Sept. 17, 1868.
40. Cushing to Kate, Sept. 17, 1868.
41. Cushing to Kate, Sept. 17, 1868; Arlington and Lewisohn, *In Search of Old Peking*, 244–45.
42. Cushing to Kate, Sept. 17, 1868; Ho and Bronson, in *Splendors of China's Forbidden City*, include two revealing pictures of the Summer Palace — one before its destruction and the other afterward (36), whereas Guada-

lupi's *China Through the Eyes of the West* has an informative account of the decline of Manchu power during the regime of Dowager Empress Cixi, (321–33).
  43. Cushing to Kate, Sept. 17, 1868.
  44. Cushing to Kate, Sept. 17, 1868.
  45. Cushing to Kate, Sept. 17, 1868.
  46. Cushing to Kate, Sept. 17, 1868.
  47. Cushing to Kate, Sept. 17, 1868.
  48. Cushing to Kate, Sept. 17, 1868.
  49. Cushing to Kate, Sept. 17, 1868.
  50. Cushing to Kate, Sept. 17, 1868.
  51. Cushing to Kate, Sept. 17, 1868; Arlington and Lewisohn, *In Search of Old Peking*, 322–23.
  52. Cushing to Kate, Sept. 17, 1868.
  53. Cushing to Kate, Sept. 17, 1868.
  54. Cushing to Kate, Sept. 17, 1868.
  55. Cushing to Kate, Sept. 17, 1868.
  56. Cushing to Kate, Sept. 17, 1868.
  57. Cushing to Kate, Sept. 17, 1868.
  58. Cushing to Kate, Sept. 17, 1868.
  59. Cushing to Kate, Sept. 17, 1868.
  60. Kwang-Ching Liu, *Anglo-American Steamship Rivalry in China, 1862–1874* (Cambridge, MA: Harvard University Press, 1962), 35–111.
  61. Cushing to Kate, Sept. 17, 1868.
  62. Cushing to Kate, Sept. 17, 1868.
  63. Cushing to Kate, Sept. 17, 1868.

Chapter 7

  1. The French and Indian War had one of its origins in Chautauqua County when a young Virginian, George Washington, attempted to dislodge the French from a primitive stockade that had been constructed to protect a portage trail from Lake Erie across Chautauqua Lake on the escarpment above the Erie shoreline. The southern end of this lake spills its water into a small river that empties in the Allegheny by which the French could reach Fort Duquesne. However, the rapid spread of rail lines several decades later, symbolized by the transcontinental railroad, greatly diminished the importance of water communication.
  2. Cushing to Kate, Oct. 7, 1868.
  3. Cushing to Kate, Oct. 7, 1868.
  4. Cushing to Kate, Oct. 9, 1868.
  5. Cushing to Kate, Oct. 1, 1868.
  6. Cushing to Kate, Oct. 1, 1868.
  7. Cushing to Kate, Oct. 1, 1868.
  8. Cushing to Kate, Oct. 1, 1868.
  9. Cushing to Kate, Oct. 1, 1868.
  10. Cushing to Kate, Oct. 1, 1868.
  11. Cushing to Kate, Oct. 1, 1868.
  12. Cushing to Kate, Oct. 23, 1868.
  13. Cushing to Kate, Oct. 23, 1868.
  14. Cushing to Kate, Oct. 9, 1868.
  15. Cushing to Kate, Oct. 23, 1868.
  16. Cushing to Kate, Oct. 23, 1868.
  17. Cushing to Kate, Oct. 9, 1868.
  18. Cushing to Kate, Oct. 9, 1868.
  19. Cushing to Kate, Oct. 9, 1868.
  20. Cushing to Kate, Oct. 9, 1868.
  21. Cushing to Kate, July 5, 1868.
  22. Cushing to Kate, Aug. 8, 1868.
  23. Cushing to Kate, Aug. 8, 1868.
  24. Cushing to Kate, Aug. 8, 1868; Kevin C. Murphy, *The American Merchant Experience in Nineteenth Century Japan* (London: Routledge-Curzon, 2003).
  25. Cushing to Kate, Aug. 8, 1868.
  26. Cushing to Kate, Aug. 8, 1868.
  27. Cushing to Kate, Aug. 8, 1868.
  28. Cushing to Kate, Aug. 8, 1868.
  29. Cushing to Kate, Aug. 8, 1868.
  30. Cushing to Kate, Aug. 8, 1868.
  31. Cushing to Kate, Aug. 8, 1868.
  32. Cushing to Kate, Aug. 8, 1868.
  33. Cushing to Kate, Aug. 8, 1868. Murphy, in *American Merchant Experience*, uses the appellation "Battles" to define this category of servant.
  34. Cushing to Kate, Oct. 9, 1868.
  35. Cushing to Kate, Oct. 9, 1868.
  36. Murphy, *American Merchant Experience*, 79.
  37. Cushing to Kate, Oct. 9, 1868.
  38. Cushing to Kate, Oct. 23, 1868; Stella Dong, *Shanghai: The Rise and Fall of a Decadent City* (New York: HarperCollins, 2001), 18, 22–25; Liu, *Anglo-American Steamship Rivalry in China*, 192, chapters II and III; Gardiner, *Conway's All the World's Fighting Ships*, N. J. M. Campbell, "USA The Old Navy, 1860–1882," 114–15, 125, 129; and Donald L. Canney, *The Old Steam Navy: Frigates, Sloops, and Gunboats, 1815–1885* (Annapolis, MD: Naval Institute Press, 1990), Vol. 1, 129–32, 91–94, 103–8.
  39. John H. Schroeder, *Matthew Calbraith Perry: Antebellum Sailor and Diplomat* (Annapolis, MD: Naval Institute Press, 2001), 255–59.
  40. In 1883 the Navy Department introduced a construction program for iron-hulled ships that relied on steam as their normal method of propulsion. The wooden-hulled steamers that relied on sails to move across long stretches of water were abandoned. In 1859–1860 the British introduced the celebrated *Warrior*, an iron-hulled, steam-propelled ship

that made other capital ships obsolete. However, this revolutionary ship did carry two iron masts for sails. In 1908 the Great White Fleet championed by Theodore Roosevelt completed its world tour, which announced that the United States had become a leading world naval power.

41. Cushing to Kate, Oct. 25, 1868.
42. Cushing to Kate, Nov. 5, 1868.
43. Cushing to Kate, Nov. 5, 1868.
44. Cushing to Kate, Nov. 5, 1868.
45. Cushing to Kate, Nov. 13, 1868.
46. Cushing to Kate, Nov. 13, 1868.
47. Cushing to Kate, Nov. 13, 1868.
48. Cushing to Kate, Nov. 13, 1868.
49. Cushing to Kate, Nov. 13, 1868.
50. Cushing to Kate, Nov. 13, 1868.
51. Cushing to Kate, Nov. 13, 1868.
52. Cushing to Kate, Nov. 13, 1868.
53. Cushing to Kate, Dec. 1, 1868.
54. Cushing to Kate, Dec. 1, 1868.
55. Cushing to Kate, Dec. 1, 1868.
56. Cushing to Kate, Dec. 1, 1868.
57. Cushing to Kate, Dec. 1, 1868.
58. Cushing to Kate, Dec. 1, 1868.
59. Cushing to Kate, Dec. 1, 1868.
60. Cushing to Kate, Dec. 1, 1868; Stephen Turnbull, *Samurai: The World of the Warrior* (Oxford: Osprey, 2003), 167–208.
61. Cushing to Kate, Dec. 1, 1868.
62. Cushing to Kate, Dec. 2, 1868.
63. Cushing to Kate, Dec. 2, 1868.
64. Cushing to Kate, Dec. 2, 1868.
65. Cushing to Kate, Dec. 2, 1868.
66. Cushing to Kate, Dec. 2, 1868.
67. MBC to Cushing, Oct. 7, 1868.
68. Cushing to Kate, Dec. 2, 1868.
69. Cushing to Kate, Dec. 2, 1868.
70. Cushing to Kate, Dec. 2, 1868.
71. Cushing to Kate, Dec. 2, 1868.
72. Cushing to Kate, Fredonia, Dec. 2, 1868.
73. Cushing to Kate, Dec. 2, 1868.
74. Cushing to Kate, Dec. 2, 1868.
75. Cushing to Rowan, Dec. 2, 1868.
76. Cushing to Kate, Dec. 26, 1868.
77. Cushing to Kate, Dec. 26, 1868.
78. Cushing to Kate, Dec. 26, 1868.
79. Cushing to Kate, Dec. 26, 1868.

Chapter 8

1. Cushing to Kate, Jan. 6, 1869.
2. Cushing to Kate, Jan. 6, 1869.
3. Cushing to Kate, Jan. 6, 1869.
4. Cushing to Kate, Jan. 6, 1869.
5. Cushing to Kate, Jan. 6, 1869.
6. Cushing to Kate, Jan. 6, 1869.
7. Cushing to Kate, Jan. 6, 1869.
8. Cushing to Kate, Jan. 6, 1869.
9. Cushing to Kate, Jan. 14, 1869.
10. Cushing to Kate, Jan. 14, 1869.
11. Cushing to Kate, Jan. 14, 1869.
12. Cushing to Kate, Jan. 14, 1869.
13. Cushing to Kate, Jan. 14, 1869.
14. Cushing to Kate, Jan. 14, 1869.
15. Cushing to Kate, Jan. 14, 1869.
16. Cushing to Kate, Jan. 14, 1869.
17. Cushing to Kate, Jan. 14, 1869.
18. Cushing to Kate, Jan. 14, 1869.
19. Cushing to Kate, Jan. 23, 1869.
20. Cushing to Kate, Jan. 23, 1869.
21. Cushing to Kate, Jan. 23, 1869.
22. Cushing to Kate, Jan. 23, 1869.
23. Cushing to Kate, Jan. 23, 1869.
24. Cushing to Kate, Feb. 11, 1869.
25. Cushing to Kate, Feb. 11, 1869.
26. Cushing to Kate, Feb. 11, 1869.
27. Cushing to Kate, Feb. 11, 1869.
28. Cushing to Kate, Feb. 11, 1869.
29. Cushing to Kate, Feb. 11, 1869.
30. Cushing to Kate, Feb. 11, 1869.
31. Cushing to Kate, Feb. 11, 1869.
32. Cushing to Kate, Feb. 11, 1869.
33. Cushing to Kate, May 4, 1869.
34. Cushing to Kate, March 2, 1869.
35. Cushing to Kate, March 7, 1869.
36. Cushing to Kate, March 7, 1869.
37. Cushing to Kate, March 7, 1869.
38. Cushing to Kate, April 17, 1869.
39. Cushing to Kate, April 17, 1869.
40. Cushing to Kate, May 4, 1869.
41. Cushing to Kate, May 4, 1869.
42. Cushing to Kate, May 4, 1869.
43. Cushing to Kate, May 4, 1869.
44. Cushing to Kate, May 4, 1869.
45. Cushing to Kate, May 12, 1869.
46. Cushing to Kate, May 12, 1869.
47. Cushing to Kate, May 15, 1869.
48. Cushing to Kate, May 20, 1869.
49. Cushing to Kate, May 20, 1869.
50. Admiral Rowan, USS *Piscataqua*, to Lieutenant Commander W. B. Cushing, USS *Maumee*, Nagasaki, May 31, 1869.

Chapter 9

1. Cushing to Kate, June 21, 1869.
2. An excellent description of the meeting of the ocean and the Yangtze River is presented by Simon Winchester in *The River at the Center of the World: A Journey Up the Yangtze, and Back in Chinese Time* (London: Penguin Books, 1998), 3–61.

3. Cushing to Kate, June 21, 1869.
4. Cushing to Kate, June 21, 1869.
5. Robert Blake's *Jardine Matheson: Traders of the Far East* (London: Weidenfield and Nicolson, 1999) provides a review of the history of this remarkable mercantile company.
6. Stella Dong, in *Shanghai: The Rise and Fall of a Decadent City*, has written a fascinating account of the evolution of Shanghai; the first three chapters of her book focus on the time period that Cushing surveyed.
7. Kwang-Ching Liu, in *Anglo-American Steamship Rivalry in China*, narrates the sensational rise of Russell & Co. as a successful competitor to British mercantile interests in Shanghai.
8. Blake, *Jardine Matheson*, 4–7. Jonathan D. Spence's *The Search for Modern China* (New York: W. W. Norton, 1990), chapter 9, discusses the inadequate response of a Chinese bureaucracy dominated by Confucian thought.
9. Blake, *Jardine Matheson*, 120–37.
10. Kaoru Sugihara, in *Japan, China, and the Growth of the Asian International Economy, 1850–1949* (New York: Oxford University Press, 2005), offers a very detailed discussion of the textile industry in China and Japan (23–50).
11. The *Warrior* has now been restored, and is presently anchored at the Portsmouth Naval Base close to the HMS *Victory*.
12. Liu, *Anglo-American Steamship Rivalry*, 69–111.
13. Cushing to Kate, June 22, 1869.
14. Cushing to Kate, June 21, 1869.
15. Cushing to Kate, June 21, 1869.
16. Cushing to Kate, June 21, 1869.
17. Cushing to Kate, June 21, 1869.
18. Cushing to Kate, June 21, 1869.
19. Cushing to Kate, June 21, 1869.
20. Cushing to Kate, June 21, 1869.
21. Cushing to Kate, June 21, 1869.
22. Cushing to Kate, June 21, 1869.
23. Cushing to Kate, June 21, 1869.
24. Cushing to Kate, June 22, 1869.
25. Cushing to Kate, June 22, 1869.
26. Cushing to Kate, June 22, 1869.
27. Cushing to Kate, June 30, 1869.
28. Cushing to Kate, June 30, 1869.
29. Cushing to Kate, June 30, 1869.
30. Cushing to Kate, June 30, 1869.
31. Cushing to Kate, June 30, 1869.
32. Cushing to Kate, June 30, 1869.
33. Cushing to Kate, June 30, 1869.
34. Cushing to Kate, June 30, 1869.
35. Cushing to Kate, June 30, 1869.
36. Cushing to Kate, June 30, 1869.
37. Cushing to Kate, June 30, 1869.
38. Cushing to Kate, July 28, 1869.
39. Cushing to Kate, July 28, 1869.
40. Cushing to Kate, July 28, 1869.
41. Cushing to Kate, July 28, 1869.
42. Cushing to Kate, July 28, 1869.
43. Cushing to Kate, July 28, 1869.
44. Cushing to Kate, July 28, 1869.
45. Cushing to Kate, July 28, 1869.
46. Cushing to Kate, July 28, 1869.
47. Cushing to Kate, July 28, 1869.
48. Cushing to Kate, July 24, 1869, and July 28, 1869.
49. Cushing to Kate, July 24, 1869.
50. Cushing to Kate, Aug. 12, 1869.
51. Cushing to Kate, Aug. 12, 1869.
52. Cushing to Kate, Aug. 12, 1869.
53. Cushing to Kate, Aug. 12, 1869.
54. Cushing to Kate, Aug. 12, 1869.
55. Cushing to Kate, Aug. 17, 1869.
56. Cushing to Kate, Aug. 20, 1869.
57. Cushing to Kate, Aug. 20, 1869.
58. Cushing to Kate, Aug. 20, 1869.
59. Cushing to Kate, Aug. 28, 1869.
60. Cushing to Kate, Sept. 7, 1869.
61. Cushing to Kate, Sept. 7, 1869.
62. Cushing to Kate, Sept. 7, 1869.
63. Cushing to Kate, Sept. 7, 1869.
64. Cushing to Kate, Sept. 7, 1869.
65. Cushing to Kate, Sept. 13, 1869.
66. Cushing to Kate, Sept. 17, 1869.
67. Cushing to Kate, Sept. 17, 1869.
68. Cushing to Kate, Oct. 6, 1869.
69. Cushing to Kate, Oct. 6, 1869.
70. Cushing to Kate, Oct. 6, 1869.
71. Cushing to Kate, Oct. 6, 1869.
72. Cushing to Kate, Oct. 6, 1869.
73. Cushing to Kate, Oct. 6, 1869.
74. Cushing to Kate, Oct. 6, 1869.
75. Cushing to Kate, Oct. 6, 1869.
76. Cushing to Kate, Oct. 6, 1869.
77. Cushing to Kate, Oct. 6, 1869.
78. Cushing to Kate, Oct. 18, 1869.
79. Cushing to Kate, Nov. 13, 1869.
80. Cushing to Kate, Nov. 13, 1869.
81. Cushing to Kate, Nov. 13, 1869.
82. Cushing to Kate, Nov. 13, 1869.
83. Cushing to Kate, Nov. 13, 1869.
84. Cushing to Kate, Nov. 13, 1869.
85. Admiral Rowan, USS *Delaware*, to Lieutenant Commander W. B. Cushing, USS *Maumee*, Nagasaki, November 12, 1869; James Fleden, Chief of Bureau, to Cushing, Navy Department, Washington, DC, January 19, 1870.
86. Z. L. Tanner, *A Memoir for Capt. Dorr*, n.d.
87. Cousin Elliot to Cushing, Colorado, Korea, June 9, 1871.
88. *Fredonia Censor*, March 2, 1870.

Bibliography

Alden, John D., Commander, U.S. Navy (retired). *The American Steel Navy: A Photographic History of the U.S. Navy from the Introduction of the Steel Hull in 1883 to the Cruise of the Great White Fleet, 1907–1909*. Annapolis, MD: Naval Institute Press, 2008.

Arlington, L. C., and Lewisohn, William. *In Search of Old Peking*. New York: Paragon Book Reprint Corp., 1967.

Bell, John. *Travels from St. Petersburg in Russia to Diverse Parts of Asia*. London: John Murray, 1806.

Black, Jeremy. *The British Seaborne Empire*. Cambridge, MA: Harvard University Press, 2004.

Blake, Robert. *Jardine Matheson: Traders of the Far East*. London: Weidenfeld and Nicolson, 1999.

Canney, Donald L. *Lincoln's Navy: The Ships, Men, and Organization, 1861–1865*. Annapolis, MD: Naval Institute Press, 1998.

———. *The Old Steam Navy: Frigates, Sloops, and Gunboats, 1815–1885*. Annapolis, MD: Naval Institute Press, 1990.

Chengbei, Xu. *Old Beijing: People, Houses and Lifestyles*. Beijing: Foreign Languages Press, 2001.

Clowes, Sir William Laird. *The Royal Navy: A History from the Earliest Times to Present*. Volume 6. London: S. Low, Marston, 1897.

———. *The Royal Navy: A History from the Earliest Times to the Death of Queen Victoria*. Volume 7. London: S. Low, Marston, 1903.

Corbett, Sir Julian S. *Principles of Maritime Strategy*. Mineola, NY: Dover, 2004.

Dong, Stella. *Shanghai: The Rise and Fall of a Decadent City*. New York: HarperCollins, 2001.

Downs, Jacques M. *The Golden Ghetto: The American Commercial Community at Canton and the Shaping of American China Policy, 1784–1844*. Bethlehem, PA: Lehigh University Press, 1997.

Edwards, Eliza Mary Hatch. *Commander William Barker Cushing of the United States Navy*. London and New York: F. Tennyson Neely, 1898.

Fairbank, John King. *Trade and Diplomacy on the China Coast: The Opening of Treaty Ports, 1842–1834*. Cambridge, MA: Harvard University Press, 1969.

———. *The United States and China*. Cambridge, MA: Harvard University Press, 1971.

Feifer, George. *Breaking Open Japan: Commodore Perry, Lord Abe, and American Imperialism in 1853*. New York: HarperCollins, 2006.

Fredonia Censor (Fredonia, NY). July 29, 1868; September 16, 1868; March 2, 1870.

Fuller, Howard J. *Clad in Iron: The American Civil War and the Challenge of British Naval Power*. Annapolis, MD: Naval Institute Press, 2007.

Gardiner, Robert, ed. *Conway's All the World's Fighting Ships, 1860–1905*. London: Conway Maritime Press, 1979.

Garrett, Valery M. *Heaven Is High, the Emperor Far Away: Merchants and Mandarins in Old Canton*. New York: Oxford University Press, 2002.

Graham, Gerald S. *The Politics of Naval Supremacy: Studies in British Maritime Ascendancy.* Cambridge: Cambridge University Press, 1965.

Guadalupi, Gianni. *China Through the Eyes of the West: From Marco Polo to the Last Emperor.* Vercelli, Italy: White Star, 2003–2004.

Guthrie, William. *A New Geographical, Historical, and Commercial Grammar and Present State of the Several Kingdoms of the World.* 13th ed. London: Charles Dilley, G. Gad, and J. Robinson, 1790.

Hearn, Chester G. *Admiral David Dixon Porter: The Civil War Years.* Annapolis, MD: Naval Institute Press, 1996.

Hendrix, Henry J. *Theodore Roosevelt's Naval Diplomacy: The U.S. Navy and the Birth of the American Century.* Annapolis, MD: Naval Institute Press, 2009.

Hill, Richard. *War at Sea in the Ironclad Age.* London: Cassell, 2000.

Ho, Chuimei, and Bennet Bronson. *Splendors of China's Forbidden City: The Glorious Reign of Emperor Qianlong.* London: Merrill, 2004.

Jansen, Marius B. *The Making of Modern Japan.* Cambridge, MA: Harvard University Press, 2002.

Keay, John. *The Honourable Company: A History of the English East India Company.* London: HarperCollins, 1992.

Keene, Donald. *Emperor of Japan: Meiji and His World, 1852–1912.* New York: Columbia University Press, 2002.

Keene, Donald, Anne Nishimura Morse, Frederic A. Sharf, and Louise E. Virgin. *Japan at the Dawn of the Modern Age: Woodblock Prints from the Meiji Era, 1867–1912.* Boston: Museum of Fine Arts, 2001.

Kerr, Phyllis Forbes. *Letters from China: The Canton-Boston Correspondence of Robert Bennet Forbes, 1838–1840.* Mystic, CT: Mystic Seaport Museum, 1996.

Kunitake, Kume, Chushichi Tsuzuki, R. Jules Young, and Ian Nish. *Japan Rising: The Iwakura Embassy to the USA and Europe 1871–1873.* New York: Cambridge University Press, 2009.

Laidler, Keith. *The Last Empress: The She-Dragon of China.* Chichester, UK: John Wiley & Sons, 2003.

Lambert, Andrew. *The Last Sailing Battlefleet: Maintaining Naval Mastery, 1815–1850.* London: Conway Maritime Press, 1991.

Lane-Poole, Stanley. *The Life of Sir Harry Parkes: Sometime Her Majesty's Minister to China and Japan.* 2 vols. London: Macmillan, 1894.

Lavery, Brian. *Empire of the Seas: How the Navy Forged the Modern World.* Annapolis, MD: Naval Institute Press, 2010.

Liang, Wu. *Old Shanghai: A Lost Age.* Beijing: Foreign Languages Press, 2003.

Liu, Kwang-Ching. *Anglo-American Steamship Rivalry in China, 1862–1874.* Cambridge, MA: Harvard University Press, 1962.

Mahan, Alfred Thayer. *From Sail to Steam: Recollections of Naval Life.* New York: Harper & Brothers, 1907.

———. *The Influence of Sea Power Upon the French Revolution and Empire, 1793–1812.* 2 vols. Boston: Little, Brown, 1898.

———. *The Influence of Sea Power Upon History: 1660–1783.* London: S. Low, Marston, 1890.

Malcomson, Robert. *Lords of the Lake: The Naval War on Lake Ontario, 1812–1814.* Toronto: Robin Brass Studio, 1998.

Mayers, William Frederick, N. B. Dennys, and Charles King. *The Treaty Ports of China and Japan: A Complete Guide to the Open Ports of Those Countries Together with Peking, Yedo, Hongkong and Macao, Forming a Guide Book and Vade Mecum for Travellers, Merchants, and Residents in General with 29 Maps and Plans.* London: Trübner; Hong Kong: A. Shortrede, 1867.

Mehl, Hans. *Naval Guns: 500 Years of Ship and Coastal Artillery.* Annapolis, MD: Naval Institute Press, 2003.

Morison, Samuel Eliot. *The Rising Sun in the Pacific, 1931–April 1942.* Annapolis, MD: Naval Institute Press, 2010.

Morris, Edmund. *The Rise of Theodore Roosevelt.* New York: Modern Library, 1979.

Moxham, Roy. *Tea: Addiction, Exploitation, and Empire.* New York: Carroll & Graf, 2003.

Murphy, Kevin C. *The American Merchant Experience in Nineteenth Century Japan.* London: Routledge-Curzon, 2003.

Paine, S. C. M. *The Sino-Japanese War of*

1894–1895: Perceptions, Power and Primacy. New York: Cambridge University Press, 2003.

Phillipson, Nicolas. *Adam Smith: An Enlightened Life.* New Haven, CT: Yale University Press, 2010.

Schroeder, John H. *Matthew Calbraith Perry: Antebellum Sailor and Diplomat.* Annapolis, MD: Naval Institute Press, 2001.

———. *Shaping a Maritime Empire: The Commercial and Diplomatic Role of the American Navy, 1829–1861.* Westport, CT: Greenwood, 1985.

Seward, Olive Risley, ed. *William H. Seward's Travels Around the World, 1873.* New York: D. Appleton, 1873.

Shulman, Mark Russell. *Navalism and the Emergence of American Sea Power, 1882–1893.* Annapolis, MD: Naval Institute Press, 1995.

Spence, Jonathan. *Chinese Roundabout: Essays in History and Culture.* New York: W. W. Norton, 1992.

———. *The Search for Modern China.* New York: W. W. Norton, 1990.

Sugihara, Kaoru, ed. *Japan, China, and the Growth of the Asian International Economy, 1850–1949.* New York: Oxford University Press, 2005.

Sumida, Jon Tetsuro. *Inventing Grand Strategy and Teaching Command: The Classic Works of Alfred Thayer Mahan Reconsidered.* Washington, DC: Woodrow Wilson Center Press, 1997.

Sutton, Jean. *Lords of the East: The East India Company and its Ships (1600–1874).* London: Conway Maritime Press, 2000.

Symonds, Craig L. *The Naval Institute Historical Atlas of the U.S. Navy.* Annapolis, MD: Naval Institute Press, 2001.

Tanner, E. Z. "Reminiscences of Wm. B. Cushing." Washington, DC, March 8, 1899.

Taylor, Robert. *The Maritime Paintings of Robert Taylor.* Cincinnati, OH: F & W, 2003.

Turnbull, Stephen. *Samurai: The World of the Warrior.* Oxford: Osprey, 2003.

Turnbull, Stephen R., and Steve Noon. *The Great Wall of China 221 BC–AD 1644.* Oxford: Osprey, 2007.

U.S. Department of the Navy. *Report of the Secretary of the Navy with an Appendix Containing Bureau Reports, Etc.* Washington, DC: Government Printing Office, December 1867.

———. *Report of the Secretary of the Navy with an Appendix Containing Bureau Reports, Etc.* Washington, DC: Government Printing Office, December 1868.

———. *Annual Report of the Secretary of the Navy Showing the Operations of the Department for the Year 1869 with an Appendix.* Washington, DC: Government Printing Office, 1869.

Waldron, Arthur. *The Great Wall of China: From History to Myth.* Cambridge: Cambridge University Press, 1997.

Welsh, Frank. *A History of Hong Kong.* Revised ed. London: HarperCollins, 1997.

West, Sir Algernon. *Memoir of Sir Henry Keppel, G.C.B., Admiral of the Fleet.* London: Smith, Elder, 1905.

William B. Cushing Papers. Chautauqua County Historical Society and McClurg Museum, Westfield, New York.

Willmott, H. P. *The Last Century of Sea Power: From Port Arthur to Chanak, 1894–1922.* Bloomington and Indianapolis: Indiana University Press, 2009.

Wiltshire, Trea. *Old Hong Kong.* Volume 1. Hong Kong: Formasia Books, 1997.

Winchester, Simon. *Atlantic: Great Sea Battles, Heroic Discoveries, Titanic Storms, and a Vast Ocean of a Million Stories.* New York: HarperCollins, 2010.

———. *The River at the Center of the World: A Journey Up the Yangtze, and Back in Chinese Time.* London: Penguin Books, 1998.

Young, Andrew W. *History of Chautauqua County, New York: From its First Settlement to the Present Time.* Buffalo, NY: Printing House of Matthew & Warren, 1875.

Index

Adams, Pres. John 6, 103
Ammen, Capt. 136, 167
Arey, the Rev. Mr. 38, 94, 120, 206

Baptist 48, 78, 94
Barker, Lt. Cmdr. Albert S. 10, 20, 168
Batavia, Australia 45–46
Beijing, China 59–60, 63, 80, 101, 103, 107, 109–114, 116, 119, 121
Bell, Rear Adm. 28, 57, 100
bells, military time 22
Boston, Massachusetts 6, 8, 16–19, 30, 62, 103, 134, 163–164, 170, 198
Brooklyn Navy Yard 18
Browne, J. Ross 128, 132
Buddhism 77, 138–139
Buffalo, NY 166, 175

Canton 51, 58, 60–62, 64, 71–74, 76–77, 80–83, 86–87, 89–90, 92–93, 95, 102, 107, 111, 122, 146, 177, 193, 202
Cape Town 11, 38, 40–42, 43–45, 66, 82
Chautauqua 3–4, 6, 170
Confucius 120–121
Constantia 40
Cushing, Alonzo 4, 7, 26, 103, 107, 129–130, 175
Cushing, Howard 7, 26
Cushing, Katherine Louise Forbes 1, 205
Cushing, Mary Barker 6–8, 104–106, 158, 167, 175
Cushing, Milton 6–8
Cushing, Milton Buckingham 6–7, 104–106, 158, 167, 175

Dahlgren (guns) 14, 27
Delafield, Wisconsin 7
Dunkirk, NY 3, 5, 21, 72, 206

East India Company 58, 61, 73
Ericsson, steam engine 27

Farragut, David 10, 14, 57, 134
Fenton, Gov. Reuben 26
Fillmore, Pres. Millard 99
Fleming, Lt. Commander 21–22
Forbes, David 19, 180
Forbes, Katherine *see* Cushing, Katherine Louise Forbes
Formosa 142, 173, 182, 190–192
Fredonia, NY 3–6, 8, 10–11, 17–21, 23–31, 33, 37, 48, 66, 80, 94, 97, 107, 132, 134, 148, 151–152, 164, 168–170, 174–175, 180, 198, 202–203, 206

Galatea, HMS 199–200
Goddard, Rev. J.R. 56–57, 77, 180
Goldsborough, Commodore John 57
Grant, Gen. Ulysses S. 26, 75, 90, 107, 129, 136, 158, 167
Great Wall 103, 122, 125–127
Gulf Stream 25

Hainan 85–87, 91–95, 101
Hawaii 15
Higgins, Charles 27, 29–31, 66–67, 150–153, 191
Holmes, Oliver Wendell 38
Hong Kong 21, 28, 45–51, 53–54, 56–58, 60, 63–68, 71–73, 75, 77–79, 82–87, 89–94, 96, 101, 103–105, 117, 129, 131, 134, 140, 142–143, 165, 168, 170, 177, 180, 188, 190–196, 198–200
Hudson (class of paddle streamer) 178
Huntingdon, H.H. 11

Japan 11, 13–14, 42, 57, 67–68, 81–82, 85–87, 89–91, 96, 98–103, 106–107, 118, 130–131, 133, 135–145, 147–151, 153–157, 159–163, 165–167, 169–171, 173, 177, 182, 191, 195–196, 198, 203
Jardine-Matheson 50, 58–59, 62, 73, 177, 179

Kansas (gunboat class) 26
Keppel, Adm. 65, 67–68, 90, 200
King, Ellis 82
Kyoto 98–99, 147

Lee, S.P. 28
Lin, Commissioner 60, 62
Lincoln, Abraham 9–10, 15, 63, 73, 117, 158
London, England 15, 55, 58, 61–62

Mahan, Alfred Thayer 10–11, 101
Mohammedan 41–42, 121
Morris, Robert 60

Nagasaki 81, 89, 99, 101, 129–131, 134, 140, 143, 158, 172–173, 202
New Bedford 45
New York City 87
Norfolk, Naval Yard 11, 18, 31–32

Oliphant & Co. 74
Osaka 57, 96, 100, 131, 141, 143, 146, 158, 161, 165, 167, 172

Pacific Mail Steamship Co. 90, 131, 147, 154
Palmer, Adm. 22
Palmerston, Viscount Henry 89
Parker, David 11, 37, 97
Parkes, British Consul Harry 72–74, 80, 147, 154, 156
Peking *see* Beijing
Perkins Brothers 61
Perry, Commodore Matthew 13, 67, 87, 99, 142
Plymouth, NC 9
Prince Alfred 40, 199–200
Prince of Wales 67

Queen Victoria 15, 40, 52, 68, 195, 199–200

Rio de Janeiro 21, 27–29, 35–39, 44, 47, 66, 83, 87, 105, 189
Risley family 29–30
Robeson, George 90–91
Rodney, HMS 90

Roman Catholicism 77–78, 198
Roosevelt, Theodore 10–11, 15, 143
Rowan, Adm. Stephen 49, 57, 58, 71, 74–75, 78–81, 85–86, 96, 107, 134, 141, 172–173, 190, 195–196, 198, 202
Russell & Company, opium 61–62, 73, 129, 141, 177–179

St. Francis Xavier 199
St. Paul Island 44, 104
St. Thomas, Virgin Islands 21–22
Salem, Massachusetts 6, 18, 20–21, 23, 30
San Francisco 11, 15–16, 66, 89–90, 98, 102, 104, 106, 131, 143, 157, 169, 170, 172, 175, 179, 186, 188, 190–191, 195, 198, 202
Seward, William H. 63, 73–74, 87, 117–118
Seymour, Horatio 136, 158
Shanghai, 60, 63, 101, 129, 131, 141–142, 175, 177–180, 195
Smith, Adm. Josh 28, 194
Starr, Miss 31, 145, 167, 171, 183, 187, 198
Stewart, Col. Scott 163, 165
CSS *Stonewall Jackson* 100, 154

Tanner, Commander Z.L. 65, 117
Treaty of Kanagawa 14
Treaty of Nanking 62–63, 72
Treaty of Vienna 88
Treaty of Wanghia 62–63
Trinity Episcopal Church 8, 18, 206

Van Valkenburgh, Robert 57, 89, 98, 100

War of 1812 67, 88
Washington, George 4
Washington, Navy Yard 26, 29–30, 46
Welles, Gideon 10, 89–90
Wheelock, Sally 48, 152
White, Squire 25

Yeddo, Tokyo 68, 90, 96, 98–99, 101, 103, 131, 136, 147–148, 153–155
Yokohama 12, 66, 81, 85, 89–90, 96–97, 100–102, 107, 134–135, 138–139, 141, 143, 147–148, 155, 166, 169–170, 195